HEALING AND TRANSFORMATION:
Moving from the Ordinary to the Extraordinary

Eric Alsterberg, Ph.D.

Strategic Book Publishing and Rights Co.

Copyright © 2009 Eric Alsterberg, Ph.D. All rights reserved.

No part of this book may be reproduced or transmitted in any form or by any means, graphic, electronic, or mechanical, including photocopying, recording, taping, or by any information storage retrieval system, without the permission, in writing, from the publisher.

Strategic Book Publishing and Rights Co.
12620 FM 1960, Suite A4-507
Houston, TX 77065
www.sbpra.com

Hardcover version published in 2009.
Softcover version published in 2011.

ISBN: 978-1-61204-981-6

Book Design: Bruce Salender

For my son Justin,
who provides me with
immeasurable joy

Biography

Dr. Alsterberg is a licensed psychologist in the State of Michigan. He has been a practicing clinical psychologist for the past 32 years. He currently provides custody and parenting time evaluations and interventions for a local Court. He provides counseling and evaluations for our elders in nursing homes, and treats clients at an outpatient clinic focusing on various clinical issues.

Over the years, Dr. Alsterberg has worked with all age groups, from young children to our elders. He has treated both emotional problems as well as substance abuse problems. Increasingly he has blended metaphysical and spiritual approaches with psychological approaches when appropriate. He provides clinical hypnosis with some clients, which includes past memory regression and what he calls "vision hypnosis." With vision hypnosis, clients sometimes connect with deceased relatives, their Angels or Spirit Guides, Angels or Archangels, or Ascended Masters.

As a metaphysical explorer he hosts healing circles twice a month, focusing on how to help humanity and Mother Earth move toward ascension. He is certified as a Teacher I with the

Rocky Mountain Mystery School. He also participates with the Astara Mystery School. He practices Reconnective Healing I/II.

Dr. Alsterberg's first book is *Life IS An Adventure: a Guide to the Path of Joy.* Part psychological, part self-help and part metaphysical, it explores understanding and applying basic truths to achieve joy.

INTRODUCTION

We have a spiritual ego and a psychological ego that keep us trapped in dysfunctional patterns of thought and behavior. The spiritual ego promotes separation, differences, and spiritual pride that become the antithesis of walking a true spiritual path. The psychological ego prevents us from healing the emotional wounds and traumas we experience in life, preventing us from creating a path of joy, seeing harmony and unity in all, and progressively learning to walk the spiritual path. Ultimately both egos prevent us from increasingly choosing who we are and who we want to be, moving beyond the illusions of separation and limitation, and toward unity and spiritual transformation, or ascension. The processes of healing both egos lead to transformation, to truly manifesting and walking the spiritual path and eventually back to oneness with God.

Truly walking the spiritual path is more than just believing in a particular path or tradition. It is a process. While a particular path or tradition may outline a core belief system, it is putting the spiritual path into action that allows us to evolve. Being spiritual transcends religion. It is nice when they are one and the same, but more often they are not the same. Some of the most spiritual people in the world do not follow any particular religion or tradition. Some of the most religious people in the world are not spiritual at all.

The spiritual path requires three very difficult and challenging actions to accomplish. The first is to practice complete and unconditional love. The second is to practice complete and total forgiveness. The third is to practice complete and total nonjudgment. Since none of us are perfect, how can we possibly achieve these? Perhaps it is not so much achieving these as it is continually striving to accomplish these.

Adding to the challenge of striving to become more and more spiritual, each of us has a spiritual ego and a psychological ego. With the separation that took place, and that we all chose to participate in, both egos came into existence. Before this was complete and total Oneness with God. In the moment we asked, "What if?" different dimensional realities burst into existence. We began to create without God. Along the way we began to miscreate. Ultimately, on this planet, we created the world we live in now. We continually create the world we live in now. The mess we are in is the collective result of creating without God.

We again have the opportunity to become co-creators with God. We again have the opportunity to walk the spiritual path, creating our lives as masterpieces of joy. Again we have the opportunity to make better and better choices about who we are and who we want to be. Again we have the opportunity to achieve ascension.

The exciting thing about this point in place and time is that we can choose to ascend individually and collectively. We can help the planet to ascend as well. We can collectively create a different world, a world of peace, love, forgiveness and tolerance. We can collectively and individually move into higher dimensional realities.

Have you noticed that time seems to be speeding up? Have you noticed that time is more fluid, sometimes seeming to pass very quickly and other times being active and yet time has moved hardly at all? Have you noticed that the gifts of spirit in

Introduction

you are increasingly manifesting? Have you noticed how much more intuitive you seem to be? Have you noticed that you can no longer tolerate dysfunction as easily as you once could?

There is a shift in consciousness that is occurring. More and more people are striving to learn and apply spiritual truths in their lives. There is a hunger, a thirst, to know more and learn more. There is a greater desire to experience genuine oneness and connection to all and to the divine within. The increasing awareness and sharing of many spiritual and metaphysical systems and technologies is helping to facilitate a greater understanding of who we are and who we want to be.

With our current age we have at hand information and healing technologies like never before in the past 12,000 years of human history. We can find information and read about many spiritual and mystery school paths that were once only available to a very select few. With our increasing sophistication psychologically we are able to access many self-help books, alternative healing technologies, and forms of counseling and therapy that can heal us psychologically and emotionally.

With all the healing technologies, all the psychological technologies, and the entire spiritual and wisdom information available, we can heal at any and all levels. We can heal physically, mentally, emotionally and spiritually. We can resolve the emotional wounds and traumas that keep us in separation and limitation. We can relinquish the spiritual ego and the psychological ego, and be guided by our inner wisdom, walking more in harmony with the divine within each of us. We can choose love to guide us in all actions.

We can heal and transform our lives, and collectively heal and transform the planet. We can no longer survive as a species and a planet if we continue down the destructive path of separation and fear. We can no longer act out the ego's dramas and dysfunctions, creating disharmony and conflict at every level, including at its worst at war with one another. We are at a crossroads. Each of us has the opportunity to heal and transform our lives, and to accelerate our return to Home/Heaven where we really belong.

Healing and Transformation

This book provides direction on how to heal and transform your life. It guides you on how to return to and re-connect with the divine core within you. The importance of slowing down and going within helps set the stage to relinquish the ego. Understanding we are moving into higher dimensional realities, healing at all levels becomes ever more essential. Learning to create balance again leads to greater peace and harmony within and without.

With healing and transformation there is a new understanding of masculinity, and what real masculinity is. The return of the feminine is equally important for healing and transformation to take place.

Within everyday life, our intimate relationships, roles as parents, and learning forgiveness all help healing to occur. The result of the transformational process is the gifts of spirit more readily emerge and become a part of our lives, and we understand what prophecy is all about. The future is not meant to be left to chance, and dire prophecies need not come true, for we can use our free will to change course.

We can heal our selves, our communities, our nation and our world. We can all return to the spiritual path. We can live the spiritual path. We can let the divine meet our humanness. We can remember and live that we are spiritual beings having a human experience. As we fix ourselves, divine love flows through us and we become a radiant light, for ourselves and for others.

There are many paths, yet one path, to heal and transform our lives. It is not easy to honestly look at ourselves, to face the emotional wounds, hurts and embarrassments that we want to keep hidden from conscious awareness, and to move through these to release the negative and fear-based emotions attached to these experiences. Yet remaining unresolved, we only stay in misery and fear at best. This book guides you to make other choices, so that you can live more and more manifesting positive and love-based emotions, living joyfully, and moving back to unity and oneness with All-That-Is. Each of us will do this sooner or later. Why not now?

Table of Contents

Chapter 1 Return to You 1
Chapter 2 Slowing Down and Going Within 27
Chapter 3 Relinquishing the Ego 42
Chapter 4 Healing at All Levels 58
Chapter 5 Creating Balance 76
Chapter 6 Real Masculinity 92
Chapter 7 Return of the Feminine 108
Chapter 8 Healing and Transformation within the
    Intimate Relationship 130
Chapter 9 Parenting: The Sacred Responsibility 153
Chapter 10 Forgiveness 167
Chapter 11 The Gifts of Spirit 189
Chapter 12 The Purpose of Prophecy 205
Chapter 13 Healing the Community, Healing the Nation,
    Healing the World 224
Chapter 14 Return to the Spiritual Path 242
Chapter 15 Living the Spiritual Life 257
References 272

Chapter 1
RETURN TO YOU

We are privileged to now be living in one of the most exciting times in the history of the world. Each of us has the opportunity available to return to our true divine heritage, while living in physical reality. The time has come when healing and transformation are readily available to each one of us. We have the opportunity to heal and transform individually and collectively. We live in a time when healing technologies are increasingly available to all, whether at the physical, mental, emotional or spiritual level. Beyond this, what were once only available to a few initiates in select Mystery Schools, are now becoming available to any who want to enter the path of spiritual growth and transformation.

While the path is no less difficult to master, the path is no longer shrouded from all but a few select initiates. A wonderful and incredible opportunity is at hand, to reunite with your Higher Self while living in the physical. As a spiritual being having a human experience, you now have the unique opportunity to readily remember and live life, consciously aware of your connection to your divine self. It is now, more than ever,

Healing and Transformation

possible to return to You, to reconnect with your Higher Self and walk in harmony with the divine wisdom that is at the core of your being.

This is a time of transformation for you and for the world. We have the opportunity now, more than ever, to collectively create a shift in consciousness that will transform the world. This planet is about to advance from a preschool civilization to a more advanced civilization in "the twinkling of an eye." We can either do it willingly, peacefully and cooperatively, or it will be forced upon us as the result of catastrophic change, war and economic chaos.

We are increasingly experiencing an expanding consciousness. We are moving from five sensory to multisensory awareness and consciousness. As Gary Zukav has presented in his book, *The Seat of the Soul*, we are moving into a time in which multisensory awareness and consciousness is increasingly happening. You may have noticed you are experiencing more déjà vu experiences, that sense that you already lived a particular moment, yet know you have not. You may be experiencing a sense of knowing or familiarity with a place you have never visited before or a person you have not met before. You may be experiencing precognitive dreams. You may be experiencing increased intuition. You may be experiencing with significant others moments when, what you thought the other person spoke aloud, or said to each other "I was just thinking that" or "I was just about to say the same thing." This is a form of mental telepathy. You may be suddenly, or more frequently, experiencing lucid dreaming, where you know you are asleep and yet you are consciously aware of the dream and even its message or meaning to you. You may be experiencing so-called psychic gifts, such as clairaudience, clairvoyance, automatic writing, or mental telepathy to name just a few. You may be experiencing prophetic visions, personally or planetary. You may be experiencing contact with your Spirit Guides or Angels. I prefer to call all these things the "gifts of the Spirit" and would suggest to you that these are natural, innate abilities we have not been in touch with, used or developed for some time.

As we move into a time where we go from one age to the next, as the planet moves from third dimensional to fourth and higher dimensional vibrations, these gifts of the Spirit more readily return. As we move into the spring of the universe, and as our solar system is bathed in increased energy and light, we move into a time where it is easier to return to our true heritage. The long dark winter for the planet is over, and you now have the most wonderful opportunity presented to you. While living in your current everyday world of career and responsibilities, you get to embark on the most glorious of adventures, returning to conscious and direct contact and awareness with your Higher Self.

You get to re-establish your divine connection, to "hear" the gentle urgings of Holy Spirit, and simply re-connect to the "still, small voice within," your direct communication with God.

You agreed to come and partake of this wonderful experiment that is taking place in all of creation, on this very planet. You get to experience an opportunity to achieve your ascension through healing and transformation. You get to heal your embodiments from all time and space: to move beyond the need to live in worlds of physicality, to move beyond the cycle of death and rebirth, to move beyond the need to live in cause and effect realities.

Collectively, we get to participate in the grandest experiment yet undertaken in the universe, together creating the ascension of humanity, without the need for catastrophic change to "shock" us into higher dimensional consciousness and being. You have labored long and hard to be alive in this time of healing and transformation, to seize the new day. You have certainly "chosen" to be here to at least witness the healing and transformation that can and will take place on a planetary basis, or witness how transmutation can and will occur if we choose not to live in the old paradigm of hatred, judgment, and limited awareness and consciousness.

Why just be a witness when you too can participate in this grand vision and this grand adventure? You can choose to take

Healing and Transformation

the healing methods and technologies that are now readily available and learn more of the paths of initiation, which can lead to ascension. You can choose to heal and transform your life and return to You.

As a spiritual being having a human experience you have existed long before this moment in time and space. Your soul currently inhabits a physical body long after God created it. When this physical body is given up, through the process we call death, your soul continues on. You just simply shed the current physical body you need while existing in physical dimensional reality.

You continue on after your return to spirit. You go on to other adventures and classrooms of learning. You even get to return to another physical body, if and when it serves your further soul growth and development. You also may return to balance out karma, to balance what you have previously created, both positive and negative. You meet the consequences you have created for yourself. You truly do sow what you reap. What goes around does indeed come around, until you release yourself from the wheel of life. Do you think it is coincidental when a person wins the lottery? They are having the good return to them that they created in other times and places.

This particular time in history is even more important because the opportunity is afforded to balance out karma all at once, in a relatively short period of time. As you embrace basic truths and practice these laws in your life, the transformation that takes place heals all levels in this lifetime, as well as heals all time and space. This frees you to live in the higher dimensions, the higher planes or spheres of existence, and to be co-creators with God.

Fortunately, the law of grace super-cedes the negative side of karma. As you learn to manifest positive and love-based emotions, and truly enter a place of complete unconditional love for all, no matter what their outer behavior or appearance, then your own negative karma is released. As you learn to truly forgive any and all that harmed or wounded you and practice grace, you release negative karmic debt. As you release feelings of resentment and bitterness, you release negative karmic debt.

As you learn we are all one, unconditional love or *agape* love, is our true heritage and only way of being, we all advance. When judgment is released into unconditional love, we are all set free. We are all truly One Son. *A Course In Miracles* reminds us continually that we are one Son-ship. We are not the poor, hopeless sinners divided from each other and separated from God except for the one Son, Jesus, who came to give us salvation. Salvation is the recognition we are all one, and that we can and will walk the same path of ascension, as did the Master Jesus, as well as many other master teachers sent to guide us home.

When you entered your current physical body, the veil of forgetfulness came over you, so you would learn to return to your true divine Self through the process of ascension. You have to remember who you are and where you want to be, which is to return to You. As you learn and grow; as you heal the past hurts, traumas, emotional scars and spiritual wounds from this life, you regain an increased awareness that heals at all levels and leads to transformation. With increased awareness you begin to choose who you are and who you want to be at higher and higher levels, until you ultimately choose to return to You.

What makes this time so special and unique is that you chose to come into the physical and participate in the ascension process on a massive, planetary scale. Not only did you come to decide to return to You for you, but to participate with many others who also want to return to their Higher Self. The grandest part of the drama is we all chose to be here in the physical at this time and place on this planet, to return the whole species and the whole planet back to its divine heritage.

We are here to evolve into fourth and beyond dimensional awareness and reality. Individually, as members of society and as member of the planet, we are here to ascend together. United with the living entity we call Mother Earth, or Gaia, we are moving into a New Golden Age. This is the thousand years of peace promised in the New Testament of the Christian Bible by the Master Teacher Jesus. As our elder brother, he came here two thousand years ago to demonstrate that ascension is possible. He came as a Way-Shower, to light the path, to help us remember who we really are and help us to return home, to return to our true spiritual heritage. Many other Master Teachers have also come to light the way. Moses, Mohammed, the Buddha, and Krishna are just a few of the many masters who have walked the Earth to enlighten us to our True Selves.

The New Golden Age is actually a return to previous Golden Ages on this planet. These were eras when great, grand and glorious civilizations manifested on Earth, living in total peace and harmony. They accomplished this with divine leadership, which is where the divine right of kings first arose as a concept. Except, in the Golden Ages, divine leadership directed these civilizations. These leaders remembered and practiced their connection to their Higher Self, and through humility led with Divine Guidance.

The New World Order, which the current leadership on the planet wishes to impose, is the antithesis of Golden Age leadership and structure. In the Golden Ages, evolved and enlightened beings, working in total harmony with divine order within the divine plan, created a sense of Oneness and spiritual enlightenment and attunement in all. From this, peace, harmony, prosperity and abundance flow naturally for all. Complete harmony existed within the plant and animal kingdoms, with the devic and elemental realms, and with the planet herself.

We are on the verge of creating another Golden Age, starting with each one of us who heals, transforms and moves into greater consciousness and awareness. This process of enlightenment occurs as we reconnect with our spiritual truth and manifest who we are and who we want to be at the highest levels. As we increasingly move into the Photon Belt, this process of transformation is accelerating.

You can choose not to participate. You will get many more opportunities to live in third dimensional worlds, eventually tire of the hurt and pain limited choices create and turn back home to God. Or, you can choose to be part of this great moment in time and evolve back to where you truly belong.

Life is meant to be joyous, such that you have frequent joy attacks. These are sudden moments in which you are overwhelmed with ecstasy and joy, where you feel so good you can hardly stand it. These are the opposite of bouts of depression, anxiety, or panic attacks.

Life is meant to be an expression of love. It is especially sharing the unconditional love of the One who created us. It is meant to be an expression of truth at the highest levels. It is meant to be an expression of our highest self while in human form. It is about choosing who we are and who we are meant to be at higher levels in each moment. It is about creating the highest fantasy of you, and then manifesting it in your day-to-day reality. Life is about living from the highest truths in a third dimensional world that is evolving into higher dimensional frequencies of light. As you do this you return to your true Self. We are meant to manifest our Higher Self in our day-to-day lives, creating our lives as masterpieces of joy.

To accomplish this requires a great paradox. We have to slow ourselves down in order to increase our vibration, radiation and our consciousness. We have to slow down from the constant pressure to succeed in a materialistically defined, competitive world that will never satisfy the hunger in our souls.

We have been living in the "historical period," a time in the ongoing evolution of the world when the consciousness of humanity has been very limited. It is based on believing in only a material world, as defined by our five senses and what our science has been able to discover by extension of her instruments, within the limited perception of the basic senses. It has been a time of darkness and limited consciousness, where war and vengeance, competition and power have ruled. It has been a time in which controlling others by the designated authority of the time have held sway.

With these limitations we have engaged in a collective illusion of how the world is and how to succeed in this world.

These illusions have included the belief in competition, survival of the fittest, might makes right, whoever gets there first wins, and that whoever makes the most money or has the most things wins. This is aptly stated in the bumper sticker, "He who has the most toys when they die wins." I like the rebuttal bumper sticker that instead states, "He who has the most toys when they die, still dies."

Even religions are trapped in this illusion, with their orthodoxies and theologies. These often provide limitations about what creation is, or even the time frame it occurred in, and that creation is not a continuing process. They provide limitations on when we were created and the limited options we have to get it right, or face eternal damnation. They limit the nature of God, and in what way we can relate with our Creator. Many religions have myriad legalistic rules about how we can relate to God, or whether we must have mediators to intercede on our behalf. They try to deny the freedom from which we are to joyously know God.

Most of the indigenous peoples of the world, who always maintain a direct relationship with Great Spirit, were systematically killed or their cultures deliberately destroyed, during this historical period and especially in the last two thousand years. Missionaries, who insisted their limited concept of truth was more powerful than having a direct relationship with God, attacked many.

Much of this was done so the major religions could monopolize access to God through their leaders and through the rules and regulations that came to shape the theologies and the dogmas. These dogmas limit the truth of our being and what we can become, rather than enlighten and guide us. Yet, despite this, all religions have at their core the same basic truths. Unfortunately leaders and theologians modified these basic truths, or at times eliminated the ones that were inconvenient to obtain power and control over the masses.

Our limited worldview, until this time, has been based on fear as the predominate belief. Negative and fear-based belief systems pervade the world. There is a belief in limitation and lack, and survival goes to the fittest. Fittest is defined as who is stronger, tougher, more competitive and more ruthless. They get to define the world and truth as the way they see it. Driven by materialistic beliefs and goals, the ego demands we rush around trying to get as much as we can before some one else gets it first. Life is a race and who gets there first wins.

Who gets there first or who gets the most stuff defines self-esteem, self-worth and status. Life becomes a maddening race in pursuit of the material, whether belongings, relationships, conquests, sex or any of the hundreds of external pursuits we are led to believe produce happiness and joy. Ultimately, the pursuit of power and having control over others are seen as worthy goals, producing happiness and joy. Not only are we led to believe these externals bring happiness; we all have chosen this collective illusion.

A dramatic everyday example of this is the popularity of fad toys, cleverly marketed as a must for every child. Parents get caught up in the fervor of obtaining as many of these so-called collectibles as they can. They wait in lines and even fight to get what is available. They rationalize their behavior by saying the toys will be valuable some day, so they are only investing for their child's future. Not only do they inadvertently teach their children that happiness comes from possessing stuff, they also teach material wealth combined by competition, are the goals of life and the road to joy. Now that doesn't mean there is anything wrong with getting things for your children or grandchildren, nor that there is a lack intrinsic joy and value in having things.

Unfortunately, we are in an ever increasing, maddening race. We scurry around to get more and more stuff, and get more and more depressed and anxious. There certainly is no time left for quiet contemplation. As we rush about, we do not take the time to stop and consider what is really important, what life is really about, or what we truly want for ourselves. We certainly do not take time to contemplate who we are and who we want to be. In the most important area of our lives we let others define for us what our spirituality is or should be. We let others make spiritual choices for us, without for one moment contemplating the divine within. We certainly do not take time to slow down and go within, discovering our own divine Self. Most of the time we are even told there is no divinity within us and God is external and remote.

The challenge for humanity is to slow down. Take time to truly understand our selves and respond to our own inner Supreme Court rather than external authority. The endless race the ego insists we should engage in keeps us stuck in fear and limited consciousness. It keeps us stuck in the belief in limitation and lack and the belief only certain externals create joy and happiness. As we race around endlessly seeking these externals, we become disenfranchised from our true spiritual heritage and ourselves.

Worse yet, as we obtain more and more stuff, we discover it does not satisfy or provide the joy we thought it would. There may be a momentary satisfaction, but it quickly passes. There is never a lasting satisfaction or contentedness. We may momentarily celebrate a victory or accomplishment, but soon the ego is driving us on to obtain and win more, even at or especially, at another's expense.

What is the price we pay for this endless, ego driven need to acquire more? Usually we just get more and more stressed or distressed. There is never enough time to acquire the demands the ego says we need to be happy. The ego constantly reminds us that there are others who are willing to work harder, try harder and race faster, even as you consider slowing down. Fearing there will not be enough we become even more fearful. We get depressed when we can't get enough, yet paradoxically we get depressed when we momentarily feel like we did get enough. We have depression and anxiety, even panic attacks, as we seek to compete in a giant, collective race for the seemingly limited resources available. In the race to have more, we are even willing to risk the destruction of an entire planet and the future of the next generations. Ultimately we do this in an endless rush to avoid discovering who we really are and who we really want to be.

This suits the ego fine. It doesn't want you to recognize who you are and who you want to be. It doesn't want you to remember you are a spiritual being having a human experience!

Right now we are so caught up in the human experience, we have forgotten what our true heritage is. We also allow religions to define what our spiritual heritage is, defining it as another external race we have to get into, to achieve heaven. While all religions have at their core essential spiritual truths, centuries of theology and dogma have masked these magnificent truths in rules of belief and rules of conduct that may even contradict what the Master Teacher first taught. One is only going to be "saved" and achieve a state of perfection, oneness and "be in heaven" with God, if their set of beliefs and rules are followed. At its most absurd, one will achieve instant heaven if they engage in a martyred act and commit an act of terror.

Failure to win this race and one suffers at least purgatory, if not eternal damnation in a hellish nightmare for having failed to follow the 'right' rules or system of belief. Adding to this the current consciousness of limitation and lack, only a select few will win this race and secure a place in heaven. Everyone else is doomed, but deserving to be doomed because they didn't follow the legalese of a particular religion. Any souls that existed prior to a particular religion are doomed as well, because they had the misfortune to live before that Master Teacher arrived.

In this limited consciousness there is the belief that only one religion, or type of religion, gains one's access to God's eternal love and a heavenly home. There is certainly presumptuousness and a supreme arrogance that says only we have the truth about God. Only we know how the universe works and we are the only path to salvation. Despite having many systems of understanding God and our relationship to Him/Her, religions and their follower claim their system is the only way.

Despite being on only one planet, in a Universe where there are worlds without number, we presume there is only one path

Healing and Transformation

to God. Despite probable civilizations on at least some of these planets, all with their own diversity of understanding what God is and what basic truths may exist, some still have the arrogance to say that this path or that path is the only legitimate way to God. Even Jesus, who truly is one Way, one Truth and one Light, is misunderstood in limitation and lack to mean only "Christians" may enter the kingdom of heaven. He best demonstrated the path, but there are many systems that create the same path.

Jesus came to teach many truths, the most important yet least understood being how to achieve ascension or resurrection. He came to show this is what we are all here to do. Lost in the thought system of limitation and lack is a deeper understanding that his whole ministry was rich in deep metaphysical meaning. He taught the complexity of who we are, who we are meant to be, and how to return to our True Self. This True Self is our divine heritage waiting to be rediscovered and remembered as we live, understand and apply basic truths. These basic truths come to us from many sources, including religions when we examine and try to live the core truths minus the dogma and legalese. More and more metaphysical truths come through inspired writing and the metaphysical, and even channeled material is readily available to more and more people.

The path of joy leads to returning to You. The path of joy is available to all, when followed with an adventurous attitude. By meeting the challenges and opportunities life has to offer, in a positive and adventurous manner, healing takes place physically, mentally, emotionally, ethereally and spiritually. When healing and transforming the hurts, wounds and traumas of life, true joy and happiness emerge as well. By understanding and applying basic, universal truths you can achieve joy. The whole process of taking time to reflect on what the basic truths are and how they operate in our lives leads to the path of joy. Putting basic truths into action leads to joy. Certainly and inevitably this path takes us back to our True Self, the Divine You within. It's not something you can merely believe; it is something you have to do.

As you slow down, you take the time to understand the coincidences of your life and the messages and guidance this provides. You learn to understand and cope with the painful realities we all encounter and use those events to transform yourself. One comprehends the general and specific life lessons and how they provide for learning and growth. You rediscover your mission and purpose in life and your role in the divine plan each step of the way.

As universal truths are applied, in a heightened, multisensory, contemplative state of awareness, the return to You becomes more and more possible. Right and creative thought, an attitude of gratitude, sharing love, living from the heart, developing genuine self-love and self-worth, and being of service help manifest a return to your true divine heritage.

Our Higher Self functions at a greater vibration rate. It is just as real and tangible as the physical body you experience in third dimensional reality. Raising our radiation and vibration allows us to more closely connect with and experience this higher vibrational Self. I have clients in hypnosis who look above them and see this Higher Self. We are now living in a time when all that remain on the planet will experience this greater vibration and radiation, and will have their higher self and physical self overlap, or integrate, more and more. Those who choose not to go beyond third dimensional reality will no longer be able to live here. Fortunately, they will go on to other three-dimensional worlds where they will continue to learn and grow until they are ready for ascension.

Third dimensional reality is about living in duality, being on the wheel of life, and working out all karma. With infinite patience God allows us to use our free will until we get tired of the consequences, pain and suffering, and return to love. The inevitable choice is to return to love. When and how is up to us. Even the Hitler's of the world will eventually return to love, facing the karma they create, and hopefully applying the law of grace to speed up the process. It is learning forgiveness, compassion, and unconditional love that return us all home. We are to love even the unlovable.

Healing and Transformation

The process of slowing down paradoxically leads to an elevation in vibration and radiation. All masters know this and teach truth seekers how to do this. While in the past, only a few disciples or students were allowed to enter the mystery schools. We now enter a time when this wisdom and knowledge to accomplish this are available to all.

As we choose to return to our true heritage, and as more and more choose to do this, the consciousness of all is raised. Mother Earth is already entering fourth dimensional reality. As we slow down, and go within, we also go into fourth, and even higher, dimensional reality. As we leave the so-called "historical period," a time of darkness and very limited consciousness, we move into higher dimensional frequencies, as does the planet. We again know our spiritual heritage and live in an evolved civilization on an evolved planet. We once again join our rightful place with other evolved civilizations living in peace, harmony, prosperity and abundance with God and our God-Connection at the center of all life. We rejoin the Federation of Planets, with civilizations that are already evolved.

The end of this historical period is at hand. No longer will we live in limitation and lack, concerned with only power and control over others. True freedom, especially spiritual freedom, returns. The time for the thousand years of peace promised in the Christian Bible is at hand. On August 11, 1999 a great astrological event took place. It was the Grand Fixed Cross, a time in which all the planets of this solar system were within the four fixed signs of the Zodiac. This appeared with other heavenly bodies as a huge cross in the Northeastern sky. It signaled entering into the New Golden Age.

This event further escalates the birth changes already taking place, as this New Golden Age gradually emerges. Birth occurs with spasms of pain, and this transition is no exception. It is hard to give up the old ways, the ways of the ego based on negative and fear-based emotions, and return to love. How great or how little these birth pains are depends in large part on us. We have to make the choice collectively to return to who we really are, spiritual beings operating with positive and love-based emotions at our core. It is our consciousness individually and collectively that helps shape the intensity and the amount of the disruption during this time of transition. It can be done peacefully or chaotically, smoothly or disruptively, with gradual Earth changes or through catastrophic change.

As this transition progresses, even greater spiritual experiences take place, individually and planetary. Also, greater darkness and fear arise in those unwilling or unable to slow down, go within, and allow their true Self to more easily and readily emerge. Those caught up in dogma, whether scientific or religious, close themselves off from their true spiritual heritage and evolvement.

With the changes in dimensional frequencies, and the increasing time spent each year in the Photon Belt as our solar system gradually moves more and more into this energy, greater evil and greater good are manifesting at the same time. Thus, in the same week we have the terrorist attack on America and a worldwide day of prayer for peace and harmony. Despite the great evil perpetrated on September 11, 2001, tremendous good followed. Yes there has been great fear and anxiety, moments of panic and selfish behavior, but also tremendous volunteering and the raising of money to aid the victims. It brought a great city together and united a nation.

The so-called war between good and evil has begun in earnest. As the energy level continues to increase, and as the Earth is bathed in greater vibration frequencies, time becomes more fluid. It becomes easier to manifest in the physical with our thoughts, and our thoughts in turn more readily create the world in which we live. With darkness, fear and hatred there is greater disharmony and discord, and dreadful and tragic atrocities more readily occur. At the very same time, even more wonderful good, harmonious and loving actions are also created and manifested. As we align with our Higher Self, we do indeed manifest harmony, peace, happiness and joy. As you manifest love, even in the midst of destruction and evil, you are protected.

You are meant to live here as an expression of your Higher Self. You are meant, more so than before, to return to your True Self—to YOU. We now live in a time of great change and transition to the time of peace promised by Jesus. In a channeled session the Archangel Michael told me the birthing of the new world is happening. He further shared we are past the morning sickness and into the fullness of the pregnancy birthing a new world. Interestingly, the last date in the Great Pyramid at Giza is September 17, 2001. The last date on the Mayan calendar is 2012. We are in the final period of healing and transformation. The date line in the pyramid ends because the outcome of how this transition would occur could not be predicted 12,500 years ago. We create this transition as we heal and transform, moving from fear-based thoughts and emotions into love-based thoughts and emotions.

It is no longer the saints and sages, or the few disciples in mystery schools, who learn to live at the highest levels of consciousness. Everyone now gets to learn and live at these higher levels of consciousness. To have all the gifts of spirit manifest as part of everyday living. We get to live at higher vibrations and radiation, to move into fourth and fifth dimensional awareness and functioning. We are all meant to resurrect or ascend. We are all meant to overcome the world. This is the whole purpose of Jesus' ministry, what he came to teach us. It is not the crucifixion but the resurrection. That is why he says over and over in *A Course In Miracles* to focus on the resurrection. He tells us in the Course to make his crucifixion "the last useless journey" anyone has to make.

Unfortunately, most of Christianity is focused on the crucifixion, the idea of original sin, and telling us we are all useless sinners who deserve the wrath of a judgmental God unless we follow certain rules and creeds. The focus has been on fear, the natural focus of third dimensional reality and of the ego during the historical period. Ironically, the original meaning in translating the word sin from Hebrew to Greek is simply error or mistake. It is that as we become aware of errors or mistakes, we are not to persist in these errors, but rather to move forward beyond them. It is to choose over and over at higher and higher levels, who we are and who we want to be right into fourth and fifth dimensional reality. It is to transform us to no longer live in judgment and fear, to instead be love and practice forgiveness.

So-called original sin is simply the first error we all made as spiritual beings when we came to the Earth plane. We came to experience third dimensional reality and to help God know and create in this reality. We were meant to go back and forth from spirit to physical without permanently residing here. We agreed to not experience all there is here, nor to remain here. Once here we did experience the sensual world, and got gradually caught up in it. So much so we forgot we are spiritual beings having a human experience. We became enmeshed in the law of cause and effect, or karma, and could no longer freely return to spirit. We cannot move on without resolving the debt we created for ourselves. Thus began the cycle of birth, death and rebirth or reincarnation.

This original error or mistake interfered with our ultimate destiny of helping God to continue creating physical universes. It is still our destiny to do this, but we get sidetracked along the way. While it was not meant for us to become sidetracked, we have free will and God will never interfere with this. However, God creates solutions even as we make the mistakes. Thus, the divine plan was and is continually modified to account for the mistakes we continuously make, individually and collectively.

God knows all the endless probabilities of all our choices. He continuously modifies the divine plan to account for these probabilities, yet waits for each choice we make. There is no need for guilt or unworthiness, just remembering who we are and making better choices of who we want to be. When Jesus said "Go and sin no more" he was telling us to simply make better choices with the mistakes we have made as we gain increased awareness and understanding.

It is time to return home to your true spiritual self. Inevitably, we will all return to God. Why not do it sooner rather than later, especially since remaining in third dimensional worlds leads to so much pain and suffering?

We all chose to come to this planet and participate in this wonderful drama of using our free will in the physical dimensions. We came to create not miscreate. Once the first error was made, we chose to "forget" our true spiritual heritage, to forget the connection that exists with our Higher Self. We have also all chosen to be here at this time of great transition, to slow down and remember who we really are, and to reconnect in a conscious awakening to our Higher Self.

You have chosen to return to YOU, to slow down and reconnect to your Higher Self. You have chosen to live your life in such a way, and to have the experiences you need to have, so that you can elevate your consciousness, increase your vibration and increase your radiation. You have chosen to be here now to consciously and willingly move to fourth dimensional beingness individually and collectively. You have come to ascend.

We have all chosen to be here to move with Mother Earth into higher dimensional reality at this time. The more we choose this individually, the more it happens collectively and thus the more harmonious and peaceful the transition will be. The more we are able to release and heal our individual karmic debt the more we are able to help humanity peacefully release its karmic debt. Collectively, from a heightened and awakened being, we manifest the law of grace and create heaven on Earth.

As we collectively manifest the gifts of spirit, and truly practice love, compassion, and forgiveness, we help usher in the New Golden Age as easily as is possible. Unity is all of us as one Sonship living our divine partnership with God.

There is a wonderful Unity hymn that goes like this:

> It's in every one of us
> To be wise
> Find your heart
> Open up both your eyes

> We can all know everything
> Without ever knowing why
> It's in every one of us, by and by.

As you find your heart, your connection to your Higher Self, wisdom returns. You begin to heal the pain, hurt and anger within that keeps you in conflict, disharmony and discord with others. As you heal your karmic debt through the law of grace, and by meeting life's challenges with gentleness and forgiveness, then you allow collective healing to happen as well. As you let go of fear and embrace love, the transition into the New Golden Age more peacefully arises. It is inevitable we are going into this next Golden Age. How peacefully and smoothly this occurs is up to each one of us.

There are many dire prophecies and predictions that have been made based on the many probabilities we collectively choose. Even the Y2K predictions created enough fear to cause some trouble to arise, although the collective celebration of the new millennium led to a joyous and mostly trouble free transition.

The more we honor the return to our True Self, the more peaceful and gradual the transition can be. We can have sudden catastrophic change, or we can have gradual geographic change with ample warning so people can move to places of safety. We can have a world war, or we can have individual Armageddon's where we heal and transform the anger, resentment and aggression we still harbor within. We can have disease and starvation, or we can learn to live in harmony with Mother Earth and the animal and devic kingdoms. We can create a new Eden with our collective Higher Selves partnering with the divine plan at all levels.

The noted national columnist, Leonard Pitts, Jr. asks, "Can a people be whole by feeding the body, but never the soul? By fulfilling the demands of immediacy while ignoring those of Infinity? Truth is to be human is to need both." The world calls out for change. The world as it is must change. We can no longer go along with the same old, limited values. We can no longer stay the same. As the birthing process continues to the New Golden Age, we are now in a time of chaos and confusion that will not let us live the same way. Yet the changes we seek cannot come from without. They can only come from within, as we begin to discover, live and be the truth of who we really are. The change is a spiritual change, a time to return to the true Self, living a heart-centered life, connected to the divine wisdom within.

It is time to attune your mental, emotional and physical bodies to their spiritual source. It is time to let the etheric pattern manifest from your spiritual truth. It is connecting the bodies to their Maker. We have been rebellious, moving away from the consciousness that our identity is spiritual. We let ego and our personality divorce ourselves from our True Self. It is time to move away from seeing ourselves as only physical, based on a five sensory awareness, and return to what Gary Zukov describes as multi-sensory awareness. In limited consciousness we have only occasional insights or experiences of being spiritual beings living in the densest physical realms.

Without mental and spiritual well-being, there cannot be health and wholeness. With a state of consciousness in which we truly embrace ourselves and who we really want to be, we can fearlessly embrace the present and the future, heal the past and heal physically. Our consciousness is the critical factor. All of our ways, our thoughts, values, beliefs, hopes, fears, planning, creativity, inspiration, behavior and relations with others, and the planet, are dependent on our state of consciousness. Human consciousness is the critical factor leading to destruction or to transformation, individually and collectively.

The answer is to center your life on God, not the seeming events or realities of your life within the larger whole. When you return to your true Self you center on the eternal condition of all conditions, not on temporal circumstances.

Edgar Cayce, in reading 877-26, said

> For every spark of light,
> Whether in the spiritual,

The mental
Or the material sense must have its inception in infinity.

Creating heaven on earth is possible. Peace is possible even in the midst of chaos and uncertainty. Heaven can be gradually created for all on earth, or could even happen in the twinkling of an eye. Transformation can take place so chaos and old ways are replaced. As more of us return to our true Self, the new consciousness, which is really the ancient wisdom we already know and can remember, once again leads us into the New Golden Age.

The raising in consciousness that was once the province of a few mystics and Masters is now our collective destiny. The guides and technologies to accomplish this are there for any to use. I in You, and You in Me, Together We all will be free. Where there was once only one Christed one, now there are many Christed ones. Eventually we all will be Christed ones. In a short time only the Christed ones, those moving into ascension, will be permitted to remain on this planet. The others will still live, and will return to other three dimensional worlds to continue the journey toward choosing what can be chosen now by everyone who desires it and works to have this choice be in their life now.

Joy is the natural product of the return to You. God is the source of joy, the gladness of each soul. Within each soul there is a quiet joy—a joy born of connection with God remembered in faith. Inner joy is an attitude of love and reverence for all people and for all life. There is no room for judgment here. It is a gladness of spirit, a sense of well-being and strength in knowing our oneness with God. This heartfelt connectedness with God never fades, although it may be forgotten as we let our personality dominate. It is always there, even when we forget it is there, focusing only on the material. It is there in all situations that challenge us. It fills us with hope and faith that blesses us in each moment of life.

Our hearts have been created with an unlimited capacity to express love. At the very center of our soul, the joy of Spirit dwells at all times. There is a flame of golden light in your heart and your heart center, where your soul dwells within you. There you connect with God. God is the source of our joy, a fountain of gladness that never runs dry.

As you return to You, and you reconnect to your divine flame within, you once again become fully aware and connect to the God-Source that resides in everyone. Holy Spirit works easily in and through you. You are aware of the gentle guidance that always leads you to the right choices and the right actions. You begin to transform, to more easily and readily fulfill your part in the divine plan. You live more and more in peace and harmony. You become part of the next great adventure on this planet, manifesting the transformation of higher dimensional awareness and beingness.

The New Golden Age is beginning. To be a part of it in this lifetime and on this planet you have to return to You. This is a return to a spirit-centered civilization and consciousness. As you enter into this return to You, you not only heal yourself and move into higher dimensional consciousness; you also become part of the grand collective transformation and healing that can, and will, take place.

As we slow down and go within, we begin to bring harmony to this world of despair. The world can, and will, become a place of hope and joy as each of us return to their true self in the physical. Each of us can and will experience good humor and be joyful. You can and will have joy attacks; suddenly feeling so good you can hardly stand it. Then all of us will do it together. We will have a collective joy attack, as a thousand years of peace promised is made manifest by us together.

What is accomplished when we return to the True You present in each of us? Divine will is established in humanity collectively, with righteousness, justice and peace operating all the time. The Christ Mind is made manifest in the physical. This is a super-consciousness that establishes and maintains right doing, perfect adjustment, peace and perfection. The Christ Consciousness is a state of mind lived and taught by the Master Jesus, who became the Christ. He is the perfect example of this in action. We are all meant to become the Christ. This is a universal consciousness and beingness not restricted only to the "Way-Shower."

The Christ Consciousness is not to be confused with the man who became the Christ. As perhaps the greatest master and teacher to have walked the Earth thus far, the Christ Consciousness is universal and existed before time. Lord Matreya, a master being operating in tenth dimensional reality, is responsible for the Christ Consciousness, seeing that it is taught and shared throughout the universe. He is the guardian of the Christ Mind, known by many names. It is the Buddha Mind, the way of highest thought taught by every master, not only on Earth but also wherever civilizations exist in the cosmos.

So returning to You, the divine Self within, is a powerful and meaningful process. It is a powerful state of being. To always be in "right mind" fulfilling God's plan, creating harmony and joy, peace and justice, prosperity and abundance, perfect adjustment and right doing, are powerful yet humbling actions. In this perfection the world is healed, a new civilization emerges, and we become one. We become a highly evolved planet.

The return to You is the logical goal and ultimate choice each person makes. Now is the time to choose the path of joy, returning to your true state and your right heritage. The planet is going forward, whether or not you choose to go forward with it. It is time to live in higher dimensional frequencies and vibrations. The light is here and intensifying.

You have sensed and felt the change. Time seems to be speeding up. There is a sense of change and urgency about you and the world. We can no longer live as though the world can go on forever with the collective choices of the historical period. Advanced science and technology without corresponding maturation and evolvement spiritually and ethically will only lead to disaster and destruction. The darkness can no longer be the norm. As the energy increases the old ways will no longer work for you individually, or for the world collectively. We have been here before, most recently with Atlantis, and destroyed ourselves and almost destroyed the world. We are now in the edge of the Photon Belt, a massive wave of energy that crosses the universe, transmuting and transforming all in its path. Each year the orbit of the Earth merges with this energy. We are moving more fully into the New Golden Age.

As you return to You, and as humanity returns to its true heritage, this becomes a welcoming and wonderful epochal event. Embrace the change. Embrace the truth of who you are and who you really want to be. Walk the path of joy, healing your self at all levels. Take on the Christ Consciousness and be You.

As we assume, more and more, our True Self we increasingly see beyond the illusions of this world. We no longer see only with our mortal mind. We can see the truth that exists beyond the illusions of third dimensional reality. We develop the capacity to do what Jesus and other masters have done. With Jesus, even during the crucifixion, he could see the truth of those projecting their fear, anger and rebelliousness onto him. He knew the truth within them, beyond the surface behaviors in that moment. He did not judge their illusion. Instead he saw the True You in each one, and forgave their limited consciousness that allowed them to act in judgmental and persecutory ways. He forgave and loved them without exception. Jesus demonstrated and became a Wayshower, the Truth and the Light, because he could stay in his True Self and saw others in their True Self. Even as they murdered him, he lovingly and compassionately stated, "Forgive them Father, they know not what they do."

As Jesus fulfilled his mission he did not suffer. He gladly and willingly did what he came to do, to show us we can also achieve mastery and ascension. His mastery was such that there is no way he could or would have suffered. With pure love he could eliminate all pain. We also have the capacity, returning to our true Self, to attain the same mastery. That is one reason he said, "These things I do you can do, and even greater things than these can you also do."

In love and forgiveness Jesus taught us true compassion. He was in the Christ Mind, and could see and act on his divine vision through the Christ Consciousness. He showed us how to do the same thing. The True Self operates with unconditional love, compassion and forgiveness. An enormity of love begins to manifest such that you feel you can hardly contain it in your being. The Christ Mind exists as a universal consciousness that Jesus took on in his mastery to become The Christ. It is not limited to him only. It is not limited only to those who call themselves Christian. That is why there are many paths, but only one way. Becoming a master is the one way. It is not just belief in a particular path; it is the action of returning to your true self and eventually achieving ascension that is the one way. The labels attached to the Christ consciousness are many, but the process is about returning to You, the Divine Self within.

In the process of returning to You a change literally begins to take place within your DNA structure. You begin to take on a new physicality. A change begins to take place at the atomic level. You begin to shift into a finer vibration and radiation of your being. You begin to come closer to your higher mental body and to your spiritual DNA structure. You will find that harsh tones, sounds and music will be more unpleasant. You will find that you need to be in a softer tone environment. Sound will influence you more sensitively as you move into a higher atonement and attunement.

Atonement resolves all negative and fear-based emotions and experiences for all time and space. At-one-ment heals you at all levels, so you can experience your higher mental body, vibrate at a higher radiation, and be at one with your, I AM Presence.

As you move into your higher vibration and radiation you begin to more often experience inner peace of mind. You begin to be more centered and become intuitive. You begin to hear the messages, encouragement and guidance continually offered by your spirit guides. You begin to more clearly hear "the still,

Healing and Transformation

small voice within" ever guiding you. Higher-level beings are drawn to you and desire to work with you. Ascended masters stand eagerly and always ready to assist when called upon. Your gifts of spirit return.

With inner balance the trials and tribulations of life are easily faced and calmly dealt with. You are able to quell the raging storm within, and no longer desire to attack another or yourself. Patience readily manifests in your life. You can patiently unravel the "knots" in the emotional body you have created. You begin to come from a sense of deep humility, ready to be of service in the unfolding of your part in the divine plan. You again become a servant of the Most High.

We do have to go through the bitter and forsaken feelings. We do have to go through adversities and challenges. We do go through our own crucifixion, feeling betrayed, facing the painful realities of life. We do have to clear our karmic debt, learn forgiveness and practice grace. We begin to rise in the Light, above earthly conditions and concerns. Others can no longer pull us down.

Externals will not bring peace and harmony within or in your world. It is the return to your divine heritage, long forgotten and misunderstood during the historical period, will bring you peace, happiness, harmony, balance and joy! When we are one with our true Self, we are aligned with divine wisdom, and we co-create a life of higher choice of who we are and who we want to be. With our Creator, in perfect partnership, we manifest peace and harmony in the world. We enter into and participate in the New Golden Age. We go forward with Mother Earth into higher dimensional life, and create a highly evolved civilization.

The choice is yours. This journey, the adventure of a lifetime or lifetimes, awaits you. You can go on to other third dimensional worlds, exercising your free will cautiously, or you can go forward adventurously. You can begin to live your life from increasingly higher thoughts of who you are and who you want to be. It is time to return to You.

Chapter 2
SLOWING DOWN AND GOING WITHIN

How do we go about the process of slowing down and going within? It is certainly easier said than done. We find all kinds of ways and reasons to stay constantly active and busy, never allowing time for contemplation and quiet. The mind abhors a vacuum, so it seems. A constant, never ending dialogue goes on within, making it virtually impossible to stop and experience the great stillness, which allows us to access higher mind and higher thought.

Returning to You, returning to your center of truth, wisdom and love, requires slowing down and taking the time for deep reflection and contemplation. It is getting out of the race, at least for part of the time. It is getting out of the belief in externals. It is saying that the mindless race you are caught up in with the collective no longer serves, and never really has served you. It is saying, "I can live in this illusion of duality without accepting the illusion."

Rather than manifesting unconsciously, you begin to manifest your own reality as you re-align with your divine heritage. It involves taking the time to slow down and become reacquainted with your True Self, the spiritual You having the human experience. You begin to create your life as a masterpiece of joy consciously.

Driving home one evening I witnessed a mother duck frantically trying to revive her six dying babies. They were smashed to the surface of the road, all in a line, as they tried to cross. A commuter, in a rush to get home, and perhaps oblivious to the world around them, did not either see nor care to slow down long enough to spare the mother duck her babies. She frantically ran back and forth, desperately trying to save her family, trying not to get hit herself. How sad, and even unnecessary. We are so busy rushing around and are so unaware, oblivious to the life we share on this planet. On the other hand, we all enjoy photos or video showing a different outcome, with traffic stopped and a person or police officer safely escorting another family safely across the road. In our mad rush we not only harm ourselves, we also harm the life we share on the planet.

Another time coming home I enjoyed a better outcome. Another family was crossing the road. The car in front stopped for no apparent reason. My initial impatience (I have to keep working on patience and slowing down) quickly disappeared as I watched the mother duck lead her babies across the street. The last one struggled awhile to get up on the curb. We all waited patiently for the last one to successfully get across the street.

We are so caught up in the rush and race to accomplish things, and get so caught up in the race itself; we can no longer vacation without being "connected." Needing to be connected we carry pagers, cell phones, and lap top computers, often using these devices at inappropriate times and places, even on vacation. Now the Movie Theater asks us to turn off phones and pagers. Despite the requests, you can still hear phones and pagers at church and even during funerals. I love the story of Al Pacino receiving a standing ovation at a live performance, when he told a patron in the front row to call back later.

Slowing Down and Going Within

We live in a time and culture where faster is better, more is better, and problems are solved with pills and mindless—if not negative and dark—entertainment. Entertainment has become a way of life. Our consciousness is overwhelmed with endless information and sensory stimuli. As a result, even the well-intentioned seeker finds it nearly impossible to quiet the mind and go within. Yet the very process of slowing down and going within is necessary for you to reconnect the True Self, the divine mind within.

Paradoxically, as we begin the process of slowing down and going within, we don't immediately experience the Great Silence that connects us to Eternal Wisdom and Love. As we slow down and begin to re-experience the true Self, endless chatter seems to bubble up even more, especially as we try to meditate. This seeming chatter is the unresolved hurts and pains of the past we need to heal and release.

The chatter is also the ego trying to hold on and be in control, fearing its existence will come to an end as we go back to our true heritage. The unresolved hurts, pains, traumas and emotional scars are the negative "karmic debt," the emotional baggage of all time and space, stored throughout our emotional body, which the ego works hard to keep forgotten and hidden. It is the place of fear.

We buy into cultural demands to stay constantly stimulated and racing to accomplish whatever, so we can avoid hurt and fears. Or, we vigilantly look for the perceived slights and threats from others so we can immediately attack back, especially self-righteously, and still avoid our own hurts and traumas.

However, it is in the releasing of the fear and returning to love, afforded by and facilitated through slowing down and going within, that these old debts are released once and for all. We truly do heal physically, mentally, emotionally, etherically and spiritually. We really do release the emotional and etheric blockages, and purify the emotional body and the etheric body over time. The etheric body is one of the many bodies that simultaneously exist and overlay the physical. It is the etheric body that provides the blueprint, which manifests you at the physical level, as much as your genetic codes, both the physical strand and the spiritual strand. The etheric body provides the blueprint for the physical body.

When you slow down and go within, you once again access your true spiritual heritage. Again you can hear "the still small voice within,' your connection to God through your Higher Self. The St. Germain I AM materials show how we connect from the Higher Self to the physical. The Higher Self animates our physical being while we are alive. Other sources talk about the "silver cord" that connects our physical to the Higher Self. The St. Germain material depicts how this "Magic Presence" operates, picturing our Higher Self as a golden body anywhere between ten and fifty feet above us. Light from the Higher Self connects from its heart center through our physical crown chakra down to the physical heart center. This is our universal connection.

When you allow yourself to slow down and go within, you begin to reconnect consciously to your spiritual body. Once again you can hear as Divine Mind speaks to you and guides you. This wonderful connection is re-experienced, and you "remember" you are a spiritual being having a human experience. Ultimately, as you align your spiritual body with your physical, and gradually overlap the Higher Self within and about your physical self, then ascension occurs. It is the ability to align the spiritual body with the physical body that completes ascension, and mastery is achieved. You become an Ascended Master, conquer death, and no longer participate in the karmic cycle of birth and rebirth, cause and effect.

The first step for slowing down and going within is to make the time for contemplation and quiet. Contemplation is the allowance for reflection and review. It allows the intuitive part of ourselves to speak to us. We need to have alone time, free to think about our life, to think about what is important, and to "know" direction, purpose and mission in life. Time is needed to review how everything is going, consider alternative paths, and decide how we wish to create next who we are and who we want to be. Time for review is absolutely essential for physical, mental, emotional and spiritual growth and attunement. Ultimately, it is in the Silence that we once again connect with our Creator.

Time for quiet contemplation and connection with God is the most important part of this process. We connect with God when we slow down and go within. We become quiet enough to hear "the still, small voice within," the continual Presence with which we are always able to connect.

We can find peace and quiet inside, especially as it becomes more and more difficult to cope with whatever challenges life is presenting to us at the time. Learning to relax and be calm leads to the quietude and peace we seek. Meditation and quiet prayer are tools in this process. Meditation allows God to talk to us. Prayer is us talking to God. Properly understood, prayer isn't endless requests, but rather gratitude and acknowledgement for what is, what is to come, and how it all serves us. Intentional prayer goes a step further, and puts forward a purposeful consciousness asking for the greatest good for all concerned.

Alexia/Alhambra share that meditation is not just a quiet time to sit and daydream, although this is much better than the constant rush to fill our life with endless and often mindless stimulation. Meditation also teaches how to become calm inside and stay calm all the time. It teaches us how to cope with life and its problems and situations, and yet still maintain inner peace and tranquility. As we stay calm and tranquil, learning how to achieve and maintain inner peace, we can then create and extend this calm and peace to the world around us. We can create a world of peace.

When we are constantly busy and active, filling every moment with action and entertainment, there is no time left to think about and contemplate upon what is happening, how life is going, what to do next, and whether what we are doing makes any sense or fits with who we are and who we really want to be. If our time is constantly filled with the seemingly important events and tasks that must be done, there is little or no time left to stop and review where we are and where we want to be. We stay in a state of reaction, rather than taking time to reflect and choose to create our lives in a proactive manner.

Either way we create, either unconsciously or choosing consciously to create our lives. When we choose consciously, we can create our lives as masterpieces of joy. If all our available free time is spent filling our life with the endless pursuits that keep us from knowing ourselves, there is no time left to find out who we are and who we really want to be. We try to believe these endless pursuits will lead to joy and happiness, while avoiding the responsibility of creating consciously. Yet it is full awareness and responsible choosing which leads to the path of joy, meeting life's challenges so that true joy and happiness can emerge.

In the series of books entitled *Conversations With God* by Neale Donald Walsch, a common theme is the continual reminder that we are to experience life so we can discover who we are and who we really want to be. This is a process of experiencing and feeling life and all it has to offer. It is a process, which ultimately leads to choosing higher and higher visions of who we are and who we really want to be. While God repeatedly emphasizes through Neale Donald Walsch the need to experience life, and especially to feel life, there is also the need to stop long enough to contemplate what we are experiencing and feeling. Becoming still and spending time in quiet contemplation, allows reflection upon our experiences, and make choices on how and where to proceed and what to experience next.

Taking time to stop and contemplate life, to go within, requires first and foremost taking time to think and to review. We need "time outs" to embrace what we are experiencing, in the here and now. This is taking time to reflect on what has happened, what is valued, how did we choose, what are the alternatives, and how and what to choose again or next. This includes letting go of the past as needed, to resolve regrets, review goals as needed, all in terms of living in the present moment.

God reminds us in the conversations with Walsch that we continually have the opportunity to choose who we really are and who we want to be. The purpose of life is to create. Created in the image and likeness of God means we are given free will to be part of creation as we create our lives. As we make higher and higher choices in creating, we partner with God in manifesting our part in the divine plan, truly becoming co-creators with God.

As previously shared, life is meant to be joyful. We are meant to create our lives as "masterpieces of joy." Right thought and right action bring us on to the path of joy as we create who we are and who we really want to be from the highest choices we can make. Particularly, this is connecting with our Higher Self, our divine link with our Father/Mother God. Through this connection we create, and in each moment decide and decide again. We don't have to remain entrenched in previous choices; we are free to choose again. We certainly don't need to remain a victim of any part of our past. We have choices on how we react to the events that occur in our lives.

In working with patients about past hurts and traumas, and the dangers of repeating the dysfunction they learned from their parents and others, I remind them they can be "generation busters." They are free to make new choices and don't have to repeat the pathology they learned. Thus, they don't have to re-create their past to heal it. All of us unconsciously hope if we re-create the past, somehow this time it will be magically "cured." This explains in part how the spouse can leave an alcoholic only to find another alcoholic, repeating what it was like to live with an alcoholic parent. The abused child becomes the abusing adult. Whether great or small, the opportunity exists to overcome and to heal the past, not letting the dysfunction continue in their future. Thus the abandoned child who vows to be the nurturing, available parent breaks the pattern of abuse and dysfunction, creating new realities as they choose who they are and who they want to be at the greater level.

In order to understand how the choices we make create who we are and who we want to be in the present moment, we have

Healing and Transformation

to take the time to slow down and go within. This gives us time to discover whether our choices are working for us or not, and whether we simply want to choose again. If we are experiencing negative and fear-based emotions, we are being signaled that other, better choices are available. When depression, anxiety or fears are present, these are signals we have not made the best choices for ourselves. Or they may be a signal our egos wish to remain in control fearing the higher choices Spirit would guide us to make. As we step back and contemplate these feelings, and let Holy Spirit truly guide us as well, we can look at the kinds of choices we have made and whether to decide to choose again. With quiet time, we can truly and fully understand what has been created and which direction we wish to create in next.

Life is the product of our creations, individually and collectively. Together we create the world we live in now. It is our free will that has created the world as it currently is. God did not create our world as it is now; we did it to ourselves. We are totally and completely responsible for our lives. We are totally and completely responsible for our planet.

A student asked his Hindu Master, "How can I be responsible for war when I live a religious life?" The master asked him in return if he harbored any thoughts of anger or resentment. All war begins with the anger and resentment in each one of us. All wars begin with the resentments, angers, jealousies and hatred we carry within. War begins with the attack thoughts we feel justified in having toward one another. War begins in the lack of forgiveness we have toward anyone. War begins when we say we forgive but we will never forget. War begins when we say everyone is forgiven but this one "monster" we judge as unworthy. Jesus showed us that peace begins, when even in the midst of the most terrible things that could be done to anyone, he judged not and asked God to forgive his persecutors for they knew not what they did.

Jesus said that when two or more are gathered in his name, the world could change. When millions meditate for peace at the same time, the world changes dramatically. Many dire prophecies for our time and place have been delayed or modified by the thoughts and prayers of even a few. In peace projects where people go and meditate in troubled places, such as Lebanon, Northern Ireland, or inner city America, dramatic reductions in violence occur. The world can literally change overnight. We can enter the emerging new fourth dimensional world peacefully if we just change our consciousness.

When consciousness reaches a critical mass, change follows easily and readily, hopefully in a loving and positive way. It is inevitable that humanity and Mother Earth now enter fourth dimensional reality. We have the choice to bring this about easily, gently and peacefully if we so choose. If we choose to continue negative, destructive and fearful patterns, the change will still come. The consequences of the later choices are possible catastrophic disasters, natural and human-made. If we do not choose to return to ourselves, Earth changes and other disasters will push us to the point where the return to ourselves will be inevitable anyway. Transformation and ascension are about to occur on a mass basis, either peacefully manifested by us or manifested through mass change, which suddenly pushes the collective consciousness forward. Look at the results of 9/11.

As noted earlier, enough people have meditated for peace and harmony, that love has changed some of the more dire prophecies for global nuclear war and the subsequent nuclear winter. We came very close with our previous consciousness of hatred and fear. Breshnev and the Soviet Union Politburo seriously considered a preemptive nuclear strike on the United States in the 1980's to "win" the Cold War. Of course there would have been no winner in such an action. The same would have also been true if American leaders could have had their way when advocating for a nuclear strike on China or North Korea during that conflict, or Hanoi during the Vietnam conflict.

Taking time to slow down and go within allows for meaningful contemplation to occur. Someone once said that a life examined was worth living. It is worthwhile to examine our life, to look at the choices we have made, the results so far, and what to do next. Life is meant to be proactive, not reactive. As we create our lives as masterpieces of joy, we do so from a proactive posture. There is plenty enough to react to, without always reacting to events and circumstances. The more proactive we can be, the more we create positively and joyfully.

As we slow down and go within we are able, first and foremost, to prioritize our life. Part of being proactive is establishing goals and the order we would like to address them in. Taking time to assess our goals, keeping and changing them as we go along, allows us to take creative control of our life. Contemplation and thought about progress helps us as we advance with our healing and attunement. Personal planners are effective precisely because they facilitate organization and assessment. They are systems designed to create goals, prioritize them, and put them into action. Transforming systems, such as Master Minding, do the very same thing for personal goals and planning. Slowing down and going within affords us the opportunity to create proactively.

Life doesn't always go as planned. In fact, if your life is a lot like mine, it often ends up differently than planned. As we work to heal and transform our lives we need the still time to sort out where we are and where we hope to go next. As we contemplate goals to achieve, already in the process of being achieved, or new ones we hope to achieve, taking time to evaluate and reconsider is absolutely essential. Recognizing that all doesn't go according to plan, and that other life experiences and events may emerge as part of our divine plan, developing patience is important. Patience is one of the general lessons on this planet, and a part of third dimensional reality.

Many of the elders I work with in nursing homes wonder why God won't let them come "home" already, especially when they are dealing with physical disabilities or limitations. Understanding they are still learning patience helps them immensely in coping with why they are still here. Other lessons they may be learning include dealing with a body that doesn't work well, long suffering, learning to be dependent when they have always been independent, and learning to let others help them. They may also still have wisdom and purpose, especially sharing the love they have and the wisdom they have learned.

Even when we are proactive in the creation process, life may not unfold, the way we think it should, nor may it follow the timetable we have in mind. The very processes of slowing down and going within helps us to learn from the process as it unfolds as well as practicing patience. As we get still and learn to listen to our God Connection, we are better able to have our creation be in harmony with Divine Wisdom and our part in the divine plan. With patience, we are better able to understand what the divine plan is, and our part in this magnificent creation process, both individually and collectively. We are then truly able, developing and practicing patience, to more fully partner with God.

Marianne Williamson writes in her book *Enchanted Love* how she began to see more her prayer and meditation times as opportunities to commune with God regarding all, not just some, of the issues she was dealing with in her life. She states that spiritual practice rests on inner stillness, and this stillness is the root of personal power. She tells us that from within this space, we visit the inner temple of God. She describes it as an underground sanctum that exists in all of us because He placed it there. When we pray and meditate, the mind is naturally drawn to its Source. She tells us that there we find strength, serenity, guidance and love. Just spending time there brings love to us. Stillness draws love to us.

Prayer is an important part of this process of slowing down and going within. Prayer is our place where we talk to God. While it can be a place where we give God a long laundry list of what we think we need and want, it really is a place we can go to thank God for what we already have and what is coming to us. He already knows the answer to our prayers, yet sends us the experiences and the opportunities, which are most beneficial to us. While we may ask to win the lottery, She already knows this may be the worst thing that could happen to us. This does not mean we aren't entitled to abundance, but creative thought in harmony with divine understanding brings ample abundance, as we are able to best use it to create and be of service. The prayer that already thanks God for all the good He/She brings allows abundance to come in ways that best serves the creative process and us. As we continue to live by spiritual law and truth, the abundance is already coming, and already acknowledged by prayer.

As we get still and go within, we also use affirmations. Affirmations are a particular form of prayer. This is creation and the right use of mind of the highest magnitude. With this form of prayer we command the universe to bring us our good. The universe always answers. The most powerful affirmations, stated as "I Am…" statements, literally command our God Self to bring us our good. They are effective when spoken at any time, but by the process of slowing down and going within, affirmations become even more powerful prayers.

Sometimes we ask why a prayer was not answered. It is not that prayers are not answered; just the form of the request may not be in our best interest. It may interfere with lessons and experiences we have to go through. It may interfere with our divine plan, or the Divine Plan. Finally, it may produce results that set us back rather than propel us forward.

Prayer is a powerful means of communication with our Creator, particularly as we express gratitude for all that we have, and all that comes to us. As a tool for slowing down and going within, prayer becomes an equally powerful process for becoming still and connecting to All-That-Is. It is a great opportunity to enter the great silence within, allowing for spiritual attunement, and with that facilitating awareness that leads to spiritual growth and soul growth.

Taking time to slow down and go within is not only a process of contemplation and of listening; it is also a time for visualization as well. It is an opportunity to envision who we want to become and what kind of a world we want to live in. We are creative beings. The gift God gave us is to be creators. This is what is meant when we are told we were created in the image and likeness of God. Along the way we "forgot" this, buying into one of the many negative messages our egos give us, that we are unworthy of being considered a god. When Jesus came, as an elder brother, to remind us of this truth, we elevated him to deity status as the "only Son of God" instead of remembering and embracing our creative heritage, which he demonstrated for us, so we would remember we could do this too. As *A Course In Miracles* reminds us, all of us are the Son of God. Jesus tells us in the Course that the Sonship is One. Our heritage and our truth are co-creation.

When we envision who we are and who we want to be, with ever increasing levels of consciousness, we are living and being our true heritage. The time outs we take to go within give us the opportunity to create who we are and who we want to be. As we visualize, imagine or see ourselves, as we want to be, we then create or manifest this in our everyday lives.

Envisioning also gives us the opportunity to create the world the way we would like it to be. Starting with our own goals, in harmony with the divine purpose and mission each of us has at any moment in time, we begin to manifest what we want. This is why affirmations are so powerful. This is why our thoughts are so powerful. If you affirm prosperity and abundance, these will be made manifest. If your thoughts are "I want…" you will get all the want you are asking for. If you think and affirm "I Am…" you will get the creation you affirm.

Beyond our personal mission, purpose and goals, we can also envision the world we want to have become manifest. As each person envisions peace, prosperity, harmony, balance and joy for the world, the world transforms for all. The power of individuals coming together to visualize, imagine and see a world of peace, harmony and joy manifests this process more completely and in a more timely manner. Individually and collectively, we can envision a world in which there is no more war, violence, discord, and where we can agree to disagree while working toward common solutions.

We can envision a world in which everyone's need are met, where there is no more poverty, hunger, starvation, and lack. We can envision a world in which there is no more illness or disease. We can envision a world where differences are celebrated, where it is recognized there are many paths and understandings about God, where ethnic and racial differences are respected and celebrated, and a world where everyone is respected and honored and seen as valuable.

We can envision a world in which life is joyful, and where we all work together to manifest joy for all. We can envision a world in which together we remember our true heritage as spiritual beings having human experiences, working together to gain in knowledge. We can envision a world where there is no fear, and only love rules the hearts and minds of all. We can envision a world in which love creates our relationships with others and with all the other kingdoms on this planet and the planet itself.

We can create positively or negatively. We can create a world based on positive and love-based emotions. We don't have to continue to create a world based on negative and fear-based emotions. We can create our lives based on positive and love-based emotions, rather than on negative and fear-based emotions.

As we get still and go within, creating with and from our partnership with our Higher Self, our God connection, we manifest love, joy and peace in all we do. We return to balance and harmony, and the peace that passes all understanding. As we connect with our intuition, "the still, small voice within" can be heard. When we take the time to slow down and go within on a daily basis, we are truly guided to be and fulfill our divine mission and purpose. We walk the path of joy.

There is a hymn which sums up this process. It goes like this:

> "I release and I let go.
> I let the spirit run my life
> And my heart is open wide.
> Yes, I'm only here for God.
> No more struggle, no more strife.
> With my faith, I see the light.

I am free in the spirit.
Yes, I'm only here for God."

Allow your self to be still and go within. Reconnect to your Higher Wisdom. Make the time on a regular and consistent basis to be reflective and envision your life and the world you want. Return to your true heritage—creation. This is an essential part of returning to You.

Chapter 3
RELINQUISHING THE EGO

The following statement of being from Unity summarizes who we really are. It states:

> GOD IS ALL
> Both invisible and visible.
> One Presence, One Mind, One power is all.
> This One that is all
> Is perfect life, perfect love, and perfect substance.
> I am an individualized expression of God.
> I am ever one with
> This perfect life, perfect love, and perfect substance.

It reminds us we are spiritual beings having a human experience. We are an individualized expression of God and are ever one with our Creator.

However, along the way we created our ego. In the mists of time, as we separated ourselves from God and forgot our divine heritage we created an ego. We did this because fear entered in, and the ego's main purpose is to protect us from fear, hurt, humiliation and embarrassment. With each subsequent incarnation we created another ego to navigate life in third dimensional reality. While the ego protects us from physical harm—we know not to step in front of a car or to touch fire—it also begins to associate other fear experiences with the need for protection.

Our ego is the part of us we most identify with in the midst of the human experience. We come to identify with the ego, forgetting our true, divine nature. A metaphysical interpretation of the "fall from grace" is we began to exclusively identify with the ego, "forgetting" our true heritage. This is essentially what we did. As we became enmeshed in the physical dimensions of reality, we forgot who we truly are. We started to create apart from God's Will. As a result of universal law, we reaped the consequences of this choice; meeting again and again the results of the choice to live by the ego, separate from our God Self. We entered the karmic wheel of birth and rebirths, beginning a journey back home through countless lifetimes. Each lifetime becomes an opportunity to remember who we really are.

Initially, it seems the ego provides a valuable function. Protecting us from dangerous choices one can make in third dimensional reality. The ego came into existence to protect us from harm. It does this through the emotion of fear. Fear of acting in ways that would bring physical harm, the ego prevents us from making damaging choices. Thus, we don't walk off a cliff, put our hand in the fire or walk in front of a car. In this way the ego helps us from the dangers of physical reality.

As a psychological construct, the ego also uses fear to "protect" us from possible psychological harm. As we learn and grow from childhood on, we learn that certain behaviors or thoughts will lead to disapproval from others. We become embarrassed by the reactions of parents, caregivers, family, teachers, neighbors and peers. Anxiety and other negative and fear-based emotions are learned, to protect us from embarrassment and humiliation.

Especially, we are taught early on that intuitive and psychic experiences are not to be believed. We better not let anyone know that our imaginary friend is an Angel or other-dimensional being we can still see and hear, because we are taught to disregard these experiences as not valid or real. The ego becomes more vigilant and more powerful, seeking to protect us from potential harm of the belief in other realities.

When traumatic events do occur in our lives, the ego strives to protect us from the hurt and pain of those events. Employing a wide variety of defenses, the original trauma is diminished or forgotten, replaced by patterns of behavior removed from the original anxiety. These dysfunctional patterns protect us from the original hurt, but also try to "work out" the negative and fear based emotions in disguised but disruptive ways. We get far away from the injury, yet are left with a sense of unease in life at best. Worse, we become involved in avoidance through destructive behaviors such as addictions, food abuse, sexual acting out, or consuming behaviors that distance us from others while supposedly keeping us safe. When these behaviors are rewarded in some way, we are powerfully reinforced to stay in the dysfunction. Thus, the workaholic who is very successful in business and reaps financial success along the way, is rewarded to stay away from intimacy or the original fears and anxieties left unresolved within him.

In psychodynamic theories of psychology and personality development and functioning, the ego becomes a compromise between the Id, which is the primitive, unconscious mind and the Super Ego, which is the internalized consciousness learned from parents and others. Often, the ego is at best a compromise between the internal tensions produced by the endless conflict to contain and control unacceptable impulses on the one hand, and the sometimes rigid and harsh demands of an internalized conscience that demands adherence to a strict moral code or belief system on the other hand.

Most of us manage to develop somewhat healthy egos that help us manage the psychological and emotional pitfalls of everyday life. "Healthy" ego functioning is even necessary as a foundation on which the process of self-actualizing can take place. First studied by Abraham Maslow, self-actualizing is the process of growth and development that leads to higher and higher functioning psychologically. It is also a good foundation for spiritual growth and development, especially as higher states of consciousness begin to be accessed. When these higher states of consciousness are accessed without healthy ego functioning, psychological and spiritual emergencies can occur, often imitating psychotic breaks from reality.

The process of self-actualizing provides direction to personality functioning. It is a model of growth in which personality functioning is always moving toward higher states of integration and the development of the human potential within each person. The assumption is there is only one great force of direction and growth in life. Life is a progressively greater expression of this force, an unfolding process. With self-actualizing, this force has a tendency to express, to an even greater degree, the capabilities, potentialities or talents based on one's genetic constitution. All potentialities of humankind are in the service of the maintenance and enhancement of life. For Maslow, this force is the push toward actualizing our inherent potentialities. This insures the development of self-concept. The push to satisfy needs ensuring physical and psychological survival is part of this force to personality development and functioning.

In his classic study, Maslow examined healthy living by means of biographical examples. He studied exceptionally healthy, mature people. From this, Maslow found several characteristics of self-actualizing people. The first characteristic is the more efficient perception of reality and having more comfortable relations with reality. This is followed by an acceptance of reality as it is and not as they would prefer it to be. Next, self-actualizing people are relatively spontaneous in behavior, and far more spontaneous than that in their inner life, thoughts and impulses. He found their behavior to be marked by simplicity and naturalness, by lack of artificiality or straining of effect. In general, Maslow found his subjects to be strongly focused on problems outside themselves. They are problem centered, rather than ego-centered. Another characteristic is a quality of detachment, such that they can be solitary without harm to themselves and without discomfort. They can be alone without being lonely.

Self-actualizing individuals are relatively independent of the physical and social environment. They are dependent on their own development and continued growth of their own potentialities and latent resources. They have a continued freshness of appreciation. They have mystical experiences he called "peak" experiences. They have positive, empathic feelings for others. Ultimately, this lays a foundation for an even deeper level of love manifesting as compassion.

Self-actualizing individuals have deeper and more profound interpersonal relationships. At the same time they are democratic people in the deepest sense. They have a strong ethical sense and value system. They honor their own "inner, Supreme Court," possessing, a philosophical un-hostile sense of humor. They have a universal characteristic for a special kind of creativeness, originality or inventiveness. Finally, they resist enculturation. They can be part of the ethnic heritage or social group and yet independent of it.

At the same time self-actualizing individuals showed many of the lesser human failings, such as silly, wasteful or thoughtless habits. By no means are they perfect.

More recently in psychological theory there emerged the idea that ego not only can be increasingly healthy, but that in higher levels of functioning it can be transcended. The transpersonal model of personality development sees the striving for heightened levels of functioning leading back to spiritual awareness and development. Seeing beyond the ego, into larger dimensions of consciousness and perception. Thus, spirituality becomes part of psychology again. Since psychology was originally the study of the "soul" we now come back full circle to the original intent of the study of psychology.

While useful as a psychological construct, the ego prevents a larger spiritual construct to emerge. In this context ego represents the part of us that goes against our true spiritual nature. As spiritual beings having a human experience, we "forget" our true heritage as the ego comes into existence and demands our attention and allegiance. The ego sets itself up against our true heritage. Worse yet, having rejected our spiritual nature, it seizes upon fear to define who we are and who we want to be.

The "fall from grace" was our collective decision to forget who we really are and instead live by the negative and fear-based reality we created in place of a positive and love-based reality. We decided to Edge God Out as we bought into fear, embarrassment and humiliation. We then went a step further, and said with our egos, that God must be a fearful and judgmental being who is ready to punish us for rebelling against him.

Having recreated God in our own, ego image, we have made God a fearsome being and ourselves as worthless sinners. We then distorted the teaching of wise teachers sent to us by God, creating religions with nearly impossible rules to follow to achieve a heavenly state. Religions and their theologies took the love-based teachings of these masters and made them into fear-based systems demanding allegiance to a fear-based God. If you follow all the rules, at best you may make it to heaven. Otherwise, forget it.

Then these ego-based structures go a step further and claim they are the only path to God. Thus, in an immense universe with billions of galaxies and four billion stars in each galaxy, on one relatively minor planet, God "revealed" the only way back home to one group of billions of souls. Further we are only talking about the physical universe we are aware of, let alone other universes and other dimensions of reality.

The ego is fear-based. It is the opposite of love, even though it will adopt a loving attitude for a time. Based on fear, the ego believes you are always going to be attacked, and thus suffer humiliation, guilt, blame or shame. The ego is ever vigilant for the attack it is convinced will occur. The ego instructs you to be on guard, and ever vigilant for the harm that will inevitably be directed toward you by others. Often this will be the case because others' egos are ready and vigilant to guard against attack by attacking you.

Worse yet, the ego is at war with you, ever vigilantly scanning your own thoughts and feelings for any hint you may reject it, or try living in another way. Thus, the ego is just as ready to attack any part of you that doesn't agree with it or feels threatened by it.

The main mode of operation for the ego is always attack. It is to get back at whomever causes possible fear, humiliation or embarrassment. It is also ready to attack anyone or any idea, which challenges its right to be in complete control of your life, your thoughts and your perceptions. The ego justifies attack to protect your "integrity." Every perceived threat is pounced upon, often in dramatic fashion. Although this can be cleverly disguised to not seem to be attacking or to appear justified within the accepted thought system in the world in which you live.

This can be particularly insidious when group prejudice or belief justifies the attack on your enemies. It then becomes easy to say that another is unworthy because of their behavior or affiliation. Thus, you can attack others for their ethnicity, gender, nationality, race or religious affiliation. Certain groups within a culture get singled out as scapegoats as well, such as homosexuals in America. So individuals frightened by their own potential to even have thoughts about having sex with a same sex partner, justify attacking gay and lesbian people and attributing all kinds of false beliefs about them, such as they want to molest children.

From the ego perspective, anyone who violates societal rules and engages in criminal conduct is deserving of attack, to be incarcerated and to do hard time. Murderers are to receive the ultimate attack, to be killed for taking a life. Justification

Relinquishing the Ego

for this even comes from the Bible, which says an eye for an eye is justice. Never mind the Master Teacher came along and suggested a more enlightened approach— based on love.

Interestingly, societal rules change from moment to moment. Sometimes a whole society may be "insane," such as Nazi Germany. Jesus demonstrated the courage it takes to go against the societal and religious rules of his day, to demonstrate what spiritual love and "law" truly is. In *Conversations With God,* God suggests the Ten Commandments become the Ten Commitments when the spiritual path is naturally followed.

The most extreme form of fear is anger and hatred. Again, the ego justifies these emotions as legitimate and to be acted upon. Themes of revenge are particularly part of ego belief. Movies in which the "hero" gets revenge on those who harm him are particularly popular. Vengeance is an important ego belief. The ego even distorts God to be a judgmental and vindictive God.

The power of anger and vengeance as vehicles for attack cannot be under estimated. Even the slogan "I don't mad, I get even" summarizes the belief perpetrated by the ego that attack is always justified. Who does not, when angered, want to get revenge? However, when someone goes too far, we are appalled they acted on fear and anger to the extent they did. Yet any one of us is capable of acting with extreme vengeance if our ego justifies it in our mind. Tragedies such as school shootings or disgruntled employees shooting up the work place, or terrorists are simply the more extreme responses the ego is capable of leading us to. On a national scale, hatred for the Jews could allow the egos of the Germans to justify horrible actions against others. Our collective egos in America, at times, have argued for "nuking" those we disagreed with at the time.

Ultimately, the ego fights to stay in control of your life by cleverly arguing that you are a worthless sinner who rejected God during the fall from grace. You better not take any chance on rejecting the ego, because then all you will be left with is

Healing and Transformation

God, and boy is he ever going to get you for misusing your free will.

The paradox here is that God doesn't punish us for our so-called sins. We are allowed free will in a cause and effect dimensional reality. We then get to experience the effects of our choices. We create our own consequences, positive and negative. We live in a lawful universe, and truly what goes around comes around. We create our reality and we collectively create our world.

While I am citing dramatic examples of the justified destructiveness of the ego based on fear, it is the subtle forms in which the ego attacks and seeks to preempt the expected attack from others that operates most of the time. Control dramas are one of many ways the ego looks to be in control of every situation and to guard against fear and possible attack from others. These manipulative systems of ego operation, learned from our parents and other significant people in our life, lead to ways in which we can control our life and protect ourselves from others' control dramas. There are many ways to describe these patterns of control. One of the better examples is James Redfield's outline of four basic dramas found in *The Celestine Prophecy*. He calls these dramas the "intimidator," the "poor me" or victim, the "aloof," and the "interrogator." Each of these dramas is a way to control others and to take energy from others without having to relinquish any of their own energy.

The ego is created out of fear and operates out of fear. Control dramas or manipulative styles arise from fear—fear of humiliation, fear of embarrassment, fear of attack, fear of hurt, and fear of pain. Essentially, the ego is very judgmental, constantly scanning the world looking for potential harm and embarrassment, ready to react and to defend from this potential harm. Judgment is the constant way the ego operates in the world. Ever vigilant, the ego judges everyone and every thing, even itself.

Judgment is not to be confused with discernment. Discernment is the process of evaluating and responding to the world

Relinquishing the Ego

about us from love and compassion. It may say that a certain behavior, action or thought does not reflect our highest good of who we are and who we want to be. It may say that an option is not a choice you wish to make. However, it is not a value-laden conclusion based on negative and fear-based emotions. Discernment is an honest attempt to evaluate a situation and the potential harm that may exist without being judgmental or condemning. Thus, we may say that a serial killer is dangerous, very distorted in their thought process and needs to be locked away to protect the rest of us. Or, the spouse may say to the alcoholic that they love them and want them to get help, but will no longer live with their destructive behavior or be enabling to help perpetuate that destructive behavior.

The ego constantly judges, usually in a condemning manner. It fully justifies this judgment in a self-righteous manner. How dare someone else say or do those things to us? Anticipating the worst, the ego judges, based on past experience, and is ready to respond in kind. The response is always one of attack. Getting back at another for real or perceived harm is what the ego is all about. The ego simply can't comprehend loving others or "turning the other cheek." According to the ego, only a fool allows himself or herself to be harmed without getting retribution for what was done to them.

Everything and anything is judged by the ego. Ultimately, even the person themselves is judged by the ego. We often become our own worst critic, harboring for a lifetime regrets and remorse for behavior and thought that wasn't worthy of who we truly are. We often have the most difficulty forgiving ourselves. And the ego constantly reminds us of how unworthy we really are. So much of negative self-esteem is tied up in our own self-condemnation and ultimately our own self-loathing.

The ego would rather have us be miserable and feel unworthy, than begin to experience the possibility of who we really are and who we are meant to be. When we begin to contemplate and even become slightly aware of our own true, "divine" heritage, the ego steps up its attack on others and ourselves. We put onto others our own unworthy thoughts and feelings, motivation and agendas, and say how awful it is that they think and feel this way. The ego fights hard when we attempt to heal and then relinquish its importance in our lives, often in the subtlest ways.

One of the ways I continue to struggle with this is when I am driving. Almost unconsciously, I find myself in a continual dialogue about what other drivers are doing wrong. As I try to be more consciously aware of these thoughts I am amazed how much time and energy I devote to judging others and finding fault for their "poor" driving habits. I find myself irritated and annoyed at the person who won't turn right quickly enough on a red light when traffic clears. Further, I think how selfish and inconsiderate they are for other drivers, especially me! Yet, what is my big hurry and who am I to worry, much less judge, how they are doing with their driving? What is wrong with my own impatience and my need to have everyone drive the way I think they should drive? What unnecessary stress do I put myself through in my judgments about another? Finally, what is the fault I perceive in the other that is really my own fear based emotion and perception?

Whole systems of thought, such as the control dramas or manipulative styles, develop out of the need to judge others. The more limited the ego functions, based on the traumas we all experience with and from others, the more the ego operates in dysfunctional patterns. Growing up in toxic environments, whether they be poverty, ghetto-like communities, alcoholic and drug abusing families or abusive families, further adds to the pathological ways ego functions in the world. At its worst, fearful experiences lead to the development of mental health and personality disorder problems, with an ego that functions in a very constricted manner.

Despite the many traumas that fear creates in our lives, most of us are able to overcome these events and are able to strive to more healthy ways of ego functioning in the world. Increasingly, as we heal the ego, we are able to move more and more into the self-actualizing state of awareness and personality functioning Maslow studied and shared with the world.

Relinquishing the Ego

How is the ego healed? By releasing the negative and fear-based emotions that arise from the traumatic emotional events we all experience. Not only is it releasing the negative and fear-based emotions that arise in our formative years, but also the ongoing traumas we experience as adults. It may seem that the word trauma is a strong word to use here, but to the ego every hurt and slight, no matter how minute, is traumatic to the ego.

To add insult to injury, the ego creates its own trauma by constantly judging the present based on the past. It often projects, or "puts on to," the other person or event the hurt and pain of previous experience. The judgment is that the same thing is happening over again, even if to an independent observer there is no connection between the events and what the ego concluded took place. Convinced that pain is coming or that the other is attacking, the ego readily interprets everything based on past events and not necessarily what is taking place now.

Complicating this even further, based on the ego system we develop to protect ourselves, we unconsciously choose over and over again to put ourselves in similar situations. We hope that somehow this time we will get it right and be healed without any effort to change how our ego operates. We certainly never have to look to relinquish the ego.

Often the ego reacts with various versions of anger. This is what fuels attack, whether overt and obvious or covert and passive. Beneath anger is always hurt. To protect ourselves from even recognizing the hurt beneath, we stay with the anger and ways to get back at the person who hurt us. Even the driver, who cuts us off in a reckless manner, producing an angry reaction in us, has hurt us at a deeper level. At the deeper level, this person is saying they don't care or don't consider that they could physically hurt us. Our anger is that they consider our safety and well being unimportant as they rush to whatever they see as important for them.

The ego is born of fear. It is born of our separation from who we really are. It even convinces us there is a judgmental

Healing and Transformation

God ready to punish us for violating His laws and misusing our free will. Feeling guilty for choosing without God, the ego says we are better off with out it, because if we choose to let our Higher Self be in charge of our life again, we are really going to get it. The ego offers an out by saying if we follow this or that fear-based religious system, we will get to heaven without the need to learn and be love.

The Christian faiths have even taken Jesus' example for us and said we really cannot do that; only he could because he was really a Deity, the "only" Son of God. So the ego says it is okay to follow this or that fear-based system, rather than heal and ultimately release the ego by learning to do as Jesus and every other master teacher taught and lived—to be love.

Following external systems will not get you back to You. Learning to operate from positive and love-based emotions will get you back to You. To do this we do have to begin with healing the ego. Psychotherapy is one place this can occur. Certainly, self help books give tremendous guidance in healing the ego. The many religious retreats, healing seminars and spiritual growth groups also guide the process of healing the ego. Mediation and prayer, reconnecting to the God Power within also helps with the healing of the ego.

While the work of healing the ego is important as an initial step and is necessary to prepare for the larger work of expanding conscious awareness, the ultimate goal is to relinquish the ego. *A Course in Miracles* states that the ego is suspicious at best and vicious at worst. It is dedicated to chaos by seeking to judge and then blame others, to always find fault and to attack-attack-attack. Part of the process of returning to You is to relinquish the ego's control of your mind, your thoughts, your actions and your life. It may have a limited role of protection for a very short while, until you let your Higher Self and Holy Spirit have total charge of your life.

When I first started to write this book I wanted this chapter to be about healing the ego. While healing the ego may be part of the process of getting to the point where it is no longer needed or desired to be in control of your life, the truth is the

Relinquishing the Ego

ego must be relinquished. True spiritual freedom, healing at every level and between bodies, can only occur when we consciously choose to release and let go of ego-dominated thinking and doing. To return to You, the ego has to be relinquished. The choice has to be made to let go of the ego. Letting go and letting God is relinquishing the ego. We allow ourselves to align with the greater wisdom within, to the part of ourselves that is always and eternally connected to God. The return to You is made possible as healing takes place, leading to the moment when you decide you no longer need or want the ego to be in control of you. The ego is ultimately the attachment to separation, rebellion, judgment and fear.

Relinquishing the ego allows us to return to love. Returning to love becomes the focus of your being. It is allowing positive and love-based emotions to take control of your life. It is truly healing all the wounds, relinquishing the negative and fear-based emotions attached to those wounds, and allowing forgiveness to truly take place. It does release the negative and fear-based emotions within. It does release the emotional blocks at all levels that prevent energy from moving freely, between and within, all bodies and levels of being. Freely moving energy is what allows miracles to occur.

As we relinquish the ego, self-healing and self-attunement once again occur. As we let go of judgment, the need to blame and all the ways we have learned to attack and be separate from others, healing takes place at all levels. Love becomes our way of being in the world. This is the heritage we relinquished long ago when we became caught up in and then trapped in the world of physicality and three-dimensional being. The ascension process begins with releasing the ego and returning to where we belong—to love.

In the *Medicine Cards* from Native American tradition the Deer represents gentleness, in the legend from this tradition. One day Fawn heard Great Spirit calling to her from atop Sacred Mountain. She immediately starts up the trail; not knowing a horrible demon guards the way. The demon (fear) was trying to keep all of the beings of creation from connecting

Healing and Transformation

with Great Spirit. He wanted all of Great Spirit's creatures to feel that Great Spirit didn't want to be disturbed. This would make the demon feel powerful and causing all to fear him.

Fawn was not at all frightened. This was curious, as the demon was the archetype of all the ugly monsters that have ever been. The demon breathed fire and smoke and made disgusting sounds to frighten Fawn. Any normal creature would have fled or died on the spot. However, Fawn said gently to the demon, "Please let me pass. I'm on the way to see the Great Spirit."

Fawn's eyes were filled with love and compassion for this oversized bully of a demon. The demon was astounded by the Fawn's lack of fear. No matter how he tried, he could not frighten Fawn. Her love had penetrated his hardened, ugly heart.

Much to Demon's dismay, his rock-heart heart began to melt, and his body shrank to the size of a walnut. Fawn's persistent love and gentleness had caused the meltdown of the demon. Due to this gentleness and caring, the pathway was cleared for all of Great Spirit's children to reach Sacred Mountain.

Deer teaches us to use the power of gentleness to touch the hearts and minds of wounded beings, ourselves included, who are trying to keep us from Sacred Mountain. Like the spots in Fawn's coat, both the light and the dark must be loved to create gentleness and safety for those who are seeking peace.

Love is the gentleness of spirit that heals all our wounds. Ego wants to change others and demands we push hard to make this happen. Instead we are to love them as they are. With love guiding us, we can apply gentleness to our present situation. We become warm and caring. Serenity and the peace that passes all understanding enter into our lives. Love will always truly guide us.

As we relinquish the ego and allow love to guide our lives, there comes a willingness to serve. There comes a willingness to learn. There comes a willingness to gently transform our lives, giving others the chance to transform their lives and to see all as one. For we are all one.

Relinquishing the Ego

Relinquishing the ego allows the human personality to cooperate with its soul through willingness and understanding. It is also about respecting the rights of others. In, *New Teachings For an Awakening Humanity*, The Christ tells us the personality is not to do just as it wishes. He says, "When an adult is asked to surrender to God it does not mean to become a vegetable without purpose or goals. It means that the little human personality becomes viable and useful to the soul without the fears and anxieties, guilts, and uncertainties that plague an individual's habits—habits created by those early conditionings and personality tendencies."

As we relinquish the ego, we allow love, gentleness, tenderness, and our greater wisdom to come forth and manifest in our lives. We become open to hear our Greater Self and Holy Spirit to guide us. We can hear the answer to the question, "What would love do?" We begin the journey back home. You begin the journey back to You.

Chapter 4
HEALING AT ALL LEVELS

We are composed of many bodies. Healing and transformation does encompass these many bodies. We assume there is only the physical body because it seems this is the only body we are aware of as we live in this world. Coming into a world of three-dimensional reality, we assume we are the sum of the physical body we experience ourselves in. Relying on the five physical senses, we conclude this is all we are.

As our intuitive side develops we begin to grasp a larger reality exists. Yet it is easy to believe only the physical, as we sense it is "real." Science suggests larger realities beyond our normal sensory comprehension, but since these are detected by instrumentation that relies on the physical senses, we still conclude this is the only reality. However, our scientific instruments do comprehend a larger realm of being. We can only infer by these instruments and their measurements the extent of reality. As science advances the extent of reality broadens even more.

As the world already begins to shift into fourth dimensional reality, there is increasing recognition even greater realities may exist. Certainly many religious traditions imply there are greater dimensions of existence than are accepted by the limitations of third dimensional perception. Altered states of consciousness also suggest larger realities exist. When people experience so-called "psychic" phenomena, they begin to grasp the larger possibilities of existence.

Psychic is a limited explanation of the greater abilities all are capable of as we grow in spiritual wisdom and open to greater conscious awareness. New Thought Christianity explores and accepts the larger perception and truth of how complex, rich, varied, and multidimensional life is within the Supreme Intelligence and Mind that is our Father-Mother God. Metaphysics certainly explores the larger realms of existence we simultaneously live and operate in, as well as the scope of all creation and the possibilities of where we are and where we may go as we return to our true Self. The various mystery schools, and the process of mysticism, also present the vast multi-dimensional realities that exist.

Interestingly, physics is increasingly saying the same things about "reality" that metaphysics has been stating for some time. The truth is what seems to be supernatural, miraculous, or beyond physics, is in reality laws of understanding yet to be discovered and explained by our science.

What is called psychic is what I prefer to call "the gifts of Spirit." The natural abilities we all have that increasingly emerge as we grow spiritually. These are the gifts that occupy the 90% of the brain we don't seem to use. These are telepathy, clairvoyance, clairaudience, "déjà vu" experiences, lucid dreaming, telekinesis, and prophecy to name just a few.

More and more we are coming to the understanding we are spiritual beings having a human experience. We are beginning to conceive and believe there is more to us than the seeming physicality of third dimensional reality. The density, which humanity has found itself trapped in resulted when we allowed ourselves to choose to separate ourselves from the Creator and decided we could create on our own without divine guidance and direction.

We became trapped in the wheel of life, of cause and effect, having to learn and experience over and over again the consequences of our creations. What we put out in thought and action is returned to us. Even nature reflects back to us our miss-creation for anger, revenge, discord and disharmony. This miss-creation is returned to us in storms and cataclysmic events, ultimately restoring Mother Earth and Nature back to their pristine, pure states. Think of the balance that is lacking in the world now; especially as we cling to the old thought systems of the ego, rather than let love guide all our actions.

When we refuse to forgive and to not see the God Self in others, we create disharmony. When we focus on judgment and condemnation of the surface, fear-based behaviors of others, not only do we create disharmony and discord in human affairs, but also in the world about us as well.

As noted in the preceding chapter, the ego is the fear based and motivated way of being that keeps us separate. It keeps us separate from each other, the world and all its kingdoms about us, from the higher dimensions and all the beings that reside there, and from our own Higher Self—our direct connection with God. There are at least seven spheres of existence. There are at least twelve dimensions of existence.

The ego has no interest in these larger realities. It continually tries to convince us that all that exists is the three-dimensional world we live in as the physical universe. From even the next sphere that encompasses the entire universe we live in, as immense as our universe is, looks but like a mere speck as one looks back and down upon it. Of course the ego argues this is all nonsense. Nothing exists unless it can be experienced only by a physical body, and by the five senses that allow us to perceive physical dimensions of reality. Yet Helen Keller, with only two senses, could remarkably perceive three-dimensional reality. She could also perceive beyond third dimensional reality. The ego continually fights to preserve a world of limitation and lack, to argue, "show me." Yet even when three-dimensional reality suggests larger truths, the ego fights to say we misperceived or misunderstood the data.

Perception is necessary to even make sense of the data streaming in at all times from the five senses. Discrimination is learned, based upon the combined agreement of everyone, with only "accepted" ideas allowed. The history of science is replete with phenomena and data that could not be identified and accepted until the *zeitgeist* of the time was ready for acceptance.

Studies that showed visualizations of healthy tissue in place of cancerous tissue could cure cancer, could not even be published until we were all ready to experience this could happen. Researchers were reluctant to publish such findings for fear of ridicule and being discredited until we were collectively ready to hear data supporting this.

While I was in graduate school, one of my professors shared the pioneering work he and a physician were doing with visualizing cancer disappearing with terminally diagnosed patients. This was in the mid 1970's. He shared; they didn't dare publish the astounding results they were getting. Ironically, the mother of a resident of the group home I worked at was one of the subjects. She shared how her liver cancer was in complete remission using the methods of visualization she was taught in one of the studies.

When collective egos are ready to accept new information, it is always within a context in which the ego can accept this larger truth and incorporate it in its own deceitful web of fear and judgment. A tragic outcome of this process of ego deceit has been people blaming themselves for developing their cancer or their inability to cure it through visualization or alternative means. However the cancer may be the experience that soul needs for its growth and development regardless of the seeming miraculous ways it disappears in others. Or, the cancer may be the way that person is to exit this physical incarnation and go on to the next dimension. We have to be very careful of the judgment we assign to our experiences as well as the experiences of the other. We don't always know the larger wisdom or divine plan at work in each situation.

As we learn to transcend the ego, and live more and more from a love-based center of ourselves, the more we can experience, directly and indirectly, that other bodies and levels of existence are there. Already we are moving as a species and a planet into the early levels of fourth dimensional reality. There is still physicality, but it is more fluid and subject to the manifestation of mind. That is why time now seems to speed up. Yet, at other times we feel like what must have been a longer period of time turned out to be only minutes.

We retain physicality in fourth, fifth and sixth dimensional reality. What changes is an increase in radiation and vibration so that at each level we are no longer perceived, or as easily perceived, at the next lower levels. Yet, a sixth dimensional being is just as real and tangible as you are at upper third dimensional, lower fourth dimensional reality. A sixth dimensional being may be in the room with you and just as real as you are, but you can't see them with your lower five senses.

Often, as conscious awareness expands, we begin to sense the presence of these beings, even though we can't literally see them. At the fifth and sixth dimensional levels we have a physical-etheric body. It is a body that vibrates at a higher frequency than the third dimensional, or even the fourth dimensional level.

As we progress into higher dimensional realities, humanity will become a physical-etheric species. Humanity returns to the original blueprint for existence on this planet, known as Adam Kadmon. It is a body that is physical-etheric, in which all 24 strands of DNA are activated, filled with light and fully operational. By point of reference, currently humanity has only two strands of DNA activated. In these two strands, only some of the twelve levels within each strand are activated. Full DNA activation allows for all the gifts, especially spiritual gifts, we are capable of manifesting to come forward.

Adam Kadmon is the original divine blueprint for the human body and for humanity to exist on this planet. With the collective choice to begin creating without remembering the connection to God, humanity became trapped in physicality and more dense physicality emerged over time. So-called "original sin" was the decision to create without co-creation with God. As a result, humanity became further enmeshed in the lower vibrations of existence, ultimately trapped in the third dimensional body and limited sensory perception currently in operation for most of us.

With this increased separation from our true self and our divine heritage, we also became enmeshed in the karmic wheel of life, and could only leave and enter a physical body through the process of birth and death. Having lost our connection of who we really are, we became separated from our Higher Self, the You to which we wish to return.

As we became enmeshed in the cause and effect reality, the wounds, emotional scars and traumas we experienced along the way became part of the emotional body. Ultimately they became part of the seed atoms of each incarnation, bringing forward the unresolved issues we have yet to work on or resolve. As we clear out our emotional, mental and physical bodies, we resolve for all time and space, the negative karmic debt we have accumulated. We also resolve any blockage or darkness in any body, allowing ourselves to heal at all levels. Gradually we begin the process of ascension in earnest.

With increased physicality and becoming limited in denser physicality, strands of DNA were no longer activated. In choosing to create without God, still retaining full spiritual gifts, the capacity for miracles, would have led to even greater miss-creation and desecration. Look what we have already managed to create with our limited awareness and limited uses of spiritual gifts. We can already see the dangers when gifts of spirit are used for darkness rather than light. However, those who choose to miscreate at this level only harm themselves. The law of cause and effect is not suspended and harm returns to the person sending it out.

Imagine the destructive impulses the ego creates out of its own system of attack and revenge, linked with a vastly more powerful mind, misguided by the loss of co-creation with the Higher Self. I suspect atomic and biological weapons would be child's play compared to the havoc we could create. I suspect we would have already brought on cataclysmic change or created such a consequence for ourselves collectively we would be mourning for billions of years the consequences we would have brought upon ourselves.

There was a planet in this solar system that did just this. Where the Asteroid belt is now was once the planet Maldek. They took the path of miss-creation, ultimately blowing them selves up. Since life is abundant at higher dimensional levels, not only did they harm themselves, they also harmed others in the universe. Since that catastrophe, the misuse of free will, collectively, has never been allowed. That is part of the reason this planet has been quarantined from the other planets in the galaxy.

It is also why the Pleiadian fleet and the Ashtar Command stand by to assist us if we go too far, as well as keep the energy grid of the planet in place from the destruction we would have otherwise already caused it. While we have come close to being more destructive, there will be an intervention that prevents us destroying this planet. Mother Earth herself will bring on cataclysmic change if we don't begin the journey back to our true Self, and bring as many along as we can.

Those born before 1975 came in on what is known as the fifth root race of humans. Since then, the majority coming in has come in on the "indigo blue ray" and they are the sixth root race humans. They are here to change the world. They do not function in the same way as the preceding humans. They are not interested in or bound to the same old ways of doing things. Already their presence is impacting schools and the work place. Aware teachers are changing the way they structure the classroom. Many places of employment are implementing flexible schedules or paying for production, not just time spent on the job. They have literally come in to change the world and the structure of human society.

The seventh root race is Adam Kadmon, the original human. As the world increases in energy and vibration, as the light intensifies and grows, the seventh root race will emerge. In a very short time, the new human will return. This is what the return to You is all about. As we increase in radiation and

Healing at All Levels

vibration and progress from third to fourth to fifth dimensional existences, we return to Adam Kadmon, the divine human. The balance of spirit and physical returns as we return to our true Self. Currently we have over-emphasized the physical and nearly forgotten the spiritual part of ourselves.

Fortunately, the technology to achieve Adam Kadmon is now given to us once again. It has always been there in the teachings of the mystery schools, especially in the Kabbalah. The teachings of Jesus demonstrate this. His life demonstrated how to achieve this. Living in pure love, unconditionally applied to all, with forgiveness for everyone is the path that leads to the divine human and the ascension process. It is misunderstood that Jesus suffered on the cross. He had such love for all, even his persecutors and the forces of darkness; he could easily overcome the physical. The point of his death was not the crucifixion but the resurrection!

Humanity has begun the shift to a higher vibration existence, as has the planet itself. Already the planet has moved into lower level fourth dimensional reality. Some of humanity has fully moved into fourth dimensional reality. In the more advanced countries of the world, lower levels of fourth dimensional reality is where people are functioning. This is, in part, why there is renewed interest in spiritual growth and development, and why so-called new age interests have emerged. We are returning to another Golden Age, as has existed on this planet before. What is coming, hopefully as peacefully and as gently as we can choose it to be, is indeed a New Golden Age. The thousand years of peace Jesus and many other prophets have predicted.

The road to this destination begins with understanding the various bodies we have and how to return them to balance. It is about understanding and healing the wounds that trap energy in the various bodies and how to bring about balance so the energies in the various bodies can flow freely between them. There are membranes that separate the various bodies. Wounds left unhealed turn these membranes into barriers AND prevent the free flow of energy between these bodies. This leads to limitation and lack, experienced by all.

The increased vibration and light coming onto the planet further aggravates this bound-up energy, intensifying the damage these unresolved wounds do to our ability to be creative and fully functional. This also intensifies the fear and can lead to increasing insanity, as the light increases the vibration to which we are all exposed. Without a freeing of this energy, increased distress and occasional tragedies come about. The increase in violence and destructive acts are partly related to the inability of some to handle the increased light, radiation and vibration we are all now experiencing. Thus we have random acts of violence, increased conflict where long-standing grievances have not been resolved, and hateful confrontations within families.

This is continuing to intensify as Photon Belt energy bathes the planet as well. The increased light and radiation is part of the transitional process initiating us into higher dimensional awareness and functioning. The movement to fourth and then fifth dimensional reality is occurring.

Releasing the density in the various bodies becomes part of the process of healing and transformation. In doing so, we create our light body which allows us to move forward into the higher dimensional frequencies coming in at this time. As we are inundated by the greater light energy coming in to the planet, healing becomes necessary to absorb this light and to remove the dark spaces in the various bodies. If we remain in the darkness and our chakras remain closed, we have difficulty assimilating the light and releasing the density. The transformation emerges as we move the energy through ourselves and hold that energy within our various bodies.

As we assimilate more energy and freely move it between the bodies, we can focus on joy and higher consciousness. We experience bliss and higher wisdom. If we stay closed, with pockets of darkness in the bodies and unable to assimilate the light coming in, fear is intensified, and turmoil and chaos are experienced.

Healing at All Levels

Healing the wounds that bind energy and prevent advancement easily and readily to higher dimensional realties is now a necessity. Without this healing and freeing of energies which are trapped by old wounds and traumas, you will not be able to advance with the planet and the part of humanity that goes forward into Adam Kadmon.

This requires an active and proactive approach to your own healing and transformation. Belief in a religious ideal will not get you there. Simply proclaiming a belief in a particular religious figure and following external rules and structure will not get you there. You have to live the spirit of the law, not just follow the law to get there. Your have to begin the journey back to You, to literally transform yourself. Healing the wounds, releasing the past, and freeing the energy between the bodies are a vital step in this process.

There is a physical body that we live in and function with in third, and now early fourth, dimensional reality. In addition, there is an emotional body, a mental body and an etheric body. The emotional body is the place where many of the emotional hurts and wounds become trapped. These hurts and wounds also have physical locations and correlates in the physical body as well. Anyone working with the multitude of body interventions can tell you about these. Therapeutic massage for instance, often finds the hurts and wounds reflected in the physical body. Reiki work also finds emotional energy blockages and tries to release these.

With deeper work, the therapist begins to release these wounds at the physical level. The energy bound in the physical body often brings up old memories of the trauma and embarrassment that led to the bound energy at the physical level. Clients even remember past life trauma that is reflected in their current physical structure. It all remains with us, from all time and space. The beauty of this is we can heal all time and space. We don't even have to remember or relive the past. In many of the healing circles I currently participate in, we are able to simply work with the energy of the physical body and other bodies, helping the person to release and let go of all negative and fear-based emotions at all levels, healing all time and space.

Recently my right shoulder has been in pain, with restricted movement as well. As I have worked to heal this shoulder, in part through therapeutic massage, both the masseuse and I have become aware of at least two past lives that affect my current physical condition. In one past life I was an Arabian assassin and lost my arm in a battle with another. It appears that in another lifetime, perhaps on another planet, a rod was inserted into this shoulder and an electric current was run through it causing severe damage and debilitation. Whatever resentment and bitterness I still carry from those lives has to be released in love and forgiveness if my shoulder is going to heal in this physical body.

Releasing the negative and fear-based emotions in the emotional body is essential. Consciously choosing to let these go, allowing forgiveness to take place, heals us. Forgiveness is the way we really let go of the wounds and emotional scars that bind us to lower dimensional reality, and bind us to continuing ego beliefs and functioning. Jesus emphasized forgiveness unconditionally and completely. This is truly the way we return to our True Self. Love really is the answer. Love that sees all, as part of divine creation that looks beyond each of our miss-creations to behold the truth of another is the pure love of God reflected in our life. Forgiveness allows us to heal the emotional wounds. Forgiveness is an important process psychologically and spiritually.

Everlasting forgiveness of others, and your self, releases the anger stored in the emotional body. It releases the pain, rejection and hurt from others that didn't understand you or seemed uncaring.

The mental body houses our belief system, the accumulated, often ego-based thought system that keeps us in limitation and lack, and that also binds energy as well. Since our thoughts create the world we perceive and live in, any negative or fear-based thoughts bind us to a world of limitation and lack. Doubt, distrust and suspicion contribute to thoughts of limitation and lack. As the ego reigns supreme, the emotional body becomes distorted by the thought and belief systems we learn along the way, especially those that keep us from love-based thoughts and perceptions.

Mind is the creator. Repeatedly, Edgar Cayce reminded us in his readings of the powerful nature of the mind. The distortions in the mental body, from the wounds we all experience, as well as from the thought systems it is demanded we believe in, give rise to miss-creation. Since we have free will choice, we decide based on the belief systems and distortions at the emotional level. As Divine Mind is allowed to guide and direct us, we can make better choices of who we are and who we want to be, overcoming the wounds and the errors residing in the mental body.

The etheric body is the blueprint for what manifests in the physical body. At the higher dimensional level it creates the manifestation of what we become in the physical. When separated from the other bodies, the perfection that potentially exists at the etheric level is unable to manifest in the physical. Healing the wounds and distortions at the mental and emotional levels allows the etheric to manifest in the physical the way it is meant to be. Energy from the etheric freely moves through the other bodies to the physical, creating harmony and perfect health.

Emotional wounds and psychological scars in the emotional body manifest as pockets of darkness. They block out the light that naturally is within us. Bitterness and resentment, harboring feelings of hatred and judgment, further darken the emotional body. Not only are there blockages in energy flow between bodies there are also blocks preventing the etheric blueprint from manifesting in a perfect physical form. Negative habits and addictions further add to the blockages between bodies, and add darkness that interferes with the etheric blueprint functioning at the highest level.

As we heal the wounds, release and let go of negative and fear-based emotions, allow Holy Spirit and Divine Mind to guide us, get still and go within, the membranes between the

Healing and Transformation

physical, mental and emotional bodies become permeable. As each body is healed it becomes filled with light, replacing the darkness as it is released. Energy then can move freely within and between bodies. The abundant energy of the universe can also move freely within and between bodies, from us to others. One gift of love is channeling the light and energy of God to others and the world around us. Energy is meant to be shared will all there is. This is one aspect of true giving.

When emotional wounds are healed and negative and fear-based emotions and beliefs are released, we increasingly become joyful and more at peace. We gain the capacity to create miracles as energy flows freely through us, and with divine direction, extends out to heal others. As we begin to master peace and joyfulness, we can easily and readily extend love to others. We no longer need to hold grudges, see differences and judge. We can truly begin to forgive others, knowing their truth lies beyond the illusion of the external appearance made manifest by their wounds, distorted and ego-based thinking, darkness in their emotional body and blocked energy.

All of the Masters were able to release the negative and fear-based emotions, and release the judgments about others. In gentle service and humility, they taught and continue to teach humanity the truth of life and of God. Freed of the emotional wounds and bound up energy in their bodies, they could and did extend light and love to others. They are not the exception to the rule. It is your heritage to do the same.

The Master is able to feel the full range of emotions. He/she can experience sadness and anger. He/she can go into the experience and discharge the feeling. He/she does not deny the anger, but instead can acknowledge the anger. He/she can say, "I am angry this has occurred. This does not serve the highest good of all involved." In releasing the anger, energy associated with the emotion can then be directed to the highest good of the person and others.

Numerous techniques are available to begin the process of healing. There are many traditional means of healing, such as psychotherapy, support groups, twelve step traditions, self-help books and technologies, seminars and workshops. There are increasingly available alternative healing methods to free energy and release wounds, traumas and emotional scars through massage therapy, Reiki and other methods. There are practical methods one can use on a daily basis to release negative and fear-based emotions and thoughts from the various bodies. Meditation and prayer are powerful methods to achieve this.

As energy begins to flow freely between all bodies and all levels, true inner balance and harmony is achieved. Reactions of the moment are readily transformed into energy that is available to be used in positive and love-based ways. The Master is capable of experiencing the emotion of the moment and yet readily transforms this energy to be used for the greater good of the individual and then by extension to others.

One method to heal wounds and to remove all negative and fear-based emotions comes to us by way of St. Germain. It is to spend ten minutes or more a day visualizing yourself in a cone of white light. Then surround this cone of white light with a blue silver light for additional protection. Then, visualize, imagine or see a violet consuming light throughout this cone of light. This violet consuming flame removes all disharmony and discord from all bodies. When practiced regularly and consistently, healing takes place at all levels. This can be extended to others, putting the violet consuming flame through ourselves and those we are in conflict with or those who have harmed us. The flame removes the disharmony and discord between two or more.

Another method for healing and transformation is using Liquid Golden Light. This light, which comes from the very heart of God, is a powerful means of healing. In a relaxed state, visualize, imagine or see a liquid golden light enter and gradually fill your entire body. It is the color of honey. It is a thick, slow moving light and looks just like honey being poured from a jar. You may experience a tingling sensation as this light moves through your body. This light releases negative, fear-based emotions and thoughts from your bodies. It can also be used to prevent engaging in harmful activities and temptations.

Healing and Transformation

I have successfully used this with those suffering from addictions, preventing them from continuing to feel and act on the urge to use. It is very effective in breaking habits and destructive patterns of behavior.

The liquid golden light can also be used to heal relationships with others, even when they are not present or from a distance in time or space. It can even heal relationships with those who have passed on into other dimensions. With the light fully visualized within you, extend the light form your heart center to the other person's heart center. Once the connection is made send your forgiveness. Then, ask for their forgiveness. This releases negative karma for all time and space with the other person.

A more proactive way of releasing negative and fear-based emotions involves the following procedure. Becoming aware of the emotional wound with the other, state out loud the following (quietly if necessary), "I release the…" and list each and every negative and fear-based emotion you are aware of that goes with the incident. After all are listed then say, "I release all these negative and fear-based emotions into the light." Then visualize, imagine or see these negative and fear-based emotions leaving your body and going up a shaft of light into other dimensions.

Then state, "I replace these with healing light, love, joy, peace, happiness, forgiveness and…" listing the entire positive and love based emotions you can think of opposite the emotions just released. Then visualize, imagine or see these positive and love-based emotions coming back into your bodies on the same shaft of light from other dimensions. With most wounds, several or even many repetitions will be necessary to release the old wounds and hurts. Over time you will begin to notice the negative and fear-based emotions are gone. You will feel freer and less bound to the past.

Healing the wounds and resolving the negative and fear-based emotions attached to the wounds, creates open boundaries between the various bodies we possess. Then energy can freely move between these bodies. It is no longer bound or trapped in any one body. With the gift of free will this energy becomes accessible for use in creating harmony and peace at all levels.

The peace that passes all understanding begins to permeate our entire being. Energy can also be directed by conscious will easily and readily shared by others. Forgiveness, the key to freedom from judgment and unloving thoughts, is more easily possible. Fear diminishes and no longer has power to distort our thoughts and feelings, our perceptions of others and limit the possibilities the creative mind is capable of.

Letting go of limiting thoughts also opens the boundaries between the bodies, again allowing energy to flow freely. The energy can now also be directed where it can provide the most good. Free of thoughts of condemnation and judgment, and the need to attack and find blame, one can truly react with peace to the attacks and provocations that come from others. One can stay centered in their truth and truly "turn the other cheek." No longer invested in defense and projection, one can see the pain in another and not accept as real the distorted and fear laden way it is expressed.

Recently I was verbally attacked by a patron at a service station/convenience store who was convinced I had given him a "dirty look" when he suddenly stepped in front of my car and I had to brake sharply so as not to run over him. I was able to calmly respond to a provocative diatribe that included many nasty names being directed at me. It was clear, as he raged; he was trying to intimidate me with threatening behavior. I was able to calmly respond, making direct and unwavering eye contact, asking him why he was so angry. I was able to respond to his control drama without reacting to it. He clearly hoped I would respond in kind or go into a victim drama. Quite possibly he wanted to physically attack me.

Yet I absolutely did not feel any fear, nor did I feel a need to attack back or in kind. My ego did not need to engage his ego. Mastery is the capacity to control and direct energy appropriately, even directing negative and fear-based emotions in the moment and readily transform these to positive and love-based emotions. I could respond in the moment to the behavior, setting limits on the control drama of the other and stay at peace. I could understand how Jesus could remain calm and at peace even as they crucified him. Never did he judge or condemn anyone. His response is a shining example of what we are all able to do.

As we remove the blockages in each body, we free ourselves to use and control energy at all levels. This allows us to manifest what we want in life and to truly create at higher levels, who we are and who we want to be. Using affirmations like the following on a daily basis help to create the permeable boundaries between bodies that lead to healing and attunement at all levels. One affirmation is as follows: "I call upon my own Mighty I AM Presence, the Goddess of Purity and the Elohim of Purity to remove all blockages from my emotional body and fill my emotional body with peace; and, to remove all blockages from my etheric body and fill my etheric body with peace." A second affirmation goes as follows: "Beloved Mighty I AM Presence; purify my emotional body and fill my emotional body with peace; purify my mental body and fill my mental body with peace; purify my physical body and fill my physical body with peace; and, purify my etheric body and fill my etheric body with peace."

Healing the wounds and changing the thought systems, creates permeable boundaries between all bodies that allow the mastery and control of energy at all levels. Forgiveness is easier to do. Love is easier to share. Peace comes into our lives. We no longer need or want to react to the fear in our brothers and sisters. Healing takes place at all levels and in all time and space, letting us to return to our true Self.

It is our destiny to become physical-etheric beings as we free energy to use at higher dimensional levels, going from the third dimensional reality to fourth and fifth dimensional reality. We are to become the Adam Kadmon, the Galactic Human. This is where we have been meant to be all along. The historical period humanity has been in is the detour into third dimensional density, resulting in limitation and lack, limited consciousness, and forgetting our true heritage we have experienced in the recent history of the world.

As we actively heal and transform, at the energetic level and the body's level, blockages become transmuted through permeable boundaries between the bodies. We move a step closer to our divine heritage, while living in physical realities.

Chapter 5
CREATING BALANCE

We are out of balance within ourselves, with one another and the planet. A return to balance within and without is an important part of living, of healing and of transforming. Life is an ongoing process, especially for healing and transformation. Ultimately it is a process of building your light body and achieving ascension. Ascension is ending the need for physical incarnations on this planet and moving forward into other dimensional experiences, as well as other higher dimensional planetary experiences. The return to You is this process of healing and transformation, and ascension.

An essential part of returning to You is establishing, manifesting and maintaining, balance. As we learn to be quiet, to be still and to go within, we increasingly find that balance becomes an important part of everyday life. Achieving balance allows us to further create harmony and peace, even in times of stress and painful realities. Finding balance between all levels of experience and existence helps us to more fully understand and allow attunement and alignment with the Higher Self to take place. Balance allows love and light to enter at all levels and in all bodies.

Balance occurs on many levels. There is a need to establish balance between our emotional, physical, mental and spiritual bodies. It is having balance between and within the physical body, between and within the emotional body, between and within the mental body, and between and within the etheric body. It is having balance between the human side and the spirit side of our being. It is having balance between self and others in all the differing ways we have relationships in the world. It is having balance between work and play, responsibilities and leisure. It is having balance between freedom and responsibility.

Having balance allows us to be who we are and what we want to be at every level. Ultimately, creating balance facilitates the building of our light body, moving toward ascension as we align more fully with the Higher Self. Balance allows love and light to manifest as you build your light body.

First and foremost is to create balance emotionally. It is in the arena of emotions where we mostly get into trouble at the third and fourth dimensional levels of existence. Since there are two basic emotions operating on this planet, creating harmony and balance emotionally are essential in overcoming what holds us back from remembering and aligning with our true heritage.

The two basic emotions are love and fear. Being human we most often operate from fear. Negative and fear-based emotions are predominating in the planet and in all of us. The ego operates from fear. Learning from moments of embarrassment, hurt and trauma, the ego quickly becomes vigilant in scanning the world for potential attack from others. However, to protect you even further, the ego learns not only to anticipate attack, but also to also readily strike back. Ever vigilant to any and all potential harm to the integrity of the ego, the ego perceives in others attack and often strikes first to get them before they get us. All negative and fear-based emotions are readily available

Healing and Transformation

to the ego in its never-ending quest to perceive attack and attack others in kind.

The ego even goes so far as to create a vindictive God ready to strike any that may differ from us in any way. Anyone who disagrees with us in any way, whether politically, philosophically, differing value systems, the differing particular creed or theology practiced, differing moral choices, or any of the many arbitrary ways we separate ourselves from one another must be on the wrong side of God.

Unfortunately, the natural conclusion of fear is a vindictive God is ready to strike us for even the smallest deviation from the "right way." Thus sin, which in the Greek translation was simply error, becomes the place that God will get your enemy, but also you. The ego's ultimate argument to keep you in fear and limitation is to suggest that God will get you, because you long ago chose to rebel against God. Thus, the fall is the original sin for which you will pay according to the ego.

One of the most powerful negative emotions is guilt, which prevents you from recognizing, or even taking a chance, God is really Pure Love. We persist in error, at the ego's prompting, because it seems better than taking a chance on finding out that God is anything but vindictive and really angry that we chose to create without Him/Her.

Thus, creating emotional balance is a daunting task at times. To move through the negative and fear-based emotions and increasingly embrace the positive and love-based emotions is hard work. It means gradually releasing the hurts, pains, traumas, and bitterness and resentment the ego easily creates and feeds upon. Especially through the process of forgiveness, emotional balance is achieved leading to an inner peace and sense that all is well with life. Increasingly you experience joy attacks, those sudden moments of overwhelming happiness and sense of connection with all of life. Much better to experience joy attacks rather than panic attacks, let alone feelings of sadness and dread.

As we grow and mature, this doesn't mean we are free of negative and fear-based emotions. They are going to still arise.

This is not a perfection model where we never experience moments of anger, fear, guilt or embarrassment. Yet, what changes with emotional balance is that we can take the negative emotion, acknowledge its existence and then move back into positive and love-based emotions. The negative emotions do not rule your life. Balance is an acknowledgement of the full range of emotions, experiencing and expressing them appropriately, not being stuck in any one them.

Everett Shostrom, Ph.D., a clinical psychologist, wrote about basic polarities at the core of personality functioning. He stated these polarities were love/anger and strength/weakness. When personality functioning is in balance you can experience each part of the polarity and flexibly move from feeling to feeling. When personality functioning becomes constricted due to emotional hurts, embarrassments and traumas then the full range of the polarities is either not experienced, or one area of a polarity is over-emphasized, and the opposite polarity is under-emphasized.

Love and anger are opposites, which is why we commonly think of love and hate as opposites. Hate is an extreme form of anger. The love side of the polarity is the feelings of liking something or someone, through all the gradations of love, all the way to the deepest *agape* love. This includes love of family, friends, significant others, favorite activities and love of the world we live in.

It includes romantic love from the initial stage of falling in love, to the soft gentle place of being "in love" with the person we want to be significantly committed to. This love recognizes the other isn't perfect but still the one we want to spend our intimate life with. Transcending this love is the deep, abiding love that emerges with genuine partnership with another. The product of direct and honest communication, sharing expectations and negotiating to get to common ground, partnership creates a love that evolves that is so profound it makes the initial falling in love feel like preschool in comparison.

Ultimately, this love dimension includes having compassion for all others, even enemies. This is the true expression of love God eternally has for all of creation. It is the love that sees the good in all and beholds the Christ light in everyone.

The anger polarity is the opposite dimension, from feelings of minor irritation and annoyance all the way to feelings of deep explosive anger and rage. It includes the distortions of anger that occur when it becomes bitter and resentful, when the anger becomes all consuming. Vengeance is an extreme form of anger. Certainly the anger that becomes violence is a distorted expression of anger.

The strength polarity is the capacity to experience and express feelings of confidence and competence, through all the gradations in between, to a powerful sense of being able to stand on your own two feet and handle all that life sends your way. In a distorted form it is the macho/macha, bullying stance that rules through toughness and a willingness to go to any extreme to get your way. The most distorted form of this is the dictator, who has a whole nation live in fear of their power and the ruthless way they will express that power.

The weakness polarity is the capacity to experience and express minor feelings of disappointment and an inability to adequately accomplish something, through all the gradations in between, to feelings of complete vulnerability and failure. In a distorted form it is the person who always settles for the "victim" drama, claiming they are worthless and incompetent about everything. Unfortunate forms of this are feelings of helplessness, hopelessness and worthlessness that go with various forms of serious depression.

Operating from the defensive stance of the ego, letting negative and fear-based emotions control their life, exaggerations of any polarity distort personality functioning. Being constricted in one dimension and overly exaggerated in the opposite dimension, can lead to distortion in personality functioning and certainly a lack of balance. So the person who can never admit to vulnerability and weakness, and over relies on a false sense of strength becomes a controlling, dictatorial individual. On the other hand, the individual who over emphasizes weakness and vulnerability and can never accept they may be competent and strong becomes endlessly trapped in victim dramas and being seen by others as a loser.

The person who over emphasizes their loving side and can never be angry results in expressing hostility often in passive-aggressive ways. They will "kill" you with kindness. You will feel like you will develop diabetes if you stay near them too long. On the other hand the person who is always angry and hostile, and takes offense at every perceived slight, over emphasizing their anger dimension and never allowing their love feelings to emerge is also out of balance.

As we strive for self-actualizing, the tendency to allow our innate potentials to emerge in higher and higher expressions of who we are and who we want to be, the more we are able to be in balance. We are able to fully acknowledge and express the full range of emotions and flexibly respond to others and the world we live in. In the moment we are able to experience and express the full range of emotions for each polarity. We then go beyond that; to readily transform the more negative emotions by acknowledging we have them and express them appropriately, never denying them. As noted in the previous chapter we learn to master our emotions, transforming the energy and using it in a positive way.

As balance is achieved emotionally, we increasingly move in the direction of self-actualizing. Personality functioning becomes more balanced. Abraham Maslow, noted psychologist, describes the characteristics of self-actualizing. Maslow developed a psychology of the healthy person, healthy being, and healthy living. Self-actualizing is the full use and exploitation of talents, capacities and potentialities in each person.

Mallow's study of psychological health resulted in a description of self-actualizing individuals. The first characteristic is a more efficient perception of reality and more comfortable relations with it. They more readily see the world the way it is, without the filters of judgment and prejudice of the ego. This is followed by an acceptance of reality the way it is and not as they would prefer it to be. Dr. Phil McGraw talks about this as getting "real" with you and the laws of life.

The next characteristic is relative spontaneity of behavior, and being far more spontaneous in inner life, thoughts and impulses. There is less need to be in roles or present one self to the world other than what you really thought and felt. Behavior is marked by simplicity and naturalness, and by a lack of artificiality or straining for effect.

Self-actualizing individuals are strongly focused on problems outside themselves, in general. They are interested in working to change the world and to help others in myriad ways. They are problem centered rather than ego-centered.

These individuals have a quality of detachment, such that they can be solitary without harm to themselves and without discomfort. They are "ok" with their alone time. They are also relatively independent of the physical and social environment. They don't need the approval of others or the need to belong, such that they sacrifice their own self-worth and self-identity. This is not selfishness, but instead is honoring who they are and who they want to be. They are dependent on their own development and the continued growth of their own potentialities and latent resources. Thus they strive for greater and greater awareness and manifestation of who they are and who they want to be.

Another characteristic Maslow found with self-actualizers was a continuous freshness of appreciation. They constantly delight in the world about them; enjoy others, nature, arts and knowledge. Above that, they have mystical experiences which Maslow called "peak experiences."

Individuals who are self-actualizing have positive, empathic feelings for other human beings. They have deeper and more profound interpersonal relationships. They are without exception, democratic people in the deepest sense. They have transcended their control dramas and manipulative styles, and work for consensus and common ground.

These individuals have a strong ethical sense and value system. Yet they don't readily accept imposed values, but instead develop a sense of ethics and values that are carefully thought

Creating Balance

out, corresponding to higher truths, and developing their own "inner supreme court."

Self-actualizing individuals have a special kind of creativeness or originality or inventiveness. They resist enculturation. They are not prisoners of the culture they are raised or find themselves in. They can appreciate what is good in all cultures, without being stuck in any particular culture or class of people.

Yet as we achieve self-actualizing, this doesn't make us perfect in any way. We can still exhibit many of the lesser human failings, such as silly and wasteful habits. We can still be thoughtless at times.

With the process of self-actualizing, we increasingly experience all of the polarities, express the full range of emotions, and yet are balanced in the dimensions of the polarities. The dichotomies of the polarities are resolved; they disappear. Synergy happens, which is the process of the merging of desires. The paradox is, the pursuit of selfish ends automatically resulting in helping others. Selfish enjoyment results from contributing to the welfare and happiness of others.

As we increasingly become self-actualizing we are more aware of our self, others and the outside world as we strive for psychological survival. High self-regard results from accepting responsibility for our behavior and taking charge of our life. It is being proactive and not passive and reactive. Awareness, accepting responsibility and taking charge leads to self-actualizing behavior. The capacity to make choices is part of accepting responsibility. It is truly choosing who we are and who we want to be.

Ultimately, these opposites are transcended when we are balanced and increasingly self-actualizing. These are love of self/love of others, child-like behavior/adult behavior, and subject/object. In this way we are able to honor divine order: God—-self—-others. We can understand what Jesus meant, in part, when he said "Be ye as little children." We can understand our individuality, even as we recognize we are all one.

Balance is also important at the mental level. This means learning to balance the two sides of the brain and the two sides of the mind. The left-brain is the seat of rational and logical thought. The right brain is the seat of the intuitive and creative mind. In the historical era, we have been taught to mostly emphasize the left-brain and under utilize or ignore the right brain. Intuitive knowing has not been important in general. Ironically, we give women permission to be more intuitive and use their "sixth sense" that resides in the right brain. Unfortunately we have undervalued women and thus undervalued intuitive knowing.

We have been taught to worship at the temple of the rational mind. Ram Dass called our universities temples to the rational mind. In our culture and in most cultures of the world, in recent history, the emphasis is on rational thought. A few cultures emphasize intuitive knowing over rational thought, yet they are often out of balance as well.

There is a place for reason and logic. It is the place from which we can make sound discernment about many situations and issues in life. It is important to have and utilize this ability to safely navigate life and thoughtfully make decisions about who you are and who you want to be.

Equally important is the capacity to utilize your creative, intuitive ability. There is a knowingness that just is, that can't always be proven, accurately guiding you through the tribulations, challenges and opportunities of living. Learning to be aware of and trust this intuitive ability gives you as much valuable information as any reasoning and logical thinking can do. This intuitive knowingness taps into your connection with your God Self, the inner wisdom to which all are connected.

Albert Einstein spoke of the creative, intuitive knowingness that led him to discover the theory of relativity in physics. It came in a moment, as a brilliant flash of inspiration and comprehension. It then took him a year to work out the mathematics, the logical reasoning that demonstrated what was revealed to him by his creative mind.

The importance of both minds, working in balance, helps us to navigate life and better choose who we are and who we want to be. In my own experience, I have seen many manifestations of the gifts of spirit in my work, sometimes in the least expected places. For instance, having heard about the psychic surgeons of the Philippines, I intuitively sensed there might be something to these phenomena. The psychic surgeon is able to put their hands into a body, remove unhealthy tissue, and close the wound without leaving a scar.

Many detractors claim that this phenomenon is simply the use of magic tricks to let others and the patients believe what they are doing has happened. They claim there is the use of sleight of hand; presenting animal parts as though they came from within the person.

Doing custody and parenting time evaluations for a Circuit Court clinic, I interviewed a woman whose daughter was born with a benign but disfiguring growth on her right cheek. The mother showed me a before picture of her daughter. Physicians told her, the growth could be removed, but a large scar would remain that could be just as disfiguring. Having some wealth, and the willingness to consider other alternatives, she took her daughter to the Philippines in search of a psychic surgeon. The surgery was performed, the growth removed, and her face was not scarred.

I am able to accept with my rational mind what my intuitive mind suggests is "real." I allow reason and logic to be in balance with the intuitive side, which suggested such phenomena do indeed occur. The intuitive mind "knows" there are miracles, and often we accept these with faith. Yet reason and logic can also validate these experiences.

Dad was planning a trip to Sedona, Arizona. He wanted to find the mystical experiences he wished to have there. At the church he attended, a kind and friendly woman, who told him she knew of his impending trip to Arizona, exactly where to go once he arrived in Sedona and who to ask for, approached him. He thanked her for the information and wondered about this strange woman who knew about his quest, even though he didn't know her and had never seen her before.

He decided to find her to thank her again and ask her how she knew what to tell him. He couldn't find her, and interes-

Healing and Transformation

tingly no one else seemed to have seen her. He had never seen her around before and never saw her again. Having heard about Angels coming to give us guidance, disguised in human form, I suggested this is what happened. Intuitively, in the moment I "knew" this is what happened.

In Arizona, Dad found the metaphysical store he was directed to and the mystical guide he was to meet. He was taken to very specific energy points and had the mystical encounters he was there to have. One included his chief guide, a Native American in a past life, who gave him visionary symbols he used the rest of his life, often to intuitively guide him.

I don't just accept every seemingly intuitive thought that arises; I check it out with my logical, rational mind. I don't just accept every seeming mysterious event or process without checking it out with my rational mind. I temper faith with "show me." I suggest you do the same.

Yet, I also respect my logical, rational mind isn't always truly guiding me or as well as the intuitive mind might. I will take what seems like a rational and logical thought process and check it out with what my intuitive mind suggests is the best course of action or the correct perception for me. Balance is letting both minds operate, often in harmony. To rely on only one or the other gets us into trouble. Learning to use both will guide you more truly.

Balance is also important between the emotional body and the mental body. To let only the emotions rule, or to let only the intellect rule, creates an imbalance. To always be in your head, to just think and reason, leads to distorted perception and judgment. To always be in the feeling, to just act on emotions, also leads to distortions in perception and action.

Certainly when we operate only with reason, we lack the balance that love can bring to the reasoning process. We do not experience the compassion and empathy that temper the logical conclusions we might otherwise reach. Logic can lead you into blind alleys and to dangerous conclusions when positive and love-based emotions are left out of the process. Mercy and forgiveness may even seem illogical, yet lead to right action when reason and love are combined.

However, to only operate from emotion and not use our judgment and discernment can also lead to distorted perception and improper choices for action. When we act from negative and fear-based emotions and don't allow reason to be part of the process, we may act impulsively and destructively. Even when we respond from positive and love-based emotions, without reason, we may make errors of judgment and discernment.

A dramatic example of this is what we call "falling in love." The initial stage of romantic love, which we easily mistake for being "in love," is certainly a wonderful, magical and glorious feeling. Our hearts are filled with the passion and joy of feeling romantic love with another. This time of initial romance, which lasts anywhere between six and twelve months, is certainly a wonderful experience.

Too often, however, we want to act on this initial stage of a relationship, and make major life decisions, without letting our thinking and reasoning enter into the process. While it is nice to enjoy the journey of this initial stage of love, we are not even in a position to let reason and logic become part of the process. Yet to make potentially life-long decisions without discernment and judgment of another, often leads to the dysfunctions, disappointments and failures in a relationship later on. This is why we say at this stage, "love is blind."

We have to allow ourselves to get to the next stage of romantic love, the soft gentle place of being in love with another person. Then reason and discernment are part of the process again. We see another more realistically, recognizing they aren't perfect and have flaws. Yet we can decide to commit to a longer, more intimate relationship with another knowing they aren't perfect, but differences and shortcomings can honestly be dealt with. Hopefully, we can also recognize and deal with the unconscious agendas that attract us to the other person, but may doom the long-term success of the relationship.

To have balance between the emotional body and the mental body ultimately means we are fully aware and act with both parts of our being. The extremes of overly emotional or overly intellectual responses to life and others are avoided.

Another important balance to create is between work and play. Work and the pursuit of career are important, and even necessary, human pursuits. Not working can be just as harmful to the spirit of a person as working too much. It is important to have work, to be responsible, and to take care of yourself and those who you are responsible. All work is honorable. Our society places different value on different work, believing somehow that some work is more important or better than other work. Yet everything done by everyone is essential for society to work and for all to benefit living in a safe, workable environment. We certainly can do a lot more for everyone to live in a safe world, with basic needs provided for all.

The work you do may not fit the highest vision for you or for your mission and purpose. Yet, it can provide you the means to do the other things you feel are of more service to the world and others. Be careful here, though, even the most menial and seemingly unimportant tasks may provide the most service to others and the world. When performed with an attitude of service and an attitude of bringing your best to every situation and every person you encounter, you may have an impact not known by you, but greatly revered in the eyes of heaven. That is why Gandhi took his turn cleaning toilets. That is why Jesus washed the feet of his disciples.

There is a danger in being too consumed by career and work. When done at the expense of family, friends and leisure pursuits you end up being out of balance in an important area of your life. Many stress disorders are the result of too much work, and not enough balance with other important pursuits in your life. It is necessary to have time for leisure, to have playtime. It is important to have time for your family and especially for your children and grandchildren.

Creating balance between work and leisure helps create overall balance in your life. Work is an important and necessary part of mature adult functioning. It enhances self-love and self-worth. Being responsible in this area of life helps you define who you are at higher and higher levels. Done increasingly with an attitude of service to others, customers, colleagues and co-workers, and to your employer enhances self-love and self-confidence, and adds to the overall good of everyone. Yet leisure time is also necessary and important because it helps recharge your batteries and keeps you fresh and available to others and to your work. Rest time is also important to maintain balance in life.

The need for leisure pursuits leads to another area for balance in life; balance at the physical level. Balance in the physical body means moderation in diet and moderation in exercise. It is keeping fit physically, with a balance of proper nutrition and moderation in the amount of food taken in. It is not indulging in drugs or alcohol, and avoiding the use of tobacco. Drugs, alcohol and tobacco interfere with optimal physical functioning as well as adding darkness at the mental level.

The body is the temple to the living God within you and needs to be cared for properly. It is important to engage in some physical activity on a daily basis. One of the best things you can do is walk daily for ten to twenty minutes at a relatively brisk pace. It benefits the cardiovascular system, as well as stimulating the endorphins, the natural stimulants in the brain. Walking improves your mood, and is relaxing and calming as well. It gives you time to reduce stress, and to contemplate and process daily events and issues. It is also a time to get in touch with the natural rhythms and cycles of the planet, including seasonal cycles. All benefit us at the physical level, and keeps balance and harmony at this level as well.

Having balance between the physical and spiritual is imperative to fully experience our reality as spiritual beings having a human experience. It is important to nurture and honor our spiritual heritage, to practice spiritual discipline to more fully access our divine heritage. As we practice spiritual traditions or pursuits, we remember the spiritual nature of our being.

Yet, it is also important to experience and express our human nature, as a third-fourth dimensional physical being living in a material world. We are to experience the joys of physicality. The key is to experience these joys without the carnal desires overwhelming you or ruling your life. When the physical becomes greed, avarice or lust, then we are over emphasizing the physical and not in balance between the spiritual and physical nature that is you.

Working to have balance between the physical, mental, emotional and spiritual levels allows us to function at optimal levels. Not only is it important to heal and grow physically, mentally, emotionally and spiritually, it is also important to achieve and maintain balance at all four levels of being. This allows us to better choose who we are and who we want to be, and allows us to be in greater alignment with our Higher Self.

Next, it is important to have balance between you and others. Divine order is God-Self-Others. Balance occurs when you take care of you and make time for you. Having alone time is essential in creating the capacity to be more available to others.

In the process outlined above, first is our relationship with God; however we wish to conceive and achieve that relationship. Ultimately, true partnership with God is the "God-Self" part of Divine Order.

Then as we nurture the self, as we develop and maintain positive self-love and self-worth, we bring our very best to all other relationships. Whether our intimate, romantic relationships or other love relationships, as we take good care of ourselves we then bring our very best to others. This extends to all other relationships, whether family, friends, colleagues and co-workers, neighbors and the family of humankind.

Balance is also important in our relationships. We must have time for ourselves, whether for meditation or leisure. We also must have time for our partner. We must have time for children and grandchildren. In our busy lives, some have learned to have a couple's night once a week and a family night once a week. Then finding time for each child individually, on a somewhat regular basis, is necessary. It can be quite daunting to create balance for all these competing demands; yet striving for balance lends itself to greater harmony for you and with others.

Balance is also important between freedom and responsibility. Victor Frankl suggested we needed a Statue of Responsibility on the West Coast of the United States to complement the Statue of Liberty on the East Coast. We enjoy many freedoms here, including freedom of speech, freedom of thought, freedom to pursue many activities, freedom of association, freedom of political beliefs and freedom of worship. Without responsible action these freedoms can be a license to act in excess or act irresponsibly. Balancing freedom with responsible choice and action prevents licentious behavior. Having ethics and making moral choices in thought and action add to responsible behavior.

Finally, it is important to create and achieve balance between your feminine and masculine sides mentally and emotionally, and perhaps spiritually. This will be discussed in greater detail in the next three chapters. It's a very important part of the New Golden Age and the new human.

Creating and maintaining balance, at the myriad differing levels and areas we live and function in is quite challenging and may seem overwhelming. However, while it is quite difficult to create balance, once you begin to make time for all the parts of you and their expression, maintaining balance becomes easier. In developing the habits of balance, you are more centered, more often live in the here-and-now, and experience greater inner peace and harmony.

You also begin to experience greater peace and harmony with others, the world, and your Divine Self. You begin to easily access the greater dimensions around you and begin to more easily communicate with and hear the loving support of the many multidimensional beings waiting to assist you. You begin to "hear" the guides and Guardian Angels here to assist you, deceased loved ones and the Great-Ascended Masters, ever willing to talk to you and help you return to You, and ultimately achieve your mastery and ascension.

Chapter 6
REAL MASCULINITY

Part of healing and transformation, especially for the male gender, is to move from old paradigms about masculinity and understand and manifest real masculinity. Real masculinity is allowing masculine qualities to operate, while accepting and incorporating the feminine side of our nature as well. While masculine traits are expected to manifest in the male, it is resolving and accepting their feminine side that allows real masculinity to operate.

The Living Webster Encyclopedic Dictionary of the English Language defines masculine as "of the male sex; not female; strong; robust; powerful; manly; and virile." When described for a female, they are said to be coarse, bold and mannish.

Certainly a distorted view of masculinity has existed for some time, actually thousands of years. Men have basically been in charge of the world, with a distorted sense of what it means to be powerful and strong, robust and virile. During the so-called historical period of world history, the male has been dominate and in control, with females considered to be second-class citizens, at best. This view continues with potentially destructive consequences for the world and for civilization if it persists. It is rationalized and justified at many levels and in many ways that the male gender is in charge and control in all but a few areas.

Even when we allow women to be in charge of family and children, many argue the father is the leader of the family and the final decision-maker. Many fundamental religions argue that the man is superior and the leader of the family, including the spiritual leader. This is justified by interpretations of scripture, probably distorted by male control and domination during the historical period. Interestingly, early Christian Church ecumenical councils deliberately excluded the "Book of Mary," considered by many Biblical scholars as the most authentic gospel of the many books in the New Testament.

Even our description of God is typically seen as masculine, portraying the bias of this era. A peculiarity of language, with a primary masculine description, lends to the conclusion that God must be a male energy. Since God is all, Father-Mother God is a more accurate description of what God is, although God is so much more than even this. The audiotapes of *Conversations With God* more closely suggest the all encompassing nature of God, as the voices of Ellen Burstyn and Ed Asner are used for God, changing from the male to the female in mid-sentence to depict that God is ALL.

Until very recently, males have dominated all areas of life; especially where power is concerned. They have been in control of religion, the military, business and government. Most leaders in all areas of endeavor are male. While strides have been made recently, most leadership positions still remain in the hands of men. We debate whether we are ready to consider a female president. In some religions women are still kept from spiritual leadership positions, justified on the basis of a tradition that reflects the historical period. Male control of the many Christian denominations is justified due to Jesus and the recognized disciples all being male.

With masculine control and dominance, females are expected to be in subservient roles. This is often justified on the basis of culture and tradition. Even certain professions have been mostly male or female based on the masculine bias in tradition and culture. With the added responsibility of nurturing young children, and the special bond a mother and child have, tradition and culture have the mother in the care taking role, and then dictated that women somehow are in a subservient role. Many masculine ideas even suggest that women are somehow inferior.

Often, the Women's Liberation movement has itself sought empowerment for women by adopting the masculine ideal, rather than seeking opportunity to fully participate in all areas of life by bringing the feminine perspective into equal respect and a sharing of power with the masculine. So many women seeking to fully participate in all life has to offer have to compete with the male power structure by imitating masculine values and striving. Thus, leaving subordinate the feminine values and striving, they could bring to all of society and its institutions.

The masculine domination of the last few thousand years has left us with limitation and lack, with a belief that might makes right, and with a warrior mentality that leads to the most destructive ways to resolve conflict. We have ignored the contribution the equally important feminine side has to offer humanity and society. Ironically, males have also overemphasized their masculine side, not even or barely acknowledging their feminine side. Yet, it is ultimately a balance of the masculine and the feminine in males that leads to true masculinity.

The trouble with current expressions of masculinity is the dominance by the ego. As previously mentioned, the ego seeks to protect us from perceived harm, based on the negative and fear-based emotions from earlier trauma and hurt. Not only does the ego attempt to protect us from hurt and embarrassment, it also believes in attack as the best form of defense.

Combined with negative and fear-based determined masculinity, the ego readily seeks power, control and dominance over others. Thus the male gender seeks power and dominance over others in all areas of life. Even seemingly friendly banter is tinged with a competitive desire to one-up the other person. Masculine striving gets frequently expressed in the need to put down others. Younger males, in particular, engage in almost constant one-upmanship with one another in the desire to have dominance and control over others. While there is an emphasis on dominance over other males, there is also the need to have dominance and control over females as well. Females who exert a desire for equality in their relationships with men easily threaten false masculinity.

Its feminine side frightens the male ego. It readily attempts to protect the male from his soft and nurturing side. Early adolescent preoccupation and fear about homosexuality is part of this fear about the feminine side of their nature. Later on it gets institutionalized in homophobic behavior and justification that homosexuality is prohibited by a judgmental deity.

In the world of sports, masculine striving goes beyond competition to a desire to put down and denigrate the opponent. At its worst, trash talking is seen by ego-based masculinity as a perfectly appropriate way of expressing domination and control. To gain an edge with verbal taunts or to celebrate victory by putting down an opponent replaces true sportsmanship and respect for a competition well done.

In the realm of music, certain expressions of ego-based masculinity not only are compelled to put down others, but to especially denigrate women. In certain rap videos and songs, or popular lyrics and videos, women are portrayed as second-class citizens, useful only for sexual gratification. They are certainly not to be respected. Often they are mistreated.

In some segments of the youth culture, ego-based masculinity means belonging to anti-social peer groups. Any attempt to be successful, hold a job, or strive to do well in school is perceived as not being manly. For some African-American youth, to succeed at school is to "act white."

In much of television sitcoms, adults are treated as stupid and inferior, with smart aleck children who know more than the adults. Father figures are portrayed as the most inept and incompetent. In a twist on ego-based masculinity, competent

Healing and Transformation

males are caricatured to be undesirable role models. Brash, verbally taunting young males are seen as being smarter and wiser, simply because they can seemingly put down the adults in their world with clever dialogue that is meant to be demeaning and disrespectful. The show "The Simpsons" is the best at this negative stereotyping, passed off as clever satire.

At a more serious level, many movies that portray the strong action hero getting vengeance, celebrate the ego-based portrayal of masculinity. This fits in neatly with the ego always convincing us it is justified in attacking others for some perceived slight or wrong. While getting even and taking the law into our own hands is an appealing theme, especially from the perspective of the ego, is in truth, a distorted way of operating. When combined with a false sense that this is being manly, the results can be very destructive. While in the movies, getting even with the bad guys is entertaining, because it appeals to the dark side of ego functioning; in truth it is the very opposite of practicing spiritual truth and understanding spiritual law. What goes around does come around and we don't have to be the one that gets vengeance.

I had a client recently, whose daughter was almost molested by an uncle. The daughter reported the attempted abuse right away and the parents appropriately turned it over to the police. Despite the successful prosecution of the case, the father became increasingly agitated and enraged. He felt he was somehow less a man because he didn't try to harm or even kill this relative. His conflicted feelings were exacerbated more by the idea he wasn't living up to the masculine ideal his father gave to him.

His father, who was a Detroit police officer, let his son know he had meted out street justice to the bad guys on more than one occasion. This justice included killing bad guys he determined were guilty. The son, father of the girl, felt he was betraying the ideal his father had instilled in him by not getting vengeance.

In the meantime, he risked losing his wife and daughter because of the murderous rage he expressed about this uncle.

Consumed by his rage and a desire to get revenge, he began neglecting his family, but also frightening them. He even thought at one point, it would be okay to spend his life in prison, to get vengeance in the ego-based masculine way his father taught him. It took considerable work for him to overcome this negative masculine ideal and to accept universal truths and laws, which would naturally mete out to the uncle the consequences of his behavior.

Ego-based masculinity operates, at its worst, in the realm of politics. One has to go no further than to watch two bitter, angry men in the Mideast, ready to destroy thousands of people in their desire to get vengeance on each other. Their hatred runs deep, fueled by a false masculine ideal, leading their people, and perhaps the whole world, to the brink of disaster.

In the United States, one can see the ego-based masculinity manifest in the conflict within the political arena. Politicians are no longer content to present their viewpoint, listen respectfully to their opponent and work toward compromise. Instead, they readily attack one another and denigrate their opponent or differing view. Suddenly, terms like liberal or conservative take on a condescending and demeaning meaning, with the desire to have power and control at any cost being more important than reaching reasonable compromise, or reasonably agreeing to disagree with one another.

Even in political advertising, there isn't a reasonable discussion of where candidates differ, only attack and smear campaigning. The old masculine need for dominance and control says it's good to win at any cost and manly to be as nasty as you can. Polite discourse and discussion gives way to attack and putting the opponent down. Even debates are scored on the zingers each can get on the opponent rather than on the merits of the argument.

Certain political talk shows and radio hosts take this need for ego-based masculine striving to the limit. They readily put down opponents and opposing viewpoints, rather than thoughtfully and forcefully advocating their viewpoint and what they believe are the flaws in the opposing argument.

Within the George W. Bush administration, there had been a division of thought on how to deal with the world, and apparently rogue nations and leaders. The more hardliners, advocates for military intervention and solutions, were in conflict with others who sought negotiated solutions and alternative measures. Ironically, a very successful former Army general advocated the later position. Some of the hardliners were individuals who had never served in the military, but were more than willing to commit others' sons and daughters to potential danger, which comes with war and military action. Let those who have never served in the military be the first to take up a rifle and lead the assault they so eagerly advocate.

This does not mean that tough love solutions aren't necessary at times, even at the international level. However, military action has to be carefully thought out and committed to, without ego-based macho masculine posturing. Real masculinity would very carefully consider the necessity of such action and the consequences of such action.

Retired General Norman Schwarzkopf exemplifies this real masculinity. He is very careful and very reluctant to see military action as the appropriate course of action. Yet, once the decision was made to act, he carefully planned battle to minimize risk and possible loss of life. Also, he is not afraid to share the pain his decisions lead to, especially with the wounded and those who died. He readily shares the pain with his own tears and anguish and the tragic results of military action, when necessary.

The so-called historical period has witnessed endless war and conflict, often due to the inability of people to reasonably resolve differences. When certain kings, rulers or dictators decided their masculine striving meant conquering the world and having power and domination over others, the consequences have been disastrous for their people and for the world. The endless pageant of ego-based masculinity striving to have power and control over others has littered world history with many disasters. As our weaponry and ability to massacre one another increases, we now face the potential to create massive destruction and environmental disaster, up to and including blowing up the world.

Relying on an ego-based masculinity, ignoring and disregarding the feminine, have led the world to the brink of disaster. Without a change in consciousness and without the emergence of real masculinity in harmony and equality with femininity, the long-feared Armageddon will happen. It doesn't have to be this way, but we are getting very close in the Mideast. Not only the conflict between Israel and the Arabs, but also the conflict between the Muslim world and the Western world, place us all at the edge of disaster. Fueled by negative and fear-based emotions at the heart of ego-based masculinity, the anger and hatred each of us continues to harbor within builds collectively until Armageddon becomes a possibility.

Healing and transforming old, destructive masculine striving and power into real masculine strength and determination, is the key to transforming the consciousness collectively and evolving into the higher vision of who we are and who we want to be at the planetary level. Ultimately no one wins with war. No one wins with terrorism. No one wins with continued violence, whether individual, familial, community, national, or international.

To arrive at healing and transformation, it is important to understand how masculinity develops in men and how to then achieve real masculinity versus ego-based masculinity. For this purpose, we will especially examine Jungian psychology and how the male person develops. The challenge from this perspective is to successfully separate from the mother in early adolescence, develop a more masculine identity, which does get distorted by the ego. Then ultimately allow a balance to occur, as the feminine is integrated back into personality functioning.

In a delightful book entitled *He: Understanding Masculine Psychology,* the author Robert A. Johnson explores the Jungian view of masculinity. He looks at the myth of the Holy Grail as a way to understand masculine striving that includes incorporating the feminine into the overall personality.

A central idea in Jung's psychology is the concept of individuation. This is a lifelong process, in which you become the whole and complete person God intended you to be. It involves the gradual expansion of consciousness and the increasing capacity of conscious personality to reflect the total self. This is the process of choosing who you are and who you want to be at higher and higher levels of awareness. While Jungian psychology talks about the self being the total personality, the potential person within you from the beginning and seeking expression, we take it a step further here to include re-connecting to your true Self, the spiritual You having the human experience.

The individuation process is very challenging. It involves addressing psychological and spiritual problems at all levels. In particular it requires us to address the dark side of personality and ego, the place where the emotional hurts and traumas leave us in more negative and fear-based emotional functioning. Ultimately, fear creates the unwanted side of us that conflict with our conscious attitudes and ideals. Ultimately, the process of healing and transformation lets us accept and integrate our shadow or dark side so psychological unity and balance are established. As Elizabeth Kubler-Ross said, "You have to accept your Hitler in order to know your Mother Teresa."

Part of the process of individuation is the even more difficult inclusion for the male of his unconscious feminine element and for the female of her unconscious masculine element. Men generally identify with their masculine side and keep their femininity on the inside. Inclusion of the feminine element in the male is difficult, yet if the man is unable to accomplish this, according to Johnson, then he can't enter into the full mystery of the self within him.

The process of individuation leads to completeness, where the paradoxical unity of the self is a combination of opposites. This includes combining the human and the spirit. The ego can't rationally understand or comprehend this process. Based on negative and fear-based functioning, the ego perceives seeming opposites as threats, rather than part of a continuum of being and experience.

Real Masculinity

In Jungian psychology, there are potentially three stages of psychological development for males, according to Johnson. Males go from the unconscious perfection of childhood, to the conscious imperfection of middle life, to the conscious perfection of old age. Males move from an innocent wholeness, in which the inner and outer worlds are united, to separation and differentiation of these worlds, with a sense of life's duality, to enlightenment, a place of conscious choosing to see the inner and outer as a harmonious whole.

In early adolescence, males touch their Christ nature, if only for a moment. They then become painfully aware that the world isn't always joy and happiness. Childlike beauty, faith and optimism disappear. Paradoxically, when Jesus said we were to be like children, to comprehend the kingdom of God, he was suggesting the childlike innocence has to be recreated. It is the challenge, through healing and transformation to once again get to this state of childlike joy and happiness. It requires humility, for the male, to look at his innocent, adolescent, foolish part of himself as he heals and transforms so he can once again get to his Christ Consciousness.

As males step aside from ego-based masculinity, they begin a process of healing and transformation that allows true masculinity to emerge over time. Unfortunately, as adolescent males strive to be an ego-based masculinity, it gets them in so much trouble. It distorts their views of others, especially females, and leads to much unhappiness as adults. Often they seek women who will mother them, rather than create genuine partnership with them. Hoping to find another mother, they don't have to get in touch with and balance their feminine side.

True masculinity does require the strong, virile characteristics. Males in adolescence and early adulthood have to overcome great obstacles and triumph over adversaries. Unfortunately, males come to think the only way to get this is to take it from someone else. Winning isn't any good unless someone else loses. Competitiveness becomes a part of everything for males. Yet, for a boy to become a man, according to Johnson, he also has to master his aggressiveness. Controlled aggression

Healing and Transformation

at his conscious disposal is part of real masculinity. If the male is overcome with rage and violence, then he becomes just a terrible bully, has a violent temper, or gets involved in destructive behavior. A boy on his way to manhood has to learn to master his violent side and integrate the terrible masculine power for aggression into his conscious personality.

The shadow side of masculinity must be struggled with and resolved. The male ego has to become strong enough so the male isn't overcome with rage, but can use the power in it to overcome obstacles in his path and achieve his goals. Thus, the athlete who channels his aggression into competitive zeal will succeed at competition. The scholar who channels his aggression into achieving mastery of subjects achieves his goals to succeed academically and get into the best colleges.

The opposite is unresolved aggression and rage manifested in the tragedies of school shootings, gang violence, or physical aggression directed at others or property. The local media reported the story of three 18-year-olds with long-standing conflict with another 18-year-old. They attacked him at his girlfriend's home after a party ended, and his friends were no longer there to help him. They beat him so severely for a while they thought he wouldn't live or would have severe brain damage. The three perpetrators face up to thirty years in prison for their apparently premeditated aggression. How foolish it is to not learn to master aggression and rage, to spend a significant part of their lives confined to facilities where uncontrolled rage and aggression is part of their everyday life for a long period of time to come.

Adolescent and early adult males have to learn how to win against an outer opponent or situation by being able to call upon and direct masculine energy. They also have to overcome cowardice and a longing to be protected by their mothers from the dangers of the world. Encounters with outer obstacles challenge the male will and identity and firms up his masculinity on the inside.

To develop his masculinity, the adolescent male has to be disloyal to his mother in some way. This can be very painful for the mother. She has to allow this to occur, even though it doesn't often happen in the most pleasant ways. Later the son can come back to the mother and develop a new relationship at a new level, but the male has to develop his independence and transfer his affections to females his own age. The adolescent male also has to free himself from the father, brother or substitute male authority figure in his life.

Part of male development is what to do with his inner woman, the feminine side of his nature. This is very threatening for the male as he becomes consciously aware of his feminine side. Instead of quelling the inner feminine, males seek power and control of women with false macho attitudes and behaviors, or attack homosexuals, or project onto women second-class citizenship for their obvious inferiority to males.

This gets institutionalized in cultures and religious traditions that practice discrimination toward women and treat them as inferior. It also becomes the rationalization for seeing males as superior and they have the God given right to be in control. In its worst forms, it has accounted for the witch burnings and the recent abuse of women in Afghanistan by the Taliban. In its more subtle forms, it is ministers who dictate what clothing women will wear, how much, if any, make-up they wear and whether women can be out of the home unescorted.

According to Johnson, males experience their feminine side through moods. They become overpowered by the feminine part of their nature. The male's mood is being overwhelmed or possessed by the interior feminine content of his unconscious. Women sometimes recognize this when men act bitchy. As males work on healing and transforming their lives, they have to recognize this part of themselves. They have to learn not to be controlled by their moods, affects or seductions. The initial challenge is to set this part of his self, aside, but more importantly, later on he has to learn how to relate to his feminine side. With rejection of the feminine side it will turn against him and he will continue to have moods and undermining seductions. If he eventually accepts it and relates to the feminine side of himself and life, he gains warmth and strength.

If a male has a good relationship with his feminine side he is able to feel, value and find meaning in his life. If he can't relate to his feminine side he can find no meaning and has no capacity for valuation. As he gets into moods, there is a depression that settles over him such that the world and everything is distorted to the negative. Significant others sometimes realize these moods aren't their fault, but unfortunately they sometimes react with guilt, as though they somehow caused the mood to manifest.

When the female tries to break through the males' depression there can be an awful fight, especially if the fight is between the man's moody woman and the woman's angry man. When men are in their mood, they are very critical of the nearest woman. Not aware of his feminine side or resisting this side, he becomes critical of his spouse or significant other, according to Johnson.

The good moods can be seductive for the male as well. This is the exuberant, top-of-the world, bubbling, half-out-of-control mood which men usually seek. This is to be distinguished from the genuine joy and happiness that emerges as we address life challenges and opportunities. The good mood seduction will be balanced out with depression later on.

The good mood is also not enthusiasm. Enthusiasm is the joy and creativity that naturally arises when we are in tune with our spiritual Self. If the male is filled with creativity, but is soon gone, then this is the disguised feminine coming out. Creativity that lasts is the happiness that healing and transformation lead to when the feminine is recognized and in balance with the masculine. Studies have found the brightest and most creative individuals have a balance between their masculine and feminine sides.

Ironically, women are more in control of their feelings, despite the perception they are so emotional. The female can use her moods and flexibly change moods. Men have no control over their moods. Thus females are often masters of their feelings, whereas men are not.

Finally, the male learns that when he serves his feminine side, then it serves him. By honoring this aspect of his being, he honors the beauty, inspiration, and delicacy of the whole feminine side of life. The ideal is for the masculine and the feminine sides to serve each other, for both genders.

As the process of healing and transformation takes place for the man, he is able to balance his masculine and feminine energies. Healing the early and necessary break with his mother he can integrate his feminine side into his personality. This frees him to experience all of his emotions, the full range of the love/anger and the strength/weakness dimensions discussed earlier. He can comfortably honor the moments of weakness and vulnerability, while manifesting true strength and power.

With the discovery and integration of the feminine side, the male discovers beauty, ecstasy and the golden world. With this, comes a power, a perception, strength and a vision, resulting in spiritual satisfaction and wholeness. He is able to connect to his Divine Self, and return to the You he truly is. He is able to partner with his Higher Self, no longer conflicted with his ego in surrendering to his God Self. True masculinity is the strength and power of the connection to the true Self within.

He is able to have a sense of beauty, a sense of connectedness, and a sense of at-home-ness in the universe. It is said of Jesus that he revered women and readily partook in their company. He understood their connection with the divine and the faith they could so easily have. Women are allowed their intuitive connectedness with all that is.

Men have to rediscover they have this too. With the return of the feminine, men begin to have mystical experiences. Along the way they begin to experience these brief moments of mystical awareness. These are the small moments when there was the glimpse of a joy attack, that later becomes the joy and happiness that arises when life is created as a masterpiece of joy with full awareness and choice.

As the male heals and transforms his life, he unifies his aggressive quality with his soul, which searches for love and union. Unless they are brought into balance, there is warfare within men. Often, it is the suffering brought about from acting on the aggression that leads to redemption, to accepting and integrating the personality and then moving beyond it to the spiritual level, which is our true heritage.

The process of facing and dealing with life challenges, resolving the hurt and trauma of the past allows for healing at all levels and for the stage to be set for transformation. In males, this leads to accepting the feminine side, true masculinity and then the capacity for transformation—to become the True Self.

True masculinity represents completeness, peace, stability and timelessness. Getting there manifests as urgency, incompleteness, and striving that is part of false masculinity. At the societal level, this adds to an evolution of consciousness from the nice, orderly and all masculine concept of ultimate reality, to now including the feminine. It also includes seeing the darkness within as part of the whole, even as the darkness is brought to light through the transformational process. Ultimately it is moving toward wholeness and completion. We become whole when we accept the darkness within and transform it to light.

What then is true masculinity? It is the balance of the feminine side with the masculine, creating true strength and power. It is mastering aggression. This allows for strength with compassion, power with a balance of emotional awareness and expression. It allows for the proper channeling of aggression into genuine strength that is protective and goal directed. The man can be competitive while creating win/win situations for everyone.

True masculinity is treating women with respect and dignity. It is accepting and honoring the feminine, with women and with Mother Earth. It is the combination of strength with nurturing and caring for others, especially his family. It is the softness and gentleness, a man truly comfortable with his masculinity, can express to others and the world. It is spiritually based rather than ego based masculinity.

For males, the challenge is to heal and transform their lives, including the normal developmental challenges, to arrive at true masculinity. It is learning to accept the feminine side of their nature and consciously choose this in their lives. By doing this they are able to connect to their divine truth. Not only are they in balance psychologically and emotionally, they are in balance with their human and spiritual sides.

Chapter 7
RETURN OF THE FEMININE

We live in a time where it is more important than ever to restore feminine energy to the individual and collective experience, regardless of the gender we are incarnated in currently. An important part of healing and transformation, both individually and collectively, is to return to a balance of feminine and masculine energy. For far too long the masculine has dominated, culminating in the peril that now confronts our civilization. The masculine has been so dominate, even psychological research indicates that currently females are more masculine than feminine. The Feminism Movement valuably contributes to the idea of equality of the sexes, yet even they have been more focused on masculine ideals because of the masculine domination of the world that has gone on for far too long.

It is time for a return to true balance. As noted in the previous chapter, men are incomplete without learning and accepting their feminine side. For females, there is a need to learn and accept their masculine side, and more importantly, greatly accept their feminine side as well. For society as a whole, now more than ever, there is a profound need for the return of the feminine.

Advanced civilizations balance the feminine and the masculine. They don't allow either energy to predominate. As we once again advance toward a New Golden Age, the return of the feminine will allow us to be in balance and advance into higher awareness and consciousness. We are going into higher dimensional frequencies and vibrations as third becomes fourth dimensional and higher realities on this planet. Those that make it there will be more balanced within. Society, as a whole, will be more balanced as well. It is time, once again, to honor the feminine and to let the Goddess be an equal part of life.

The *Webster's New World Dictionary of the American Language: College Edition* defines feminine as "female, of women or girls; having qualities regarded as characteristic of women or girls such as gentleness, weakness, delicacy, modesty, etc.; womanly; suitable of characteristic of a woman;" and, said of men to be "effeminate or womanish." It is important to be careful here about negative connotations or biases our culture has about weakness. With the false emphasis on strength in our masculine defined and driven historical period, we have ignored the importance of vulnerability and the dimension of weakness. As stated earlier, the weakness part of the strength/weakness polarity is equally important. The capacity to fully experience and express this dimension is not only valuable, but also necessary, if we are to evolve as a species and a planet. As Abraham Maslow rightly pointed out, as we grow, heal and transform individually, the seeming dichotomy of strength/weakness becomes an integrated synergy as we self-actualize.

From a metaphysical standpoint, the male may find love, beauty, empathy and intuition as he reaches toward the feminine aspect of Divinity. For the female, she may find strength, creative energy and power as she reaches toward the masculine aspect of Divinity. Positive male and negative female energy, from a duality standpoint, blend together which creates mutual progression, beautification and gratification. This occurs between us and within us. It is important for us to recognize the female and male aspect present in each soul and in each person.

It is even more vital to understand it is time to let the feminine return and be in balance with the masculine. The very survival of humankind is at stake. As noted in the previous chapter, this means males have to nurture their feminine side to create true masculinity. For females, this means allowing their feminine side to re-emerge and emerge more powerfully, in balance with their masculine side.

While the Women's Liberation movement has done much to bring females forward from second-class citizenship, an unfortunate emphasis has been on mimicking false masculinity, negating or diminishing the true power of the Goddess within. While it is important and necessary for full equality between the genders, let alone within all of humanity, females imitating false masculinity will not get humanity to the necessary balance between the feminine and the masculine that will heal and transform it. It is vital for true femininity to emerge once again, to help the planet and humanity evolve into higher and higher expressions of who we are and who we want to be as a civilization.

Already, we can see the positive influence of women in formerly male careers, and also the positive influence of men in formerly female careers. We see police work evolving from false masculine needs for dominance and control to the feminine influence of managing and resolving conflict in non-authoritarian ways. We see medicine evolving as female physicians bring feminine values into patient care, treatment and research. We already see the positive influence of women in the legal profession, moving from an always-adversarial approach to conflict resolution and negotiation in the interest of all parties approach. We already see the positive influence of men transforming the nursing profession as they bring the masculine perspective to patient care.

In his book, *SHE, Understanding Feminine Psychology*, the author, Robert A. Johnson examines the development of femininity from a Jungian psychological perspective. He tells us that women have a psychological masculine minority component within them, that Jung called the *animus*. In his book, he examines the myth of Amor and Psyche, and how the myth reveals the female task of becoming whole, complete and individuated. This process of healing and transformation overcomes the false femininity of the helpless, dependent, and subservient individual who must defer to the male hierarchy of the current world. True femininity moves beyond all the stereotypical roles, such as the dumb blond or the Southern belle to name a couple.

In graduate school, I remember a fellow female student who played the dumb blond role, despite being an intellectually gifted woman in a graduate psychology program. It was fascinating to watch her manipulate the males around her; especially male faculty members who one would hope would know better, or would want to nurture her more authentic feminine self. While she was often the center of attention, and no doubt used her feminine wiles beneficially for herself, it was distressing to watch this control drama play out effectively.

In mythology, Aphrodite represents primitive, oceanic femininity. This is the femininity that reigns in the unconscious mind. Johnson tells us one can admire, worship or be crushed by this aspect of femininity. Psyche represents evolving to the new femininity. Every woman has an Aphrodite in her. Her chief characteristics being vanity, conniving lust, fertility and tyranny when she is crossed. Johnson tells us it can be very embarrassing for modern, reasonably intelligent women to discover their Aphrodite nature and all her primitive, instinctual tricks she plays.

In the process of healing and transformation, women evolve their femininity. To do this they have to recognize the part of themselves that will use any means at their disposal to down an opponent. Yet the primitive feminine side is also valuable, for it is the basic, instinctive motherhood necessary for the reproduction and continuation of humanity. Women often readily recognize when this basic, instinctive aspect of the feminine is missing. Watching the subtle, rather than dramatic, reactions of a mother who supposedly lost a child and actually suspect's foul play by the mother that harm has come to that child. Paradoxically, it is the primitive feminine nature that helps the new femininity to grow. Often the tyrant mother-in-law or the wicked stepmother represents this. Much of the turmoil for modern women is the collision between her Aphrodite nature and her Psyche nature.

According to Johnson, Psyche's nature is so magnificent, so unworldly, so virginal and pure; she is worshiped but not courted. This is the intense loneliness females experience at some point in life. For men, desire can't handle the true femininity that women can manifest. Men have not been capable of accepting the new femininity, in part because of their own unresolved ability to integrate the feminine into their personality, and then wanting to find a mother figure rather than a partner and true companion. The historical period emphases on false masculinity has also led to the fear of, even remotely, touching the Goddess in women let alone have it be a part of our world.

There is a Psyche in every woman and it is intensely lonely. Every woman is a royal daughter—too lovely, too perfect, and too deep for the ordinary world. Thus, when a woman finds herself lonely and not understood, when people are good to her but keep their distance, she has found her Psyche nature. This can be terribly painful. Yet this great beauty within, this Psyche nature, can be made conscious and a noble evolution may begin. It is vital that this true femininity begin to again emerge in greater and greater numbers.

Unfortunately, most men don't want women to be conscious and certainly not aware of their new femininity. This accounts for the strong efforts by men to control women, relying on culture and tradition, even holy books, to justify remaining with tradition. Not only in marriage, but also in all aspects of living, false masculinity would prefer to have women remain subordinate. It is this very lack of balance that has left us as a very primitive civilization ready to destroy ourselves.

In marriage, at least initially, men hope their women will not seek consciousness, do things their way. Men want the old patriarchal marriage, in which they make all the decisions. According to Johnson, for some reason the Psyche in each woman has to go through at least a brief stage, in which she is totally subject to a man. He says it is an archetypal level that can't be avoided. I would suggest, as we begin to truly honor and nurture the emergence of the true feminine, perhaps this subjugation will become totally unnecessary. What is offered in return for this is the promise of paradise, thus the myth of falling in love, getting married and living happily ever after. Yet, in truth, falling in love is preschool compared to the deep abiding love two people can share, which is the product of the hard work that makes a partnership happen.

Every immature man is a paradise maker, wanting to carry the girl off and promise her she will live happily ever after. Men secretly want their paradise without any work to develop a true partnership, because they want no responsibility and certainly no conscious relationship. They certainly don't want to have to go through the process of healing and transformation in the relationship, to become more aware, to then responsibly choose who they are and who they want to be creating genuine partnership with another person.

The feminine demand is for evolution. Most evolution comes from the feminine element in the myths. This is terrifying to men, who would rather live in the paradise they control. Yet, paradises are always suspect, as they don't work well. There is something in the unconscious of a man that wishes to make an agreement with his wife that she will ask no questions of him. Men prefer marriage to be a place to come home to but not a bother. He wants to be free to not focus on the relationship while he focuses elsewhere. This is a great shock for most women. They see marriage as a total commitment, whereas for men, this is not so. Again, the return of the feminine will require men to be more committed to their partner, while balance is achieved by women not buying into the paradise promise and bringing their talents to a wide variety of opportunities in the world.

As feminine consciousness evolves, there is a criticizing element toward the masculine, often expressed toward the significant other in venomous ways. On the positive side, this ability to look at the masculine in a more critical manner allows for consciousness to evolve. Love can either become a devouring dragon or a process for increased awareness. Commitment to a significant other leads to mature womanhood. A man is death to a woman in an archetypal sense, for the maiden quality gives way to the mature feminine consciousness.

If women see themselves consciously as pure loveliness and gentleness only, they overlook their dark side. As that side emerges, it pushes the woman out of a self-satisfied, naïve paradise into new discoveries about their true depth and true femininity, according to Johnson.

When the woman looks at her masculine side and challenges it, no longer dominating her and often a terrible loneliness sets in. According to Johnson, when the woman faces her masculine side, it can no longer be dominant in her psyche. When she relates to her masculine side, she is no longer subservient to it and can bring it into balance in her life expression.

Increased awareness and consciousness for the woman allows the truly feminine side to emerge. This helps men too, for that feminine consciousness calls upon men to live up to their own consciousness and their own increased awareness. Men require feminine acknowledgement of their worth. Terrible things happen to men who are deprived of the presence of women. Apparently it is the presence of women, which reminds each man of the best that is in him. Imagine the growth in men when they are acknowledged by fully, conscious, aware females. Imagine the power of true femininity in allowing women to truly be equal partners in all areas of life, intimately and in all other relationships.

Think about this on a planetary basis. For so long, women have been kept in subservient and often substandard roles, with disastrous consequences to the religion, culture or society where this occurs. One need only look at the male dominance of the Catholic Church and other Christian denominations, or what happens in Islamic societies. One only has to look at what the historical period has brought to the world, with women barely acknowledged, let alone being able to bring the increased awareness and consciousness that would benefit us all, men and women.

Most men get their deepest conviction of self-worth from a woman, their wife or mother, or if they are more aware, from their own feminine side. Women are often the light in the family, helping men to find meaning as they often have trouble doing that for themselves. The touch of light, or acknowledgement, is a fiery thing. It often stings a man into awareness. This is partly why he fears the feminine so much. On a planetary level, keeping women in their place protects men from increased awareness and increased consciousness. This is why the return of the feminine is so essential and vital to the transformation of humankind and the evolution of an advanced spiritual civilization on this planet. Women are the light bearers. Feminine light is exquisitely beautiful. A return to the feminine will light up this world again, ushering in the light of the New Golden Age.

For the female to evolve, she must break the unconscious domination of her subordinate, mostly unconscious, masculine component. For her to evolve, her masculine side must take up a position between the conscious ego and the unconscious inner world. This is recognizing the godlike element within her, expanding spiritual awareness. Then the female has control over her feelings, a capacity unknown to most men. She can attune to her highly introverted, internal quality, accessing the intuitive, which is the God touch she experiences. Becoming very still, the feminine is able to "get right," to become very creative and very aware. This is a diffused awareness, rather than the masculine focused consciousness. Women only need a little of their masculine side, for the greater power of the feminine side is in the diffused awareness, the intuitive connection, the greater capacity to access the Higher Self, to listen to "the still small voice within." It is no accident that the oracles at Delphi were the priestesses.

The feminine suggests how we are to relate to the vastness of life. The feminine way is to do one thing and to do it well. It is to take one thing at a time. Yet, the feminine nature is flooded with the rich vastness of possibilities in life and is drawn to all of them. Unlike the prevailing masculine idea that more is better, the feminine approach is that a little of a quality, experienced in high consciousness, is sufficient. It really is about choosing who you are and who you want to be one moment at a time, gaining as much as you can from each experience, rather than trying to do it all at once. Is it not ironic that meditation helps us to still the mind, to focus on the experience itself and allow divine wisdom to flow into and through us?

A return to the feminine is important. The masculine and the feminine each carry one half of reality. During the historical period, we have over emphasized the masculine at our own peril. Each complements the other. Each needs the other. Each nourishes the other. Even the offices of the Archangels have a masculine and a feminine partnership. Yet, we have insisted one is more important than the other during the last few thousand years.

Transformation is a psychological death as we move from one level of development to another. One dies to the old self and puts on a new self. Ultimately it is to become increasingly involved with life's complexities, including the dark and ugly side and the potentialities. For women, this is allowing the true feminine side to emerge, embracing the masculine part of the personality and moving to higher levels of consciousness with the increased awareness that comes from going through this process. The masculine side saves the ego in the female. Each has a proper, whole and complete relationship with the other. The fruit of this union for woman is joy and ecstasy, wholeness and divinity.

The balance of the masculine and the feminine for the planet is also a union that brings joy and ecstasy, wholeness and divinity for the entire world. The crowning achievement of femininity is to be able to bring joy, ecstasy and pleasure into life. When a woman reaches her full development and discovers the Goddess within, she gives birth to the joy and ecstasy that is the birthright of all. Men value women because they have this capacity and power. Men can't find this alone. The world can't find it alone. Bringing the feminine back to its rightful place will bring true joy to the world. It is a female's supreme privilege and development to be a bringer of joy. Joy is a gift from the heart of women.

For women, healing and transformation allows the true feminine to emerge. The return of the feminine is critical to the further evolution of humanity and to the emergence of a truly spiritual renaissance on the planet.

Marianne Williamson shares, the Goddess retains all her many faces of femininity, from the material to the erotic, to the divine. She says that neither the Goddess Self, nor the Sexual Self nor the Mother Self is diminished by the presence of the others. She speaks of the Egyptian temple of Hathor as the most powerful sacred site in the world. The force of Hathor is found there in her vast feminine glory, resplendent in her power to rise up, both men and women, from the depths of their brokenness, littleness and shame. Marianne sites Jacqueline Onassis and Princess Diana as modern examples of motherhood and sexuality, not opposed, but playing off of each other.

According to Williamson, sex, mysticism and motherhood form a feminine trinity. She sees the trinity as a mystical union of three pieces of the universe that should not be kept apart. Separation of the essential parts of our humanity is the cornerstone of our fallen self.

She states that Isis, Osiris, Horus and Seth all live within us. The feminine side is Isis, breathing love into our deadened other half. Osiris is our masculine half, noble and brave, yet torn apart by attacks from a jealous world. The fear-based ego in each of us is Seth; set out to destroy the experience of powerful, total, authentic love. The highest potential in each of us, according to Williamson, is Horus, set to reclaim humanity's divine identity, nurtured by a divine mother, married to a divine Goddess, first pharaoh in the psychic land of their gods. Horus is the balance of the feminine and the masculine manifesting the love of the positive ego in alignment with spiritual truth.

Williamson reminds us, it is Horus' role to re-remember his father. This brings back together, the lost and broken pieces of the god-self within. Horus is the fully actualized self, born of divine parents, living a life of unity and integrity, here to rule and harmonize the forces of the universe. At every stage of his life there was a woman to nourish and support him. The return of the feminine allows the healing and transformation to take place individually and collectively, so we all remember and live our true God Consciousness.

Marianne Williamson reminds us, we should all feel authorized to create. We should want a world where everyone is equally empowered. We should want a world where everyone can feel equally empowered to manifest the power of good. The feminine does not just give birth to new life; it restores life where it is broken. Williamson tells us, love is a feminine force, not just in women but in men as well.

Creating occurs, not out of "doing" but out of "being." Williamson writes this is being loved, being appreciated, being honored, being wanted, being cherished, being respected, and being received at the deepest levels of our souls. She tells us that at physical birth we lie in our mother's arms. At spiritual rebirth, the divine mother reaches through a lover to hold us once again.

In her book, *The 13 Original Clan Mothers,* Jamie Sam shares how Native American feminine wisdom can be integrated into our daily lives. She shares the sacred path to discovering the gifts, talents and abilities of the feminine. She believes women have not always been trained to respect the feminine principle in them. She shares how knowing the thirteen original clan mothers help women to know how to heal themselves before they reclaim their roles of healing and nurturing others. She says the wounded feminine aspect in women will no longer need to be hostile, angry, separatist-oriented, or manipulative to cover old pain. Instead women can present the healed role models they represent, leading others through example, instead of through male conquest or competition, allowing our world to reclaim a new point of balance between male and female.

The first clan mother is, Talks With Relations and is the keeper of learning the truth. It is about finding kinship with all life. It is developing the capacity to see the interconnectedness of all life and know we are all interrelated to each other. Instead of seeing ourselves separate from the world and all creation, it is recognizing the unity in all life and respecting that unity. It is also recognizing the unity of all humanity and not seeing our selves as separate from one another. It is having a seeking mind, a willingness to learn, and an understanding of the rhythm of each life form, area of Earth and the Cosmos beyond.

This first feminine force is about having right relationships with the Creative Force, the Higher Self, spiritual beings, our bodies, family, and friends and worthy opponents. It is about having right relationships with every part of the natural world. This principle is having relationships that become loving, productive situations that offer us opportunities to exchange ideas and learn the lessons of sharing with unity, in order to grow. Certainly, our world is in need of this attitude and approach to life to heal the strife and conflict alone that exists in our world today.

The second clan mother is Wisdom Keeper, the historian of all Earth Records. She is the feminine aspect of ancient wisdom, ultimately kept alive and increasingly available in the great mystery school traditions, but not limited to these either. This aspect is about how to develop the True You through honoring the truth in all things.

This aspect also honors the truth as it is seen from each person's Sacred Point of View, because all individuals experience life's events in a different manner. There is truth is every life journey. It is going beyond the belief that a particular religion, philosophy or tradition holds the only truth or path to wisdom and understanding. It is about having an expansive view for self-development. It is honoring the truth in every race, creed, culture, life form, tribe and tradition by seeing the similarities in all, rather than the differences. We can honor others' truth, and have no need to defend our sense of truth. As we honor our own truths, we develop our sense of Self and allow others to do the same. More importantly, with every new understanding of the truths others carry, we add to our personal wisdom and knowledge.

The third clan mother is Weighs the Truth. This is the feminine aspect of Divine Law, being the keeper of equality and the guardian of justice. Is it no surprise justice is represented by a Goddess? It is Divine Law that is represented here, as our actions and choices always do come back to us. We are the ones who, in finding and accepting the truth in our actions, must decide what we will learn in order to make amends for not making right choices. It is moving beyond our ideas of our self-importance that keep human egos out of balance. It is moving beyond our own arrogance and learning humility.

This feminine aspect is about seeing all sides in any situation in order to determine the truth. It becomes self-determination to look at all sides of life, to all our talents and accept the truths found, even if we don't like what we discover. True healing and transformation is facilitated by the capacity for open and honest self-examination, especially those parts of ourselves we want to avoid or want to deny.

Ultimately, the process of self-determination allows us to accept the truth of what gives us joy and not be confused or influenced by what others want us to be. We respond to our heart's greatest desire, choosing who we really are and who we really want to be. We learn to accept the truth inside us, connecting with our true Self, and the truth of the experiences we encounter in life. By looking at our strengths and our weaknesses we can destroy the illusions that limit our potential. Finally we learn to focus on what is strong and right within us.

We learn to not be critical of ourselves and not be critical of others as well.

The fourth clan mother, Looks Far Woman, represents the feminine aspect of prophecy, which is seeing the truth in all colors. This involves the intuitive ability women more easily and readily allow to express in their lives. It is the capacity to be aware of all other dimensions of awareness. It is the feminine quality of being a seer, an oracle, a dreamer and a visionary. In Greece, the Oracles of Delphi were women. In previous times with more balance between the masculine and feminine, it was the priestesses that opened the door to greater awareness and connection to the spiritual domains.

This clan mother, Looks Far Woman, instructs humanity on how to unravel symbols found in psychic impressions. It is the ability to find personal and planetary prophecy that God in His/Her infinite wisdom leaves available to all of humanity. Thus, the intuitive abilities of a Nostradamus or an Edgar Cayce, the hidden codes in the Bible or the personal dreams and intuitive visions of each individual, the Divine Plan and the various probabilities that exist are available if we seek to find them. A key to accessing this is to seek with love and be willing to receive guidance when the heart is open.

This feminine aspect understands that all possibilities and probabilities exist in the future. Through free choice we manifest certain possibilities. We can use the intuitions and the dreamtime information to change the course of our personal experiences. The future is not meant to be left to chance. As we respond to Divine Guidance and open ourselves to the messages available to us, we can make better choices and we facilitate healing and transformation. We can learn to fully understand the intuitive signs and symbols presented in our awareness.

This aspect also warns us not to project too far in the future, forgetting our ability to use our free will. We can trap ourselves into projections, expectations and the loss of potential opportunity. It is important to develop personal clarity, allowing us to then make personal choices in order to alter our Sacred Path and grow.

The fifth clan mother is Listening Woman, and represents the feminine aspect of hearing the truth. This is the ability to access the Stillness and hear "the still, small voice within." It is the capacity to access the voice of inner truth. It is also the capacity to listen to all viewpoints in order to learn the harmony that can be found through allowing each life form to have its Sacred Point of View. This is particularly important when someone else may be telling us something we don't want to hear, which may be stopping our growth.

It is the capacity to listen with the heart, not just with the mind. This helps to discern if others are speaking the truth, especially as we listen to their inflections and feelings in their speech. Over time we can develop the capacity to detect when others are being untruthful.

This feminine capacity involves hearing every thought, sensing every feeling and receiving every impression. It can help us return to balance when we are out of balance. It allows us to see the potential in all things and sense probable outcomes. It gives us encouragement when we are walking in grace.

The sixth clan mother is Storyteller, representing the feminine quality of having faith, being humble and staying young at heart by keeping our innocence intact. It is the capacity to speak from the heart, always say what we mean in a truthful, clear and concise manner.

This aspect teaches us how to use humor to dispel our fears and how to balance the sacredness with irreverence. It is the ability to laugh at our humanness and our silly attempts to preserve our limitations, correcting the self-created demons that bind us to the negative ego, control dramas and dysfunctions. It helps us to step away from our own chaos and emotional distress.

The seventh clan mother is Loves All Things, and is the capacity to love the truth found in all life forms. It is the wisdom of compassion, the feminine aspect of loving and nurturing. This aspect honors the physical as sacred, such that there is no judgment. It is doing all actions with a happy heart. We can find joy in the physical life, without trying to escape our pain through becoming addicted to false pleasures or compulsive behavior patterns.

It is the feminine aspect of unconditional love. It is an unconditional love that allows us to go through the hard, self-imposed lessons that are the consequences of walking the path of negative ego and dysfunction. Experiencing the consequences of our unloving actions allows us to remember and avoid these pitfalls in the future as we choose higher levels of who we are and who we want to be. Learning there are consequences to all our actions, positive and negative, helps us to evolve. Healing and growth involve many cycles of experience as we learn from the actions we take and their consequences. Ultimately, we develop self-love as we learn to break the patterns of self-induced dysfunction and misery.

The eighth clan mother is She Who Heals, representing the feminine aspect of serving the truth. She represents intuition, truth, water and feelings. She is the keeper of all healing uses and of all growing cycles. Thus, the process of healing and transformation requires the feminine aspect of intuitive healing, for in the process of becoming aware of the Higher Self we can be properly guided in the healing process. It is not surprising women more readily seek counseling and therapy, as well as learn the more metaphysical paths that also lead to healing and transformation, since they already have permission in our current world to honor that part of them.

The special aspect of this feminine quality is the capacity to overcome the fear of death and accept the change as a new adventure in living. Whether the death is the end of a relationship, the end of a job or the end of physicality, we can see beyond the illusion of finality and celebrate each new adventure in life as another step that leads to wholeness.

This clan mother is the embodiment of the feminine principle that serves humanity in truth by assisting them through the healing process of being human. Remember, we are spiritual beings having a human experience. We need to embrace this human experience. In third and fourth dimensional reality, we get to experience the results of all our choices and learn and grow, ultimately at the soul level as we strive to become complete co-creators with God.

Setting Sun Woman is the ninth clan mother, representing the keeper of tomorrow's goals and dreams. She is the feminine principle of properly using our free will to insure abundance of the future. This has to do with the will to live, the will to survive and the will to be impeccable in preserving the planetary resources. It is learning the lessons of concern, dependability, nurturing, inner knowing, achievements and goals. It is doing this by being naturally intuitive and willing to be receptive, while doing this in harmony with all creation.

This principle has two aspects. The first is wisely using resources and thanking Mother Earth for our abundance. The second is learning how to go within and find our personal truths and resources. It is the capacity to meet the future without fear because we have taken steps to walk in the light. We learn preservation and inner knowing. We discover as above, so below. It is the recognition that God and the universe are within us in the spiritual essence of who we are, and thus who we can be. Finally, we remember we are not our bodies, but instead are vast beings, the physical existing inside our limitless spirits and the limitless dimensions of creation that is our Father/Mother God.

The tenth clan mother is Weaves The Web, representing the creative principle within all things. Working with the truth is the feminine principle at work here. It is the use of arts and crafts to create our ideas and dreams in the physical world. It is learning to express our creativity in a positive manner and use the energy available to us. As the keeper of the life force, it is the process of creating health, manifesting our dreams, developing and using our talents, and accessing our spiritual potentials.

This feminine aspect shows us when to destroy limitations and create anew. It is also the process of nurturing our creations. Since life is about creating our lives as masterpieces of joy, nurturing this process is central to healing and transformation, and creating who we want to be at the highest levels. We are meant to live extraordinary lives, not dysfunctional and limited lives, struggling to, but never overcoming the darkness we all must face.

When darkness and dysfunction seem to overwhelm us, our physical, emotional, mental and spiritual survival is at risk. We can tap into the life force to grow beyond the stagnation that threatens us. We can learn to manifest the inner beauty waiting in our heart to emerge, combining the spiritual truth of who we are while living the human experience.

We can bring our dreams to life, accepting completely, all the good that is awaiting us. Our connection to our True Self can emerge and gently guide us to create a life of joy. We can learn to overcome the dysfunctional patterns, control dramas, and the negative ego that would keep us trapped in negative and fear-based limitations and lack. We can weave a life of fear and attract the lessons needed to overcome that fear, or we can weave a life of love, creating the desire to share love and abundance. Giving birth to our dreams is always accomplished by having the desire to create, deciding to create, and taking the actions necessary, by using the flow of the life force, to give birth to the dream in the tangible world.

The clan mother of the eleventh moon cycle is Walks Tall Woman. She is the feminine aspect of walking our walk, which is walking the truth. It is learning to lead by example, doing as I do not as I say. It is about changing life's situations through taking action ourselves, not depending on others to do it for us.

It is the principle of being proud of our accomplishments through self-esteem, not self-importance. As we develop our skills, we learn to be happier. Since actions always speak louder than words, we learn to live examples of our philosophies and walk our personal truth. It is about integrity and inner knowing, not the opinions, jealousies or insecurities of others.

It is the value of true leadership, leading by example, being our personal best, and exploring all our options and the willingness to be innovative. Thus, we don't just accept what others say is the truth or only follow their definitions of enlightenment. We become innovative, not by destroying the traditions of the past, but rather by adding new truths to those traditions. Think of what the Buddha or the Christ brought to spiritual understanding by sharing new truths. This continues to be an ongoing process, at all levels. It is a guiding principle within us as we heal and transform our lives, and in the process, gain the knowledge and wisdom that adds to all of humanity as we all grow and evolve together.

This feminine aspect also represents the importance of physical health, as our bodies are indeed temples to the living God. Strength, flexibility and endurance gained through physical health are essential to overall well-being. Having a healthy mind is important to supporting a healthy body. A mind based on negative and fear-based thoughts will eventually create disease and illness. It is important to honor the body's needs by balancing physical activity, proper nutrition, proper attitudes, good sleeping habits and hygiene. We can persevere and meet our goals when the body is healthy. Our challenges are to be willing to drop our fears of taking action and balance our work activities with rest, relaxation and retreat.

The clan mother of the twelfth moon cycle is Gives Praise. It is the feminine principle of being grateful for everything we experience in life. It is having an attitude of gratitude. It is being grateful for the challenges and painful realities in our lives, no matter how difficult, since they show us how to develop our inner strength.

It is important to be grateful. As we show we are grateful for all that life gives, we complete the circle of blessings we receive. It is also the process of giving as we receive, learning to share all that we are blessed to have and know. We truly live in a universe that what we sow, we do reap. What goes around does indeed come around.

Blessings are not just material things; they are also health, shelter, basic needs being met, the love and friendship of others and experiencing the love and wisdom of Eternal Love. As we learn to appreciate and share our blessings, to have gratitude for these blessings, we create new abundance, new experiences and further joy. Negative thoughts and fears will attract difficult life lessons. When we discover that negativity takes from us our joy, we can then choose to learn how to change those patterns and shift our life experience. Being grateful for the truth found in our lives gives us the right attitudes and produces miraculous healing and new paths to follow. We can create magic and miracles within life.

When we celebrate who we are and give thanks for the lives we are leading, we open our hearts to continue the healing process of being human. The truth we find in every experience of our spiritual evolution marks a forward step in our individual path of joy and peace. By giving thanks for every victory we achieve and encouraging others by praising and being grateful for their victories ensures the continued movement on humankind toward unity. We truly do heal the world and ourselves. The attitude of gratitude propels us all on this path of healing and transformation, individually and collectively.

The clan mother of the thirteenth moon cycle is Becomes Her Vision. She represents the feminine aspect of transformation, especially the capacity to bring our spiritual essence into the physical form, becoming what we were intended to be. We are intended to be living vessels of love that God intended us to be. Through our personal visions and using our talents for the whole, we help heal humanity and transform all of humankind into a world of peace and illumination.

We learn how to go through every lesson and cycle of transformation in order to spiritually evolve. It is important to stay on our chosen path and not be drawn into limiting illusions. This process of change transforms the human body, heart, mind and spirit from a finite sense of self into an infinite, universal, creative extension of the love that Love created.

The process of transformation is continual with the goal of ascension being order of the day in the history of the world now. We can heal and transform through walking our life path or we can allow war, catastrophe, disease and pestilence to force the transformation upon us. As we heal and transform, we are shown the next level of understanding so we can continuously decide who we are and who we want to be.

The dreams we hold for ourselves grow and change with every decision made and lesson learned. The evolving dream is constantly present in our lives. We are who and what we are being in any given moment in time. As we make the choices that alter the course of how we manifest our dreams, we express our individualities. Our uniqueness then contributes to the overall Divine Plan and the unity of which each of us is one part. When we all realize our dream, heal and transform, and manifest our true spiritual and human potential, the world of peace and spiritual illumination will be complete. We can achieve planetary healing and transformation, and all ascend together to the greater adventures that await us in the ever-unfolding drama of creation and unity with God.

Achieving individual and planetary healing and transformation requires again honoring the feminine and bringing it into proper balance with the masculine, the true masculinity we must learn to manifest as well. God is All, both feminine and masculine. When we begin to again recognize the feminine faces of God, see the Goddesses in all life, and then we truly find balance, heal ourselves and heal the world. The Divine is both female and male. When we acknowledge that we are all divine, complex beings, both feminine and masculine in nature, we can begin to access true balance in our lives. In acknowledging these qualities exist in all of us, we begin to find balance in our relationships to our selves, our relationships to one another, and our relationship to the world in which we all live.

Isis represents the Divine Mother, as does the Blessed Mother Mary. The Divine Mother is the one who brings forth the qualities from within. As the Clan Mothers demonstrate, these feminine aspects, or principles, create the epitome of justice and wisdom, mercy and goodness. The feminine force chiefly expresses love, unselfishness and a desire to serve others. It is time to bring the feminine back into an equal partnership with the true masculine, healing us individually and collectively. Together, in balance, we achieve ascension and return to the right relationship with God as spiritual beings. We are having the marvelous human experience we all agreed to participate in. The balance of the masculine and the feminine exists throughout all creation. At the angelic level, each office of Archangel has both a masculine and a feminine counterpart. It is time for us to restore this same right balance within ourselves and on this planet.

Chapter 8
HEALING AND TRANSFORMATION WITHIN THE INTIMATE RELATIONSHIP

The challenge of balancing the masculine and the feminine within our selves naturally extends to achieving that balance between the self and another in the most important relationship in life. Learning to create and achieve true partnership with another person requires a tremendous amount of energy and work. The intimate relationship is the place where all our issues will come to the surface, the place where all of our negative and fear-based emotions will readily manifest, and the place where the unhealed parts of us will come forward, either to be acted out or to be healed.

Yet, relationships that come from mutual respect and equality, developing into true partnerships, can and do flow naturally and easily. As we heal the wounds within, and progress spiritually, relationships no longer require tremendous energy and work. With time and healing we may find another at the same level and the relationship progresses smoothly. Or, the relationship may facilitate healing and spiritual evolving and then becomes smoother with time. Eventually we can be in a significant relationship, in which there is acceptance and non-judgment.

No part of our life is more important than the intimate relationship. Even the sacred responsibility of parenting, which is being entrusted by God with the care and responsibility of a soul, is slightly less important. Parenting is best achieved when we are able to create and manifest a positive, healthy and equal partnership with a loved one, then together providing the healthiest level of guidance and nurturance to the children we hopefully have chosen to bring into this world.

Creating a successful and meaningful relationship with a significant other is a tremendous challenge. It requires considerable maturity and wisdom to establish and maintain a healthy relationship with someone else. Bringing in all our unhealed emotional wounds and combining these with all the unhealed emotional wounds of the other person, leads to a volatile mix that can easily sabotage our best efforts to have a loving, intimate, satisfying relationship with another person. Bringing in all our control dramas and manipulative styles, and combining these with all the other person's control dramas and manipulative styles, further adds to the challenge. False ideas about masculinity and femininity, and notions about who should be in charge of the relationship, also add to potential dysfunction and failure.

Is it any wonder that maybe only 10% of us seem to create successful intimacy through genuine partnership? As much as I think I know about successful relationships, it still hasn't prevented me from having my share of failures. As much as my psychological practice involves helping couples to identify what is contributing to the dysfunction in their relationship so they can move forward into teamwork with the other, I still struggle to overcome my own dysfunction to achieve true partnership with the significant relationship in my life. Not only do we have to heal the emotional wounds that hold us back from creating genuine partnership, we also have to overcome the dysfunctional ways we have related to other significant partners in our lives previous to the relationship we are now in.

Healing and Transformation

Is it any wonder so many relationships fail? Is it any wonder we often settle for second best in our relationships, figuring we can accommodate the dysfunction we are in; rationalizing this is better than being alone? So we think we fall in love, join with another person and even marry them with the hope that what emerges is at least tolerable. We learn to accept what is predictable with another person and end up living like probably 90% of couples live, dysfunctionally accommodating one another and never doing the work that can lead to genuine partnership and the deep abiding love that can result from healing and transforming this area of our lives.

While most of us profess we enter relationships because we fall in love, in truth, many other factors contribute to our attraction with another person. Unfortunately, we often are attracted to the other person based on largely unconscious motivations, finding the person who will somehow re-enact unhealed dysfunction from our past. We magically believe if we somehow keep repeating the same patterns over and over again with a new person, we will somehow overcome the dysfunction, heal our wounds without knowing it, and we will finally get our life right. The most obvious example of this is the person who keeps marrying one alcoholic after another, as though this time the issues and conflicts around alcoholic patterns will somehow magically resolve themselves.

Sometimes we are attracted to the person whose manipulative style or control drama matches our manipulative styles or control dramas, often learned as we survived our parent's manipulative styles or control dramas. That is why it seems opposites attract, because we find the seeming opposite to create an ongoing drama with them, each playing their own part in the matching dramas.

Sometimes we are attracted to the person who has qualities in their personality functioning that are missing or diminished in our own personality functioning. This is another way opposites attract. So the gregarious, outgoing individual may be attracted to the shy reserved individual, and vise versa. Or, the aggressive person is attracted to the passive individual, or vise

Healing and Transformation within the Intimate Relationship

versa. Or, the one who likes to take all responsibilities and make all the decisions is attracted to the one who doesn't want the responsibilities and doesn't want to make the decisions, and vise versa.

Add to this, past lives that must be balanced out karmically and the process of seeming unwitting attraction becomes very complicated. This is because we may have "contracts" at the soul level to connect with certain individuals in this lifetime. We may have contracts to resolve karmic debt or to learn certain lessons. We may also have contracts with those who are meant to be our soul mate in this time and place.

Whatever the reasons we are attracted to another individual, overcoming fear and overcoming past hurts and wounds becomes necessary if the relationship has a chance to succeed and evolve. However, we fear change in our self and in our relationship. Fear can be the biggest challenge in a relationship. We can be so vulnerable. We allow someone to get close to us, and see our flaws and shortcomings. When anger and hurt inevitably arise, the other person can use our vulnerabilities as weapons.

Even if we don't know at first what can push the buttons of the other person, sooner or later we are going to stumble on these. It is hard enough to work through the inadvertent pushing of buttons and to honestly identify this with another and own that the issue or behavior belongs to our past and not to the present relationship. Worse, is when one discovers what buttons they can push against the other and uses these against the other in the future, especially when being manipulative or not engaging in fair fighting.

Many relationships unfortunately end because of the pain and anger produced by fear. Since we are the most vulnerable in the most intimate of relationships, it is imperative that we heal and transform the places of fear, hurt and pain within ourselves, so we don't continually contaminate the current relationship at this point in time. Marianne Williamson writes our intimate romantic relationships will bring out all of our unresolved issues, whether at the emotional level, the psychological level, or the spiritual level. Romantic relationships are the place when the most significant healing can and will take place. It takes tremendous courage to understand this can and will happen, to not run from it, and to do what you can to heal your part in it.

It is important to keep in mind that we are only responsible for our half of a relationship. Our responsibility is to bring our very best to the relationship, including at the spiritual level. At this level, it is an attitude of unconditional love, a willingness to be as nonjudgmental as we can be and truly learn to practice and express forgiveness. As we try to bring our very best to our romantic relationships, it is important to remember we are responsible *TO* the other person, but we are not responsible *FOR* the other person. We are responsible for bringing our very best to the relationship, to be honest, have integrity and to work to make it work. We are not responsible for the other person's happiness or living happily ever after.

Several things are critical in creating a positive and loving, romantic relationship. It is important for direct, open and honest communication. We need to be clear in what we are trying to say, to be completely honest, in a kind and loving way, and not hide what we want to say. We cannot assume the other person understands what we are trying to say. We have to be sure they get it. We also have to be sure we get it as well, when our partner is trying to share with us in a hopefully direct, open and honest way. I cannot read your mind or guess what you are trying to tell me. I cannot expect you to read my mind or guess what I am saying either. The worst things we can say to one another are, "You know what I am thinking," or, "You should know what I am thinking," and/or, "You know what you did." Hopefully as we learn to express ourselves with direct, open and honest communication, the most dreaded words a couple can say to each other, "Honey, we have to talk" become instead an opportunity to share issues and concerns, to clear up areas of conflict and disagreement, and arrive at solutions and resolution.

Another critical part of creating a positive and loving, romantic relationship is sharing expectations. Each person in the relationship has many similar, but also many different ideas of how to share life and manage their partnership. It is important to share these expectations of how the relationship can work, what we want to bring to the relationship and what we want from the other person. This covers all expectations, both large and small. Even the simplest expectations can derail a relationship.

Sharing expectations can be more demanding than it may seem at first. This really requires taking the risk to share what it is you want and need in a relationship. By clearly stating your expectations, the other person may become frightened or turned off to a part of you, or you may do the same toward them. Yet if you just try to accommodate the other person or only tell them what you think they want to hear, you have already sabotaged the future success of the relationship. It is truly amazing, the number of people I work with or talk to, who discover the person they are in love with is not the person they thought they were getting.

There is a whole group of men and women out there who are very good at putting on an "ideal" persona to captivate the heart of another. Then after they are married, a whole different side emerges. This is also why taking time to get to know someone else is so important, because even the best "actors" can only put on their facade for so long. It is particularly important to be cautious if someone appears to be too good to be true. While some people exist that are truly as good as it gets, most of us are still striving to heal and transform our lives and are not there yet. A good piece of advice I frequently hear from Native American tradition is you should know the other person for four seasons before you decide, at the most serious level, commitment with them.

Sharing expectations about the large issues and the small issues allows each of you to have informed consent about the person you want to be romantic and intimate with emotionally. How else can you truly decide if this is a person you want to commit to and share your life with, if you cannot honestly tell them what your expectations are in a relationship and they cannot tell you what expectations they have. We all have needs and wants. It is important for each person to know what these are or may be.

By sharing expectations in an open, honest and direct manner, each can begin the process of negotiation to get to common ground. Common ground can even be to agree to disagree. Common ground is the place that both parties can get to when there are differences in expectations. Common ground can produce many different outcomes, as there are as many solutions to challenges as one can imagine and create. Take something as simple as how toothpaste is dispensed from a tube. One person's expectation may be the tube should always be squeezed from the bottom. The other person could care less and squeezes anywhere they wish. Multiple solutions are available. The couple could agree to always squeeze from the bottom, or to squeeze wherever, since it does not really matter. Or, there could be separate tubes so each person could squeeze the way they like. Or, a different kind of dispenser could be agreed upon.

While this may seem like such a trivial issue, such small issues can easily derail a relationship. If such small issues can derail a relationship, then what happens with major issues, such as, how to discipline children, what standards should there be for rewarding children for responsible behavior, what kind of financial plan should there be, how money is to be spent, what kind of retirement goals are there, what kind and size of house to buy, where to live, where to retire, should both parties work while raising children, or how to handle health issues may all derail a relationship.

There are solutions to the big and small issues that arise in every relationship. It is not the solution that determines whether a relationship will succeed or fail, but it is the process that will ultimately determine if you can have a sound, functional, and ultimately deeply, loving relationship. This is not to say all common ground solutions are optimal for each person's heal-

Healing and Transformation within the Intimate Relationship

ing and transformation. There can be very loving relationships where the common ground, either spoken or more often never spoken or overtly decided, where one party is domineering and the other is passive, and it works for them. However, I would suggest that as loving as that solution is for them, it still falls short of the deep, abiding love that can exist between two people when they actively work to achieve common ground in their relationships.

The active process of working to achieve common ground provides the framework to create a truly harmonious and deeply loving, intimate relationship. This process can be very challenging. There may be profound differences that need to be resolved by working to get to common ground. It can be work. It can be very emotional and very trying. Relationships may be hard work at times. I recently dated a woman who I instantly connected with and her with me. There was tremendous potential for us to develop a significant long-term relationship with each other. However, she could not accept true love would still require "work," and she chose to move on.

Her hope was true love would simply be romance and an easy effort to get to common ground and it would never be too challenging or demanding. It was understandable that the "work" to get to common ground would be too much for her, given the marriage she had been in and how hard she had worked to make dysfunction work in the past. The same also occurred in a subsequent serious relationship that had also not worked out too well for her.

She was married to a man suffering from alcohol and drug abuse, and was also suffering from Bipolar illness. This disorder involves serious to severe mood swings. It is a very treatable disorder, but her husband didn't want to take the medications which would keep his moods stable. He was also a very controlling individual. This woman had to put tremendous work into trying to make a dysfunctional marriage work. She also truly loved him and felt she had to keep trying. It was only when his psychiatrist finally said to her, she would have to move on because he was not motivated to change, and the situation would destroy her psychological and emotional integrity, finally she realized she had to move on.

Controlling men was an unhealed issue in her life, dating back to her father. Her next significant relationship also involved a man who was very controlling. Controlling partners want to decide everything, including how their partner dresses, what clothes they wear, how they appear, who they see, when they can go out with friends, if they are allowed to have friends or when and where they can work. Controllers even try to tell their partner how and what they can do, with the minutest details of everyday living. Trying to make this relationship work, but also being oppositional to the control drama became "work" for this woman.

Unfortunately, the work to keep a dysfunctional relationship together, as well as to repeat one's own dysfunctional patterns and unhealed issues, is not the same as the "work" it takes to create functional patterns and heal old wounds and emotional traumas. Unfortunately, it is still work at some level. When the potential for true love and genuine partnership comes along, the magic of love isn't going to smoothly create the new partnership. There will still be effort and challenges, but creating genuine partnership does afford the opportunity to do the "work" that leads to healing and transformation of oneself in the most intimate and hopefully safe environments in which healing can take place. As Marianne Williamson rightly points out, romantic love is a place that we can heal emotionally and spiritually.

It is worth the effort to engage in direct, open and honest communication, share expectations, and then work to get to common ground. Common ground is the effort to arrive at a negotiated settlement between expectations that differ. Shared expectations simply need to be acknowledged and become a part of the agreement a couple has about how their relationship is defined and will operate.

Negotiating to get to common ground requires having a dialogue and then working toward an agreement about differing or opposing expectations. This may get very intense at times,

Healing and Transformation within the Intimate Relationship

as each of you may have very different ideas about an issue or may even be diametrically opposed to each other. As an example with disciplining children, one of you may be very firm about having consequences for inappropriate behavior and rule violations. You may want to throw the book at the offender and be very strict. Or, you may be the one who wants to be lenient, take into consideration extenuating circumstances and temper consequences based on particular circumstances. Since neither of you agree what should be done, working in a genuine partnership, it becomes necessary to discuss the situation, differences in viewpoints and work to a reasonable solution you both can live with and agree to. Often, the benefit of arriving at such common ground resolutions are the strengths of each partner contributing to a positive solution that not only benefits the particular situation, but also strengthens the relationship as teamwork contributes to genuine partnership.

It must be understood here that common ground is not compromise, although there may be an element of compromise in getting to the solution. Compromise usually implies that one or the other gives in and accepts a solution rather than get to a common ground solution. This is accommodation, not creating partnership. Given control dramas, gender differences and unhealed wounds that contribute to dysfunction, it may seem easier to compromise and get to a solution rather than expend the effort needed to arrive at common ground. However, easier is not always better. The effort expended to arrive at common ground may be difficult, conflicted and daunting, but it leads to true partnership between equals.

It also provides a forum for each of you to examine what is motivating you to not get to common ground, create new awareness and insight into your self, and discover the unhealed wounds, traumas, and dysfunctional patterns of ego-based behavior that prevent you from choosing who you are and who you really want to be in the most significant and important relationship in your life.

The effort is worth it, although it is, at times, the "hard work" of relationships. Being in love, alone, will not do it. We don't fall into love and then live happily ever after. Yet, we can be in that soft, gentle place of being in love with the other person and choose to work to create a genuine partnership with that person. The payoff is you will develop such a deep abiding love with the other person. The first falling in love you experienced will feel like preschool in comparison to the love you now experience.

While psychologists and marriage counselors describe stages of relationships in varying ways, the following five stages of relationships make sense to me. The first stage is the magical stage of falling in love with someone. It is the stage that takes your breath away. You experience the intense desire to be with them constantly and to communicate with them constantly. It is the wonderful first stage writers describe and movies are made about. It is the stage most often described in love songs and in poetry. It is truly a magical place where our hearts swell with joy and we experience a grand feeling of love for another person. Thank God this stage exists; we don't see the flaws and negatives that would ever allow us to get together long enough to begin to establish an intimate relationship with another.

As wonderful and romantic as this stage is, and it is a grand experience every time it happens, it only lasts between six and twelve months. It is a wonderful ride while it is happening and should be enjoyed with passion, to the fullest. But, it is not the stage to make decisions about creating a committed, long-term relationship. The saying "love is blind" is true in this stage, and we simply cannot see the problems and issues that will sabotage the long-term happiness and joy of the committed romantic relationship.

We simply do not see our unresolved issues and their unresolved issues in this stage, nor should they necessarily be seen. That can and will emerge in the second stage. In fact, we may be attracted to the person for all the wrong reasons, and cannot yet see this, so we can make a more informed choice about the potential partnership we may have with this person. There are many subconscious and/or unconscious reasons we may be attracted to another, based on our past and especially the unresolved issues and conflicts within ourselves. We may be attracted to another based on control dramas that match or on neurotic and dysfunctional patterns we have yet to resolve.

We wonder why people pick relationships that re-enact the same dynamics over and over. All of us hope that if we do the same process over this time, somehow it will magically resolve itself and be better this time. Why does one enter relationship after relationship with an alcoholic or an abusing individual? The subconscious hope is somehow this time it will work out differently and healing will take place with no real effort on our part. We try to believe that love will conquer all. While love is a very powerful and healing energy, and miracles do happen, most often there has to be real work in resolving old patterns and the underlying wounds that keep us in those old patterns.

After finally leaving a marriage with a spouse that could be very critical and emotionally abusive, I "found" myself in a new relationship where the very same things began to happen. As I became aware of this, no longer wanting to live this pattern, I could recognize and make the choice to move on. I made the effort to have direct, open and honest communication, shared expectations, and tried to get to common ground. When these failed, I realized I would not be able to create a genuine partnership with this person. Regrettably with my ex-wife, I did not have the courage to engage in direct, open and honest communication more fully, did not share expectations completely and did not work to get to common ground with her. I had given up and so I moved on. Maybe if I had done that more fully, we could have healed our relationship and could have created true partnership.

There are other reasons we may be attracted to another and fall in love. We may have had other lifetimes with that person and are now inexplicably drawn to that person. Or, we may have karmic debt to resolve with them, whether positive or negative, and have a contract with them at the soul level to come together. Or, we may have a contract with them to work out certain issues or have certain experiences that are part of our own and their own soul's growth and development.

There is such a thing as soul mates. I have come to understand there is more than one soul mate. Soul mates are souls that we have been together with in other lifetimes, as well as other times and places. We tend to travel through eternity with the same group of souls, so it is natural we come together and experience life together in the physical plane as well. My first significant relationship after my divorce, a friend told me is the transitional relationship, involved a woman, who I subsequently learned though muscle response testing, I have been with in 116 married lifetimes. I recalled one of those lifetimes during a Chiropractic Network Spinal Analysis session. Another of the lifetimes I recalled while standing at a waterfall in Peru. We were previously at the waterfall during an Incan incarnation.

There are many probable reasons we are drawn to a person with who we experience the initial falling in love stage. Whatever the reasons, there are no coincidences; so there is a reason we are brought together with someone else. The falling in love stage allows us enough time to connect with them, discovering each other long enough to consider the possibility of establishing a more committed, romantic, intimate relationship with that person. It is not the stage for making major life decisions, no matter how much in love you feel with them.

The decision making stage is the second one. This is the stage of falling into that soft, gentle place of being in love with another. This stage typically lasts from the end of the first stage to about one year after the honeymoon. It is the stage where we can more realistically see the other person in their totality, especially their flaws and the not so nice side of their personality. This is the stage when the person you are in love with is no longer perfect, but is more realistically perceived by you. The beauty of this stage is moving into that soft, gentle place of being in love is very powerful and moving in its own right.

This is the stage where we see the person as they truly are, yet feel such love for them we are now willing to consider they may be the person we want to be with in an intimate committed

Healing and Transformation within the Intimate Relationship

relationship. We are able to see the possibility of commitment and sharing a lifetime together. Hopefully as we practice direct, open and honest communication, and as we share expectations, we begin to create the foundation for a successful partnership with two equals coming together as one unity.

As we negotiate to get to common ground, we begin to create the foundation for equality in the relationship and have teamwork in the expression of our love. The sum of the partnership does become greater than the two who come together. Yet each retains their identity, their individuality and their autonomy and independence. The relationship becomes the expression of two complete individuals coming together to create an interdependent relationship. This is a relationship in which each person gets their dependency needs met, while also having the freedom to express their independence needs. As this suggests, this is the total opposite of control dramas and unequal power in the relationship.

While this is the ideal to strive for, the second stage is the place that true love begins to manifest. While it is wonderful and magical to fall in love, this place of soft, gentle love with another is the place where you can be safe, where you can be vulnerable, and where you know you will be loved and can love in return. This is the place to "know" if your loved one is the one you want to spend a significant portion of your life with, if not your whole life with.

As we mature and have the experiences in relationships we have over time, we may simply go immediately into this second stage of falling into that soft, gentle place of being in love with someone else. We don't have to have that initial rush of the first stage, because our maturity and wisdom allow us to more readily move into that place with another person.

Since there is confusion about what romantic love is, we erroneously assume that the first stage is the only stage of romantic love. We become disappointed when that is replaced by the other stages of the relationship. We often mistakenly believe the romance is gone when the beauty and power of the second stage is not recognized or overlooked, because it is not popularized or romanticized.

Complicating this even further is when we get into the third and fourth stages of relationships, where love can and is often lost. We also mistakenly believe being in love is sufficient to live happily ever after, the unfortunate myth of fairy tales. We miss that the process of making a relationship work leads to such a deep abiding love; it is almost indescribable in its intensity and joy. Saddest are those of us who abandon one relationship after another, to go and fall in love with someone else, hoping to magically find the one true love we can live happily ever after with. The truth is the work of creating partnership with someone else, working though all the issues and healing all the old wounds, creates the love of living happily ever after.

The third and fourth stages of relationships are where most couples get into trouble, get stuck in dysfunctional patterns or eventually fail in the relationship. The third stage is the attempt to change the other person. Despite all the things we adore and fall in love about, we next try to change the other person to conform to how we want them to be. This becomes an endless source of frustration and conflict. This is also where the ego takes over and our control dramas, manipulative styles and gender differences come to the fore. Recalling the chapters on masculinity and femininity, since we often don't have these areas healed and in balance within ourselves, naturally the fear-based ego takes over and tries to assert what it wants and needs, seemingly protecting you from vulnerability and risk. Yet in trying to protect us the ego creates the very destructive behaviors that ruin relationships. I can't tell you the number of couples that come to see me who almost immediately state everything in their relationship was going just fine until each started trying to change the other or insist things be done their way.

Unfortunately about 90% of all couples get stuck in this stage and the next stage. Since we don't take full advantage of the opportunities the relationship affords for healing and transformation, we endlessly play out our unhealed wounds and traumas, mostly unconsciously and sometimes subconsciously. The value of therapy is the unconscious and subconscious motivations can be brought to conscious awareness so we can better choose to resolve the underlying emotional hurts and scars, then make better choices of who we are and who we want to be, especially in the most important relationship of our life. Relationship books, seminars and retreats can also help to make us more aware, so we can heal and move on, hopefully creating genuine partnership with the one we love.

Half of the dynamics couples get stuck in and eventually conflicted over involve gender differences. Psychological research is showing differences in how men and women perceive the world and operate in their relationships. John Gray has popularized the understanding of this in his book, *Men Are From Mars, Women Are From Venus.* Many couples I see for marital therapy read this book and almost immediately begin to understand what they are fighting about involves normal gender differences. When they better understand where their partner is coming from and what they need, just in this arena, there is dramatic changes and easing of conflict. Most importantly, each is able to step beyond the need to find fault and assign blame. The need to find fault and assign blame is the one of the most destructive things that people can do toward and with each other, especially in the romantic, intimate relationship in their life.

An example of this is the need for men to have "cave time," according to John Gray. Women have a hard time understanding men need time to be alone, to putz around in the yard or their workshop, to read a magazine or to "surf" the TV. On the other hand, women have the need to emotionally process their day with their partner, and most importantly, to have the man just *LISTEN* and not offer any advice or solutions. Males feel a need to offer advice or solutions, so these areas readily become ripe for miscommunication and conflict. When men understand all they have to do is listen as their women process their day, and then there is a dramatic decrease in communication problems. When women also understand men need some alone time and it doesn't mean they are rejecting or ignoring them, then there is the same dramatic decrease in miscommunication and conflict.

The fourth stage of relationships that couples also get stuck in is the stage of accommodation. In this stage we try to accept how the other person is, recognizing we cannot change them and they are not going to change. Rather than try to share expectations and work to get to common ground, we instead allow whatever dysfunction or manipulative style to persist. When conflict inevitably arises, we stay mad at each other for a while, then "pretend" nothing happened and go on as though nothing has happened, until the next incident occurs.

Sometimes we "compromise" with each other, but this is not the same as working to get to common ground. Compromise is actually accommodation, because one or the other "gives in," rather than letting there be more distress in the relationship. Sometimes both compromise, which does begin to approximate getting to common ground. It still falls short of getting, through effort, to that place where both arrive at an agreement on how the relationship will work and will proceed.

Accommodation often reflects the control dramas and/or the manipulative styles we learn from our parents and others, or begin to use to protect our selves from the emotional wounds and hurts we experience. James Redfield in *The Celestine Prophecy* shares one system for understanding control dramas. He states, control dramas protect each person and allow them to "take" energy from others while keeping their energy. This goes against the truth that there is abundant energy in the universe and each of us can be a conduit to share this energy with others, replacing energy we extend by a constant flow of energy coming into us.

Redfield describes four control dramas. The first is the intimidator drama. In this drama, the person has to have complete control and can be quite dictatorial. Whether subtle or abusive, this drama insists everything go their way. These individuals can be very controlling and persuasive; everything will go the way they want it to go. They can be very intimidating and will often bully others. The opposite drama is the victim drama. This individual always sees the world and others taking advantage of them. Their frequent lament is "Oh! Isn't it awful?" They allow themselves to be intimidated and let others manipulate and control them. They get great mileage out of how terribly they are treated. Victimizations extend to seeing themselves as at the mercy of external factors and how dreadful they are to their well-being. They often connect with intimidators so each can play out their drama with the other.

Ironically, the victim drama often has the most power in the relationship as they can easily push the buttons of the intimidator or do the opposite of what the controller wants. Often they do it "innocently," claiming they just didn't understand what was wanted or do the opposite, claiming this is what they thought was wanted. An example is the verbally abusive, dictatorial boss, whose employees react by being passive-aggressive and not getting the task done on time, if at all.

The third drama is the interrogator. In this drama, the person is always asking questions, about anything and everything. The twist in this drama is no matter what answer you give, it is never good enough. So, there are more questions to be asked. Again, the purpose of this drama is to take energy from another person, without losing any energy for oneself. The process of asking questions seems almost automatic and questions persist even when you do not give answers. The interrogator drama goes beyond a normal inquisitiveness and is the predominate behavior for this type of drama.

Opposite of the interrogator drama is the aloof drama. In this drama you can ask all the questions you want, because this individual is not going to answer. They tune out others and will barely acknowledge they have been addressed. In casual passing at work or in the neighborhood, these individuals always look away so they don't even have to make eye contact or acknowledge your presence. The value of this control drama is the individual never has to make a stand or commit to any position. They can remain elusive and even mysterious. They take energy through having others trying to get information out of them or commitment to a position.

All the control dramas are based on the belief in limitation and lack, rather than the idea that we live in an abundant universe with all the energy we need and can pass on to others. These manipulative styles keep us trapped in old patterns, based on old wounds and old survival strategies. In our significant relationships, they keep us trapped in the third and fourth stages of relationships, continually trying to change each other and then continually trying to accommodate each other.

The way out of these control dramas is to engage in direct, open and honest communication. This is also the key to moving into the fifth stage of relationships, which leads to genuine partnership. Through direct, open and honest communication others can no longer successfully cling to their control drama. They are forced to be accountable for their actions and to "get real" with you when you are direct, open and honest.

When you challenge the intimidator directly, calling them out on their behavior, even to the extent that their behavior is frightening, it takes you out of that control drama with them. When you call out the victim drama, challenging their stance that life is awful and they are always on the short end of every situation, it takes them out of their control drama, as you will not play that game with them. When you ask the interrogator, "Why are you asking me all these questions?" you challenge their method of operation and will not participate in their drama. When you directly engage the aloof drama, challenging them to deal with you directly and not hide what they think and feel, then they have to decide to become genuine with you.

Another way of looking at manipulative styles is offered by Everett L. Shostrom, Ph.D., in his book, *Man, the Manipulator*. He proposes eight manipulative styles that people engage in, which leads to a number of different manipulative ways we connect with a significant other.

The Dictators exaggerate their strength. They dominate, give orders, quote authority and do anything to control their victims. Variations of this are Mother Superiors, Father Supe-

Healing and Transformation within the Intimate Relationship

riors, Rank Pullers, the Boss, and Junior Gods. The Weaklings are usually the Dictators' victims. They develop great skill in dealing with the Dictator. They exaggerate their sensitivity, are forgetful, do not hear and are passively silent. Variations are the Worrier, the "Stupid-Like-a-Fox," the Giver-Upper, the Confused, and the Withdrawer. The Calculators exaggerate their control. They deceive, lie and constantly try to outwit and control others. Variations are High-Pressure Sales People, the Seducer, The Poker Player, the Con Artist, the Blackmailer, and the Intellectualizor. The Clinging Vines are the opposite of the Calculators. They exaggerate their dependency. They want to be led, fooled and taken care of by the stronger person. They like to let others do their work for them. Variations are the Parasite, the Crier, the Perpetual Child, the Hypochondriac, the Attention Demander, and the Helpless One.

The Bullies exaggerate their aggression, cruelty and unkindness. They control by implied threats of some kind. Variations are the Humiliator, the Hater, the Tough Guy, the Threatener, the Bitch or the Nagger. The Nice Guys exaggerate their caring and loving. They kill with kindness. They are hard to cope with because it is hard to fight the Nice Guy. Variations are the Pleaser, the Nonviolent One, the Non-offender, the Noninvolved One, the Virtuous One, the Never-Ask-What-You Want One, and the Organization Man/Woman. The Judges exaggerate their criticalness. They distrust everyone and are blameful, resentful and slow to forgive. Variations are the Know-It-Alls, the Blamers, the Deacons, the Resentment Collectors, the Shoulders, The Shamers, the Comparers, the Vindicators and the Convictors. The Protectors are the opposite of the Judges. They exaggerate their support and are nonjudgmental to a fault. They spoil others, are over-sympathetic and refuse to allow those they protect to stand up and grow for themselves. Instead of caring for their own needs, they only care for others' needs. Variations are the Mother Hen, the Defender, the Embarrassed-For-Others, the Fearful-For-Others, the Sufferer-For-Others, the Martyr, the Helper and the Unselfish One.

Healing and Transformation

We may fit one or a blend of these manipulative styles. We often find our opposite. Thus, the folk wisdom that opposite attracts arises from the attraction to the opposite. Identifying what role or roles we tend to play, we can make decisions to move beyond these roles. With open, honest and direct communication we can begin to move into true partnership and evolve into a healthy, mature, and joyful relationship that manifests love at the deepest level.

To move from dysfunction to function requires a willingness to share in an open and honest manner. This needs to be done with the rules of fair communication. We need to be kind to one another, to always use "I..." statements rather than "you..." statements and offer suggestions or another way of looking at things rather than attacking. We have to create safety with each other so that expectations can be shared and we can then work to common ground. There is no need to be hurtful and mean.

If you are in a current significant relationship, don't yet give up on it without engaging in one final effort to see if the relationship can be salvaged and move to creating a genuine partnership. It will require work and effort at times. It will require overcoming your own emotional wounds and healing your own dysfunction. It will require developing a strategy to resolve differences, honestly communicate expectations, to be clear what these expectations are for one another and a genuine effort to see if you can get to common ground with your significant other. If the effort fails, you can at least walk away knowing you gave it your best effort and it is not going to work with that person.

After we have been in a significant relationship for some time and it fails, the next important relationship will be the "transition" relationship. This is often the relationship in which the unfinished business of the previous relationship gets worked out. Often, you may become aware of this because stuff is put on you that you know is not your stuff. You will also find you put onto the other person stuff they will tell you is not their stuff. While it can sometimes work out that your transition relationship can heal and move to that Fifth stage of genuine partnership, usually it does not. Understand this relationship allows you to finish the healing that did not take place at the end of your previous relationship. Learn from it and move on with new awareness of who you are and who you want to be.

Dr. Phil McGraw's book, *Relationship Rescue,* is a wonderful source of information to help you understand how you operate in a relationship, how your partner operates in a relationship, and what you can do to develop genuine partnership. Whether trying to salvage an existing relationship, discovering why your relationship failed, or to help you navigate through the transition relationship, Dr. Phil's process is one of the best sources for healing and transforming your relationships.

We do have soul mates, and there is more than one. As I have come to understand it, these are souls we have known in other times and places, which we unite with again, to learn and grow together. We may have contracts with these individuals to become partners in this incarnation. We may accept or reject these contracts. Two of my recent significant relationships had these potential contracts. With free will, these individuals chose to pursue other pathways in life.

With increasing maturity and wisdom, we can immediately go to the soft, gentle place of being in love, readily working toward genuine partnership. With three simple, basic rules we can move forward in healthy, mature, equal relating with another. These rules are: no lying, no games and no sharing. We are to be honest with each other. We are to strive to overcome game playing that interferes with developing true partnership. We are to commit ourselves to one person, not emotionally or sexually cheat on our partner.

If we enter relationships, especially significant relationships, with integrity, character and a sense of fairness, we have the seeds for success. We can give love and can receive love. With honesty, faithfulness and communicating our emotions, we can easily have the romance and excitement that are a part of joyful living.

Healing and Transformation

Romantic love is transforming and healing. It brings up all our emotional and spiritual wounds and issues. It becomes a marvelous, yet challenging, opportunity to stretch and grow. With courage and determination, we can discover and resolve our emotional wounds, our dysfunctions, our control dramas and our manipulative styles. We can move from dysfunctional relating to others to developing genuine teamwork and partnership with another. As we do our spirits will soar, joyfully relating in the most intimate way with another. We can have an extraordinary love of our life.

Chapter 9
PARENTING: THE SACRED RESPONSIBILITY

Parenting is indeed a sacred responsibility. As a society, we do not take this responsibility seriously enough. It is the most important job in the world. Nothing else we do, or any role or occupation we pursue, is as important as this sacred responsibility, once we make the choice to be a vehicle for a soul to enter into the physical plane. While most choices in life can be and are honorable, this singular choice is of the utmost importance. When we choose to be entrusted with the responsibility of parenting, we choose to nurture and develop that child, to have them evolve into a mature, responsible adult, and hopefully give them the tools to make better choices of who they are and who they want to be. We also hopefully guide them with the least amount of trauma, and the least amount of emotional and spiritual wounds.

The side benefit is we also have another opportunity to heal our own wounds and emotional scars. The developmental stages of growth in our children will force us to face and deal with these wounds within ourselves.

As the Unity faith describes souls are entrusted to our care by God. We not only do not take parenting seriously enough, we do not even begin to understand the full extent of the responsibility there is to nurture and guide our children to adulthood. We do not seriously prepare to bring children into the world and raise them with full dedication.

Yet if we take the time to parent, we diminish the possibility of creating emotional wounds and hurts that perpetuate the same control dramas and dysfunctions we have learned along the way. Further, we are fully available to help them navigate the potential hurts and wounds that await them in the world around them as they grow. We help them to develop solutions and resolutions so they can achieve mature emotional and mental functioning. We help them to develop the capacity to more easily choose who they are and who they want to be. Hopefully, we can allow them to develop and become who they are and who they want to be, free from our specific agendas. We do want them to be mature, responsible, honest, and have integrity. We also want to create the nurturing and guided environment where they can make healthy choices for themselves, sometimes, even learn from their mistakes.

As we choose higher and higher paths of who we are and who we want to be as parents, we can choose to be "generation-busters," and not allow the patterns of dysfunction and control dramas that have existed in our families and been passed on to us, to continue. Instead, we can choose to learn from what we went through and experienced, and choose differently for our children. As we do this we heal ourselves and help heal our children. Ultimately, we help heal the negative and fear-based patterns that are no longer functional and prevent our children from creating lives of joy instead.

One of the most difficult challenges of parenting is it can and does open our old wounds and hurts as our children experience the pitfalls and adversities of life. What has not been healed in us will re-emerge and be felt again. Even if we successfully navigated some of the adversities that arise, the normal disappointments and failures of life will reawaken old feelings when we went through the same or similar experiences.

Who has not felt devastated at the end of the first love we have in early adolescence? There is no feeling like the first feeling of being in love, and there is no worse feeling than being rejected by a first love. When our children have the same experience we easily sympathize with what they are feeling, and can suddenly find ourselves reliving the same feelings. Since all feelings are stored in the emotional and the physical bodies, they can surprise us when we feel the same intensity again.

With the wisdom of adulthood, we can take these painful memories and transform them by releasing and letting go of the negative and fear-based emotions attached to these memories. As we guide our children through these painful events, and share the wisdom we have gained along the way, we further heal and transform these emotional wounds in ourselves, releasing the energy to freely flow within and between all bodies, as described in an earlier chapter. One of the gifts of parenting is to impart our wisdom and guidance to our children. Another gift is we are afforded the opportunity to become aware of old wounds so we can work to heal them as well.

Parenting becomes an opportunity to gain increased awareness. This allows us one more opportunity to use this increased awareness to make better choices of who we are and who we want to be. Our children will also question us, and what and why we do things the way we do them. We can try to say to our children, "Just do it because I said so." Or we can try to say, "That's the way it is always done." Or we can think through whether doing things the same way makes sense, or are there better choices available. Since the children now coming in are on the Indigo Blue Ray, they are going to challenge the conventional wisdom and ways of doing things, for they are here to help the world transform and heal.

Everything is a vibration of energy. When we incarnate, we burst into form on vibrations of light. During different eras in the history of the Earth, souls have come in on particular rays of light as well, each ray reflecting the evolved state of the souls entering in, and now the Earth is set to enter the next stage of its evolvement. Since the mid 1970's the children entering the Earth plane have come in on the Indigo Blue Ray. This is why children seem so much smarter. It is also why children don't just blindly accept authority nor blindly accept doing things a certain way because that is how it has always been done. Today's children and young adults are capable of moving society forward, especially spiritually. However, they are also capable of extreme negative paths, especially by the young men who shot their fellow students at Columbine High School.

Given the nature of the souls now incarnating, the sacred responsibility of parenting becomes even more important. Guiding and teaching these children to be responsible, loving and spiritually aware adults requires even more effort and awareness of how sacred and important is this responsibility.

We are very backward, as a planet, when it comes to having the proper perspective and attitude about parenting. We do not give it the priority and respect that is its proper due. We do not properly honor the importance of mothering, even as we do not properly consider the importance of fathering. We also do not always remember to include the wisdom of the grandparents in assisting in raising children.

Let's be very clear about this next point, parenting is not the sole or even primary responsibility of the mother alone. It is the responsibility of both parents. While the ideal may be, especially in the early years, for one parent to be home and the more available caregiver, this in no way negates the equally important role the other parent provides to the raising and nurturing of children.

While the parent who continues to work may have to put in long hours providing for the family, they must still muster even more energy to be available and involved in the parenting process once they are at home and available to their children.

Unfortunately, with divorce and relationship failures being so prevalent in our nation now, it is even more imperative for the non-custodial parent to be as available as possible and assist in the parenting process whenever and wherever they are able to do so. Thus, it is even more important for parents to heal and transform themselves when their relationship fails. To continue to act out bitterness, anger and hurt at the expense of the children is not acceptable. Using the children to continue the fight is detrimental to their development and places them in roles they should never be in. While the divorcing parents were not able to achieve commonality of purpose in their own relationship, somehow they must find the courage to work together for the sake of their children.

Using children to get back at one another or allowing them to manipulate you against your ex-spouse, creates further wounds emotionally, mentally, and spiritually for all involved. It can be difficult and challenging to set aside unresolved hurt and anger to work together for the benefit of the children, especially since divorce happened because you could not work as a team. This is a time when we have to do the right thing for the children. You just might end up having a successful divorce, healing yourself in the process, as well as helping your children survive, learn and grow from the painful consequences of divorce. You may also end up being a role model of how people can disagree, yet work for the common good.

While parenting is the primary responsibility of the immediate family, society as a whole has a responsibility as well. As a civilization we do not take the responsibility of parenting as seriously as we should nor do we give it the priority such a sacred responsibility implies. To nurture, guide and teach children so they can grow and evolve to healthy, responsible and mature adulthood is the most important process we can engage in, as a parent or as a society. It is a sacred responsibility that should not be entered into lightly and should involve our full decision-making ability. Once decided, we should then engage in a process of proper preparation to bring each soul into a physical incarnation so the soul can learn, grow and evolve in the most supportive and nurturing environment we can provide.

Healing and Transformation

This process is not just about helping the child become a mature, responsible adult. This process is also about nurturing the soul entrusted to our care, so they can learn and grow and evolve spiritually. Hopefully we provide the nurturance and guidance that allows for the spiritual enfoldment of the soul blessed to be in our care. We help the child to grow into the understanding they are a spiritual being having a human experience. All the challenges and adversities of life facilitate awareness and an understanding of this truth. Further, it is through these challenges and adversities our souls are stretched so we can and will move forward to higher and higher levels of who we are and who we want to be.

Ultimately, we help the souls entrusted to our care to choose to begin and/or continue the journey back home to oneness with God, no longer needing to return to the physical plane of existence. The journey "home" is to return to full and complete existence in the spiritual realms and move forward in those realms as well. Heaven has many levels of dimensional reality, each more grand and beautiful than the one beneath it. This is what Jesus meant when he said "My Father has many mansions."

While the sacred responsibility of parenting is primary within the immediate family unit, it is a responsibility that extends to the larger family as well. Ultimately, it is a responsibility that extends to all of society. While one may disagree with the specifics of how to do this, Senator Hillary Rodham Clinton has it right; it does take a village to raise a child. We all are responsible for the safety, well-being and nurturance of all our children. We all are responsible to each other in ways we haven't fully comprehended or yet implemented as a civilization.

As *The Course In Miracles* reminds us, We are all One. Jesus tells us in the Course we all go to heaven together. No one is left behind, for we are all One Sonship. When we fully realize this truth and put it in to practice as a society, we will more readily begin to create a truly evolved and spiritual civilization. This is consistent with where our planet and civilization are evolving to anyway. We can help to facilitate this rather than having this forced on us.

Do we as a society provide for all children so that all can succeed? Do we work to have safe communities and schools? Do we encourage parents to meet their responsibilities and obligations? Do we help, rather than hinder, parents as they strive to provide for their family and have time available to supervise and guide their children? Do we encourage the formulations of values, such as integrity and honesty, responsibility to self and others, and always doing our best? Do we provide educational and recreational opportunities for our youth so they can learn to relate to others in a positive and nurturing environment? Do we support our schools, whether we have children or not, so each child has the opportunity to be successful in life? Do we say as a society, no child is to be discarded and no life is to be wasted?

Do we create a safe world in which children can grow and learn? Do we provide safe schools that encourage and nurture intellectual growth and the creative use of the mind? Do we help children to learn how to think, evaluate and decide in a logical and informed manner, work to get at reasonable conclusions? Do we teach our children how to use their intuitive mind? Do we teach children respect for themselves and others? Do we teach and foster tolerance, that there are many ways of belief and how to understand the world, our humanity, and ways to live life?

Do we give our children the freedom to make choices, developmentally appropriate for their age? Do we provide guidance; yet let them make decisions they are ready to make, even if it means failure? Do we let our children experience failure, so they can learn from disappointment and adversity? Do we allow our children to earn things, rather than just hand everything to them? Do we allow our children to gradually gain responsibility and the increasing capacity to make their own decisions within reason?

It is indeed a daunting task to raise children and gradually guide them to adulthood with a minimum of dysfunction. It is indeed a daunting task to have them learn how to honestly and genuinely relate to others, without the need for unhealthy manipulations and control dramas.

It is a sacred responsibility to nurture and guide our children to learn how to honestly relate to others. It is a sacred responsibility to nurture and guide our children how to respond to others' control dramas without being manipulative and controlling in return. It is a sacred responsibility to nurture and guide our children in how to share expectations, then work to get to common ground with others.

It is a sacred responsibility to nurture and guide our children to be loving and kind. It is a sacred responsibility to nurture and guide our children how to express true love, unconditional love, love of the Holy Spirit, in all their relations with others. It is a sacred responsibility to nurture and guide our children to understand true forgiveness for others. It is a sacred responsibility to nurture and guide our children to learn discernment rather than judgment, the later implying attack and condemnation. The former helps us to choose the right path or to not be part of something that is not in our best interest or well-being.

It is a sacred responsibility to nurture and guide our children to learn how to be impeccable with their word, carefully choosing what to say and when to say it. This includes not engaging in the destructive act of gossip. It is a sacred responsibility to nurture and guide our children to not take others' behaviors personally. It is a sacred responsibility to nurture and guide our children to not make assumptions about why people do what they do. It is a sacred responsibility to nurture and guide our children to always do their best, especially guided by their intuition or how Holy Spirit would guide them. It is a sacred responsibility to nurture and guide our children to learn the spiritual path, understanding this is the ultimate purpose of life in the physical dimensions.

Having outlined many of the important responsibilities of parenting, it is obvious that the most important part of parenting is to have a vision and plan for nurturing and guiding our children. Teaching and guiding is the most important part of parenting. Unfortunately psychologists have learned that most parents' believe parenting is 75% discipline and only 25% teaching. In my practice, I tell parents that parenting is 90% teaching and only 10% discipline.

The most important part of parenting is to provide a positive relationship, in which our children trust us to teach and guide them. It is important for them to know it is "safe" to approach and talk to us, seeking guidance and direction for even the most difficult situations and challenges they face. When we provide a loving and safe relationship with them they are able to trust us with their feelings, concerns and fears. They can approach us and seek our guidance and wisdom. I can assure you that nothing is more satisfying, as a parent, then to have your child come to you and ask for your help with a problem, whether big or small.

The other important aspect of being a teacher and guide is to share sound values and beliefs about how to act, how to treat others, and to convey wisdom and truth about how the universe operates. By sharing and by example we best convey to our children rules of conduct and how to treat others with dignity and respect. We teach them the importance of respecting differences. We teach them of personal responsibility, not blaming, and not learning to be a victim. We teach them how to deal with adversity, disappointment and failure without externalizing blame. We teach them how to react to adversity and learn to gain from the experience, to see the positive alternatives or rise above the setback and move beyond it.

It is important for our children to learn right from wrong and develop a strong ethical sense. It is also important for them to understand there are competing ethical choices at times. Difficult choices need to be made between competing ethical standards. For instance, it may be important to be truthful, yet also kind. Sometimes we may have to choose how to be truthful without being hurtful.

While teaching is the most important part of parenting, it no way negates the importance of discipline. It is important for children to have structure in their lives, to clearly know what the rules and boundaries are and to have clear expectations. It is important for parents to express very clearly what their expectations are for their child. This is an ongoing process that lets the child know what is acceptable and what is not acceptable. This involves rules of conduct, but also involves the best that you want your child to do. So it is the rules and basic behaviors that are expected. It is also the very best in conduct that is expected as well. This covers a wide range of activities from school achievement, to following through on commitments in activities, to how to behave towards another.

We have primarily a teaching responsibility as we have to clearly set out what the expectations are and provide reasonable explanations for these expectations. We teach our children about proper conduct by giving them the rules, why and how these rules help them to have self-control, relate better with others and become responsible citizens. Eventually these values and rules of conduct become not only a means of having self-control, but become internalized expectations of how to behave toward others from the highest ethical sense. We don't give expectations "just because I told you so." We give expectations so the child can learn and grow, and make good decisions about themselves as they face all the temptations in the world to do otherwise. As we help them to learn self-control and the capacity to make good choices for themselves, we further help them to avoid painful experiences, in and of themselves; can create emotional wounds for themselves and others.

When expectations are not met, it is important to give out appropriate consequences so the child learns to make better choices in the future and learn poor choices result in undesirable outcomes. Better to have a time out or be grounded for small offenses at an early age, than to make more serious errors later on and have to experience more severe or dire consequences at a later time. It is essential for the emotional and psychological health of the child to experience appropriate and meaningful consequences for poor choices or inappropriate behavior.

Parenting: The Sacred Responsibility

For less serious infractions or not meeting responsible expectations, I like the "two warning" system of intervention. For instance, if your child is responsible for loading the dishwasher after a meal as one of their chores and they are procrastinating on getting it done, then you state "this is your first warning," then "this is your second warning," then state, "now you have lost this privilege." Obviously, for more serious infractions, you can immediately go to the consequence that "fits the crime."

It is important to never give a consequence in anger. As a parent you can send the child to their room or ground them until such time as you, or you and your spouse, have had time to calmly decide what the proper punishment should be. It is very helpful, as part of partnership, for both parents to discuss and decide what is an appropriate consequence for more serious rule violations or negative behaviors. Presenting a united front in a calm and firm manner is very powerful.

Most children will respond without the need for physical punishment. Limited corporal punishment may be needed at very early ages, but will not give the desired results at older ages. I can't tell you the number of clients I have treated, who were administered harsh corporal discipline for behaviors that simply did not warrant the degree or severity of physical discipline given. I often say to my clients, "What did you do that was so awful that you got the hell beat out of you?" The emotional wounds and traumas created by corporal punishment far outweigh any beneficial effect you can imagine from the use of physical discipline.

Parents will often say to me, "nothing else works," or "time outs don't seem to bother her," or "my kid says 'I don't care what you do." Children can be very manipulative when it comes to escaping the consequences of their actions and will try anything to convince you that the consequences do not mean a thing. Provide the consequences anyway. If they end up wanting to be grounded all the time, then let them be grounded all the time. Let it be real grounding, having them be in their room without their TV, stereo, video games, and whatever else they have available to amuse themselves. They do have to experience real consequences if discipline is going to be meaningful.

Be very accurate with your warnings. If you say you are going to do something if an inappropriate behavior persists, then follow through with the consequence. Do not let your son or daughter wear you down with whining, whether to get out of a consequence or to get something you already said no to. You have to say what you mean. Your children then learn they are safe with you. Help them with self-control when they cannot or will not and reassure you really do love them and care about them. Parenting is hard work. It is the hardest job in the world. It requires maximum effort and being there all the time. Children know if you really care about them and are willing to make the effort with them when you do the hard work of parenting.

A final note on discipline is the capacity to strike a balance between being too strict or too lenient. Children cannot learn self-control and how to internalize values of conduct if they don't have reasonable expectations and clear consequences when they don't measure up to those expectations. If they have little or no consequences they won't learn self-control and how to work towards the achievement of goals. They won't learn how to delay gratification to achieve goals that require effort and time. On the other hand, if they are treated in an overly strict and harsh manner, they will never learn how to develop their own inner control, but will just learn to comply based on fear. Once free as adults they may very well go the opposite extreme, with many harmful consequences that are unnecessary if not taught and guided properly along the way.

While providing discipline and structures are important, psychologists long ago discovered the importance of praise and positive reinforcement to encourage positive behavior and attitudes. It is all too easy to be critical and authoritative, but positive consequences more readily lead to desired behavior. Let your children know that they have done well, whether with grades, making mature decisions or with something as simple as remembering to do a chore or put their clothes away. We all desire recognition and praise for making the right choices and doing the right things. Focusing on what is positive and right encourages those very behaviors. Having reasonable, yet high standards, and rewarding these standards and expectations, nurtures mature behavior and taking responsibility. I cannot emphasize this enough: Praise! Praise! Praise!

As parents, we all make mistakes. We are role models for our children. When we make mistakes it is important to acknowledge we did err and to apologize when appropriate. This teaches our children we are not perfect, we all make mistakes, and there are proper ways to acknowledge and amend the mistakes we all do make.

One of the hardest tasks of parents is to gradually let go of our children, as they grow older. We have to give them increased responsibilities and increased choices. We have to give them increased choices as physical and emotional maturity allow. We have to let them make mistakes so they can learn from them. It is hard as a parent to not always be protective and try to shield them from the potential mistakes they may make. Yet failure is a part of life, and they need the opportunities, within reason, to fail as well.

At the soul level we have contracts with the souls entrusted to our care. They have contracts with us as well. They may be contracts to resolve previous karmic debt or they may be contracts to learn and grow together. When my son was six years old I was putting him to bed one night. He said, "You know what Dad? I saw you and Mom and this house from heaven before I was born." Over time I have learned about some of the past lives I have shared with my son and his mother. There are no coincidences for anything we experience in life. There are no coincidences for our parents or for our children.

As you examine your own childhood and what happened or did not happen with your parents, you all came together for many different reasons. As you examine your own children and how you relate to them, you came together for many different reasons. Parenting is the opportunity to nurture and guide souls to manifest their greatest potential in this lifetime, and to heal all past lifetimes. Parenting also affords you the opportunity to be aware of and heal your own past with your parents, to face and to resolve the emotional wounds and traumas you still carry from your own childhood. Even by simply making the choice to raise your children in a more positive and loving way from what you may have experienced helps you to heal your own wounds.

As we heal and transform our lives through the sacred responsibility of parenting, we also allow our own inner child to come forward and be a part of our present personality. If that inner child is a wounded child, we are able to heal him/her and restore the beautiful child there once was. When Jesus said, to be as little children, he was referring to the pure, innocent inner child each of us has that looks on the world in wonderment and joy, and understands life is meant to be a joyous adventure of discovery. Life is meant to be a joyous adventure of self-discovery. We remember we are spiritual beings having a human experience, and even adversity is an opportunity to stretch our soul's growth and development. In *A Course In Miracles*, one of the daily lessons simple states, "God, being Love, is also happiness." Recapturing our inner child reminds of us the love and happiness that truly is our divine heritage.

Parenting is truly a sacred responsibility. Approached in a loving, nurturing manner, we can guide and teach our children to become responsible, mature adults, able to handle the challenges, adversities and opportunities of life. We can also heal our own wounds. We can teach them and ourselves how to make better choices of who we are and who we want to be. We plant the seeds for their healing and transformation, our healing and transformation and the planet's healing and transformation. The wave of souls coming in, are here to change the world and help facilitate the coming New Golden Age. We can help facilitate this transformation with the wisdom and knowledge we have gained by learning how to heal ourselves.

Chapter 10
FORGIVENESS

Healing and transformation ultimately requires three different foundations be put in place so the process can unfold and be completed. It is these same three cornerstones that are the core aspects of living that allow us to walk the spiritual path. These three cornerstones are unconditional love, non-judgment and forgiveness. These are challenging ways of being, to strive for and to accomplish, especially since the ego works to accomplish their opposites. Yet, the very process of healing and transforming old wounds and emotional scars requires the attainment of these three conditions. Working to manifest true unconditional love, non-judgment and true forgiveness helps to heal the past, freeing us to live completely in the present, seeing each moment as an opportunity to create our lives as masterpieces of joy, harmony and peace.

The January 17, 2005 issue of Time magazine has articles on the science of happiness. In lifting the level of happiness, some practical suggestions were provided by the University of California psychologist, Sonja Lyubomirsky. These suggestions are based on research findings of her and others. The eight steps are:

1. Count your blessings.
2. Practice acts of kindness.
3. Savor life's joys.
4. Thank a mentor.
5. Learn to forgive.
6. Invest time and energy in friends and family.
7. Develop strategies for coping with stress and hardships.
8. Take care of your body.

With learning to forgive it is suggested to let go of anger and resentment. Inability to forgive is associated with persistent rumination or dwelling on revenge, while forgiving allows us to move on.

The ego is invested in holding on to and harboring resentment toward anyone or anything that has embarrassed or hurt us in the past. We are very good at justifying our resentment and why a particular person or situation should not be forgiven. The ego strives to remind us of what was done to us and to remain vigilant for any potential harm that is sure to come. Not only does the ego work to protect us, it constantly scans for potential harm and is ready to attack before you are attacked. The ego's motto is the best defense is a good offense. It readily seizes on any perceived threat to justify getting them before they get us. Whether employing the many defense systems the personality is capable of using or automatically going into the control dramas and manipulative styles you have learned to protect yourself with in the world, the ego readily goes into action.

The ego justifies the pre-emptive strike so we are not harmed or hurt again. Who wants to feel hurt, embarrassed of humiliated? Unfortunately, the ego takes this to an extreme, justifying its strategy by recalling all the ways you have been wounded or scarred in the past. It tries to protect you by avoiding the underlying trauma that is not resolved. It protects you by harboring resentment about all the bad things that have happened to you and those that did these things to you. More cleverly, the ego tries to conceal from you the real reason you are fearful, keeping you from the event that originally caused the pain and hurt. Preoccupied with perceived potential threats, it keeps you from re-discovering the original event and experiencing that hurt over and over again.

Unfortunately, it also reframes every new event in your life in terms of this past. The ego works to take the new events in your life and make them fit the original source of hurt and pain. Holding onto the emotional wounds and traumas of the past with resentment and other fear-based emotions, we project these original dynamics and resentments on the new situation and persons involved. How often have you been given feedback about you that you "knew" was simply not true about you? Have you not wondered where some reactions to you come from? Have you not wondered how someone else could experience the same event and see it totally different? Have you not sometimes found yourself seeing a situation totally different from others? These are the moments we become aware something is affecting our experience, an event or a person.

What happens is our personal past colors what we are experiencing in the present. As we gain awareness about this we can choose to see the present in a different light. As we release and let go of past hurt, trauma and emotional wounds we gain the freedom to spontaneously and authentically experience life and freely interact with others, especially without judgment. Often our judgments are colored by past experience tainted by the resentments and grudges we carry around.

The process of working toward forgiveness allows us to address our past hurts and traumas so we can release and let go of the negative and fear-based emotions attached to those events. The ego would rather we avoid even being aware of the original trauma, electing instead to stay with attack, defensiveness, manipulations and control dramas. For the ego, it is always better to place blame elsewhere than face and deal with the original hurt.

Healing and Transformation

The ego believes it is easier to cling to resentment and grudges, rather than resolve the underlying hurt that caused us to be protective in the first place. Dedicated to protection, the ego would rather attack, assign blame, or even to produce guilt within our selves rather than go back and resolve the original hurt. Forgiveness, as a process, is the antithesis of this. In the process of forgiveness we are willing to look at the hurtful and painful behaviors of others and begin to recognize and understand they are wounded spirits just as we are. Rather than going into judgment we look with compassion at another wounded soul acting out their protective drama with us, to avoid their own inner hurt, pain and trauma.

When we can begin to not take personally another's behavior toward us, we can release judgment of them. Ultimately, we also release judgment of our self. When we find fault, often the other person reflects our own inner fear and guilt. This is what Jesus meant when he said to beware of finding the sliver in the other person's eye, missing the log in our own eye.

A client of mine recently returned to see me, as her anger and verbal outbursts resulted in the end of her engagement to her fiancé. She saw me previously when this first occurred; concerned her angry tirades were damaging her relationship and putting at risk a continued commitment with her fiancé. When first seen, we talked about anger management and explored some of the reasons she became so enraged. To her credit she realized this behavior was not working for her and this was not the person she wanted to be. The initial crisis appeared to resolve, with plans to marry going forward.

She came to see me again after several months; upset she was not able to stay calm, with angry outbursts again emerging. This time the relationship ended and the engagement was broken off. She sought counseling again as she does not want to be out-of-control with her anger and her temper.

As we explored what happened, she became upset with her fiancé's decision to buy a condo, citing all the sound financial reasons why this made sense. He realized in talking with others it was a good idea to invest in property even before they were married, rather than keep paying rent. Although she agreed with his reasoning, she was upset with the manner he went forward with this decision. He informed her he was going to do this, reasonably presenting all the reasons this was a good idea. He also began to seek property and found a condo he was interested in purchasing.

Yet, what was missing was this decision was not a mutual decision, made by sharing expectations and getting to common ground. After the initial decision on his part, he did realize he needed to include her in deciding internal amenities, but he decided to find and buy a place without including her in the process.

She was reasonably upset, as he did not approach her in a genuine partnership way about how they should proceed; with his recognition there was a better way to manage their finances as they approached their marriage. His approach should have been to inform her of what he had learned, explore with her various options and then together they both decide what to do, how to do it and work together to find a place they would both agree was a good choice for them as a couple.

It appeared he wanted to be in control and be the one to make the decisions, not to operate as a partnership in deciding their future together. As she raised concerns about this he became angry with her, as he had sound reasons for deciding and proceeding as he did. There is little doubt his reasoning is sound and it is a good way to go. What he failed to understand completely was his apparent need to be in control and have things his way. He basically told her in this relationship, he would make all the major decisions, and there would not be a partnership in this relationship. Not understanding that she was reacting to his being in control and not including her in an important partnership decision, she became angry and temperamentally explosive, especially when he twisted her behavior around to make her seem unreasonable and ungrateful for all he was doing for them.

While the unrecognized reality of a one-way relationship triggered her anger and temper outbursts, unresolved emotional wounds from her past are the root cause of the behavior in the present. She grew up listening to violent arguments between her parents, with her father often demanding and having the last word. He was always right and had no regard for the opinion or viewpoint of anyone else. Interestingly, once her parents divorced and moved on, the angry outbursts and conflict did not continue with new partners. However, she had good role models for yelling and fighting as ways of coping with conflict and disagreement.

Further, her father did not tolerate disagreement from her, even if she was right. She was not allowed to have her own view if it differed from his. As a result she began to harbor a lot of resentment at not being heard and in not having a say in how her life should be. One of the most difficult tasks of parenting is gradually allowing our children to have their own views and make their own choices. Even more challenging as a parent is allowing our children to make obviously wrong choices so they can learn from their own experiences of failure. To never be allowed her own view and her own choice set her up for vulnerability when the same situation arose with her fiancé.

Developing insight is the first step in healing and transformation for her. Understanding there are valid reasons for her anger and the explosive nature of her temper helps her to be less judgmental about herself and less guilt-ridden for losing control. Although the need for power and control was subtle with her fiancé, he was not sharing power with her in the relationship and thus, there was no possibility of genuine partnership. Yet her rage went deeper, because lurking within is the unhealed anger and resentment with her father for not letting her have appropriate power for her age and not acknowledging her right to her own view.

Now she understands why the relationship with her fiancé was doomed to failure. Not being empowered in the relationship and having learned inappropriate ways to express her self, volatile and temperamental responses were inevitable. With awareness, she can now make better choices about why she is reacting the way she does, and can react firmly and appropriately when others are trying to control her.

To resolve the emotional wounds now requires acknowledging and releasing the negative and fear-based emotions from her childhood. In the therapeutic alliance we are now able to proceed to process and release the hurt, anger, fear, humiliation and powerlessness she felt. Ultimately, as we work to resolve these emotions, we get to the most challenging part of the therapy process, which is helping her to forgive her mother and especially her father. We also work to have her forgive her ex-fiancé and finally to forgive herself.

Interestingly in the forgiveness work I do with clients, they can often forgive those that tried to hurt or harm them. They have a much harder time learning to forgive their selves. Even understanding that God is Pure Love and has already forgiven them, they still struggle to forgive themselves.

People also misunderstand this about forgiveness: forgiveness doesn't give others license to continue to abuse us, or for us to remain in a dysfunctional relationship with someone else. Forgiveness is about releasing the negative and fear-based emotions within our selves, often the product of someone else's attack, cruelty or unkindness. In forgiveness we release the hurt and trauma within ourselves as the final step in healing and transformation of those wounds. Having done that we move forward, relating in a new and more effective way for ourselves and for the other. This may mean no longer being involved with the person. Or, it may mean we now develop a strategy of relating that no longer allows dysfunction or abuse. We step into a place where we can firmly and kindly set boundaries, and/or change the rules of how we relate to that person.

For my client, if the relationship with her fiancé could be salvaged, in direct and open communication, she could tell him in a calm and firm manner why she is upset and what needs to change. She could share expectations that the relationship move toward genuine partnership with decisions being made by both, then working to get to common ground. She could engage in a meaningful dialogue with him about what is happening and what needs to be different so they could ultimately be a team with deep, abiding love reflecting the unity they are able to achieve.

She can also make a number of choices on how to deal with her father, from honestly telling him how she felt as a child and how his behavior hurts her even as an adult. Having forgiven him, she doesn't need to be malicious or spiteful. Or, she can decide to have a minimal and mostly superficial relationship with him. Or, she can decide to set boundaries with him in a gentle and firm manner, letting him know she will no longer be talked down to and her views disregarded. She may even tell him it is really okay to agree to disagree. She may even tell him she has a different view and it's okay to have differing views. She has many choices she can make with painful memories healed and forgiveness achieved.

I knew a woman who grew up in a family where the father was a dictator, always had to have things his way and simply would not tolerate any deviation on how things were to be done. He was always right. Her mother dealt with him by seeming to acquiesce to his demands and then do what she wanted anyway. She also used her control drama of the victim to cope with his authoritarian demands. As a result she learned to tip toe around her father, take on the victim role herself, but also rebel by acting out in adolescence by doing the opposite without her father ever knowing she was rebelling.

Even as an adult she dared not confront her father or disagree with him in any way. When she went to visit him in Florida, she was the little girl again tip toeing around her father. If she would go the beach, he would insist she follow his directions on how to get there, knowing there was a "better" way for her to go. But, you did not disagree with dad or even dare suggest you might know a better way to go, or simply wanted to go the way you wanted to go. She would tell him she would follow his directions, knowing full well she had no intention of doing what he ordered. On return she would tell him she followed his directions and more importantly, tell him it was a great way to go.

Forgiveness

Not surprising she married three times, all to abusive and controlling men. She was manipulated to leave the first husband at her father's orders, he simply did not approve of him. She had enough sense to get out of the second marriage when that husband beat her and threatened to kill her, with his gun pointed to her head. The third husband lasted a long time, despite his controlling and demanding behavior, in part because she seemed to really love him.

Her victim control drama also served her well in tolerating his behavior for as long as she did. Complicating the third marriage was her husband suffered from bipolar disorder. His mood swings added to his abusive and controlling behavior. She constantly tried to please him without recognizing he continually changed his expectations and what he wanted her to do. She could also get him back at times with passive-aggressive behavior. She could pick the times to push his buttons and enrage him, without him ever realizing the underdog often has more power in the relationship, while seemingly being compliant most of the time.

Often people with bipolar disorder don't accept the need for medication to stabilize their mood. Despite the many effective medications to stabilize mood, they like the rush of the manic side of the mood swing. Unfortunately, they eventually crash into a deep depression and can be suicidal. Bipolar disorder also can have tremendous anger and the inappropriate expression of rage that accompanies the mood swings. A very dear friend of mine has bipolar disorder. To her great credit, she accepted her condition a long time ago and accepted the need to take the proper medication for the rest of her life to keep her moods stable. In addition, she had anger management training when she was psychiatrically hospitalized on one occasion. She learned to master her anger and to express it appropriately.

A psychiatrist treating the woman's third husband finally told her she had to leave him for her own sanity, as he was not likely to change and be compliant with treatment. Having finally had enough she filed for divorce. With the threat of divorce, he promised to change and take his medications. His behavior leveled out and she held off divorcing him. After six months of compliance he asked her to withdraw the divorce petition, which she did. No sooner did she do this; she walked into the bathroom to find all his medication floating in the toilet. He no longer intended to take his medications. The next day she proceeded with the divorce.

However, it was not long before she was in another abusive relationship. Often, controlling men present initially as very kind and nurturing, with only subtle indications of what they are really like. They are good at gaining the trust and affection of women, especially being heroic and rescuing, if these women are into the victim drama. They present as caretakers and rescuers. Once the trust is gained and the relationship progresses, then the controlling and intimidating dramas emerge.

Subconsciously we are very good at finding others who match our control dramas and dysfunctions. Our secret hope, each time, is somehow with this new person we will work out the underlying trauma magically without having to face and do the real work of healing and transformation. That is why someone who married an alcoholic, ends up with another alcoholic. We repeat our own dysfunction until we courageously face the underlying causes, heal the emotional wounds, and forgive.

This woman was eventually able to get out of the abusive relationship by finally understanding what was going on and setting boundaries and saying to this person she no longer wanted him in her life. Because of the relationship with her father, she would allow herself to be with abusive and controlling men, go into her victim drama, and rationalize staying by not wanting to hurt the other person, even though they hurt her repeatedly. She believed it was better for her to be hurt rather than say no to someone else. She would feel guilty for standing up for herself. Guilt is often an attack on us for not being able to forgive our selves.

Unfortunately, her bitterness remains toward her third husband. She shared if he was lying in the street bleeding she would step over him and continue on. Certainly she has reasons to be bitter. Not only did she endure his controlling and abusive behavior but also he legally fought the divorce until there were no remaining assets. He continually avoided paying child support and alimony payments. He did nothing to support their daughter, and worked to undermine her parenting of their daughter. She struggled to raise their daughter and survive financially.

Yet, since she is not able to face and resolve the underlying hurt and trauma with him and with men in general, she remains trapped in a pattern of relating which will never give her the happiness she wants or successfully relate in a genuine partnership. She professes she wants to marry again and be happy in a committed relationship. Yet, when healthy men come along she cannot believe they are not going to control her. She is suspicious and guarded, and cannot believe her good has really come. Her daughter even recognized that one man she dated was a "keeper," and when her mother rejected him, she shared with her mother he was not "perfect enough" for her mother.

The thought of ever letting go of the deep anger she feels toward the men in her life is too much for her to contemplate. The thought of ever getting to forgiveness is impossible for her to accept. To her credit, she finally learned not to stay with abusive men. Her new solution in relating with men is to be in control herself. Being extremely attractive, knowing how to play the single bar scene, and being very personable and outgoing, she is able to attract men, string them along, never let them get close, and lose them at the first hint they may try to control, whether they actually do so or not. For her ego is ever vigilant this will happen and misinterprets how men act toward her. Being ever vigilant, every action is perceived as control. One man asked if she wanted to go to the theatre and see a musical. She agreed she wanted to do this. The man purchased tickets for the following Saturday night. She called him at 2:00 AM the morning of the first play date and left a message she could not date him. What prompted this was his getting the

Healing and Transformation

tickets without checking with her to see if Saturday was okay, even though they were dating.

Unable to face and heal her past, and vulnerable to fears of being controlled, she has developed a system that seems to work for her. Yet, she will never feel safe enough to move into a truly committed relationship because her past is not resolved. Not only understanding the past, but facing and healing the underlying wounds are needed to free her to have what she really wants. Ultimately with forgiveness, she would be truly free to relate and gain what she wants in the present.

In my regression hypnosis work I am able to help clients get to the root causes of their depression, anxiety, fears and anger. We are able to get to the negative and fear-based emotions that affect them in the present. In a short period of time we get to the root cause, the emotional memory that is the cause of the current distress. We then go through a process of releasing and letting go of the negative and fear-based emotions associated with the memory. In the hypnotic state I have them verbalize the emotions to be released. Then I have them visualize, imagine or see these emotions going out of their body on a beam of light into the higher dimensions. I then have them verbalize the positive and love-based emotions to replace the negative and fear-based emotions. I then have them visualize, imagine or see these positive and love-based emotions coming down the beam of light, from the higher dimensions, and going back into them. In addition to specific positive and love-based emotions, I have them verbalize, "I replace these with light, love, peace, happiness, and forgiveness." I have them forgive the person who hurt them and also to forgive themselves.

This is very powerful and effective work. At times the client hesitates to forgive the perpetrator. With effort they often succeed. Even more challenging, clients often struggle to forgive themselves. It takes even more effort to forgive their selves.

I have done a lot of work with victims of sexual abuse, extreme physical abuse, or both. Even in the hypnotic state it can be very difficult to revisit the abuse. Once we are there it is very liberating to release the negative and fear-based emotions attached to the trauma of the abuse. It is even more therapeutic to replace these with positive and love-based emotions. In particular the work of forgiveness resolves the past. While emotional scars remain, the resolution of the hurt and trauma leads to feelings of peace, safety and calmness. The individual is free to be who they are and more importantly, who they want to be in the present. Clients are amazed at the peace that comes over them, as they no longer carry that painful emotional baggage around anymore. They feel free, especially when they have been able to forgive.

It has been popular among some sex abuse treatment specialists to advocate the client go back and confront the perpetrator of the abuse. While this can have some emotional catharsis for the client, often the perpetrator denies the abuse or inflicts further emotional trauma by their seemingly cavalier reactions such as saying, "you know you really liked it," or "I didn't really hurt you," or, "So what?" Confrontation feeds into the ego and the belief the best defense is a good offense. You attacked me and I am going to attack you back. Resentment and revenge may provide temporary resolution, but don't resolve the underlying hurt or release the underlying anger. Acknowledging and releasing the hurt and anger, finally forgiving, provide the healing and transformation needed to be free and move on with life.

In the current Tim McGraw song, "Live Like You Were Dying," one of the most powerful refrains in the song has to do with forgiveness. In the song, the person has learned they have a terminal illness in their early forties. Instead of feeling sorry for their selves, they embrace and live life completely and fully in the time they have remaining. In the refrain he sings, "To give the forgiveness I'd been denying." It is not an easy process to forgive. The ego fights us all the way. The person who hurt us deserves vengeance and condemnation. We are even perceived as weak if we extend forgiveness.

As much as I have come to understand the power and importance of forgiveness, it is still a struggle at times to practice this.

Healing and Transformation

It is easy for me to get caught up in my own judgment and ego condemnation when hurt or betrayed. Psychologically and spiritually, I appreciate the power and importance of forgiveness for my own healing and transformation. Recently my ego got the best of me again.

I met a woman who seemed to have all the qualities I am looking for in a life partner. She is very attractive, intelligent, outgoing and personable, and seems to have integrity. She is a successful professional and very good at what she does. As a defense trial attorney representing auto insurance companies, she has only lost three trials in a twenty-year career. She takes her parental responsibilities seriously and is very caring and nurturing of her children.

Several sources predicted this person coming into my life. These sources all stated this is the person I would marry. Needless to say, I was very excited when she arrived in my life. Although cautious, I was open to this being the special someone I was waiting to have in my life. In the three months we dated each other, there were no red flags to warn of possible issues or pitfalls to a successful long-term relationship. We seemed to be very compatible, and talked of long-term possibilities, even as we knew time would still be an important test.

We decided to travel to an all-inclusive resort in the Caribbean. Since we were already planning other vacations, including a European cruise, we both felt safe in spending a romantic week together. Unfortunately, the trip was a disaster for both of us. We were friendly with each other and chose to make the best of a difficult situation. For me, the initial shock was being with a person who became so intoxicated at the pool bar on the day of arrival, she began to flash her breasts at the bartenders. When the pool closed at 7:00 PM, she was so drunk I had to practically carry her back to the room after she wanted to pass out on the pool chair. Once at the room, she did pass out once I got her into the bed. I lay there wondering what I had gotten into, as there was no previous warning she could drink so heavily. My conservative estimate was she had at least twenty drinks. Later in the week she told me her youngest son keeps an eye on how much she drinks when they are on vacation. She consumed enough alcohol to suggest she can drink pretty heavily.

As the week progressed, she tended to be distant and somewhat aloof. One day she told me she placed men into eight different categories, but at least I was in one of the good ones. She told me she could see I was used to being alone, as I could do things on my own. Yet, when I tried to include her she would decline, such as going for walks on the beach.

We met an older couple from New Jersey and immediately hit it off with them. He and I enjoyed talking politics, business, travel and a variety of other diverse topics. Despite this, she later accused me of being boring and limited to metaphysics and football in my conversations.

After the incident the first day at the pool bar we got into a discussion about sexuality and the expressions of intimacy. While I enjoy adventure and exploration in the intimate relationship, she let it be known she is quite the sexual adventurer. She told me there isn't anything I could imagine that she hasn't done. When I reminded her one of my rules of relationships is no sharing, she assured me she could be traditionally monogamous as well.

It was increasingly obvious as the week progressed that she was not into me. It was no surprise my intuition also prepared me for the end of the relationship. The night before we returned home, I awoke to find her staring at me in the dark. Immediately my intuition told me this was over. At the airport the next morning, I watched across the room as she tried to call her parents back home. I "knew" instantly I would not be taking her home from the airport. When we arrived back in Detroit she told me at the baggage claim, "We do not fit." She thanked me for the trip, wished me well, said she would send a check (which I knew I would never see) and she would take a Metro car home.

Why did this person come into my life at this time, with the possibilities we could be life partners, and then everything go so wrong in such a short period of time? Given the universal truth of serendipity, it was no accident we came together. One option was there for us to progress and help each other heal and transform our lives. At the time, I was working on forgiveness and non-judgment. She became a wonderful opportunity to become aware of my judgment of her and others, my challenges with forgiveness and the capacity to move forward from ego dominance and control. As I had been working on, *A Course In Miracles,* which is all about forgiveness and not judging, this became another opportunity to put these principles into action. More specifically, I was also reading at the time, *The Disappearance of the Universe,* by Gary Renard, which explains the Course in Miracles and these principles of forgiveness and non-judgment in more detail. I could better understand and work to apply the principle of forgiveness.

At first upon returning, I was hurt and disappointed, and also unsettled about the person I discovered on the trip, who was so different and unexpected from what I experienced prior to the trip. Being hurt and angry, my ego got the best of me. One of the ways my ego attacks is by having the last word. I emailed her to get the address of the couple from New Jersey and let her know, I knew what she was going to do at the end intuitively. With no response, a few days later I sent another email and chastised her for her behavior on the trip.

Later that day I received a scathing email back from her. She attacked me pointedly and broadly. She bragged at one point about having over 150 partners, that basically I was an amateur sexually, and she had no interest in teaching me how to be a good partner. Thinking she was getting me good by attacking my manhood and how I may perform in the intimate relationship, she may not realize her put down of me is more indicting of herself. Sadly, she may be technically proficient, but there is much more to intimacy than physical ability and prowess. Physical connections can be superficial and lack the deep connection mentally, emotionally and spiritually that occurs when two people deeply in love connect at the most intimate level.

While painful, I had it coming. I was judgmental and attacked her, rather than going to the place of forgiveness. She started out her email saying she got drunk because of my faux pas right before we left. She said she wondered what she had gotten into with me, and got that drunk for the first time in eighteen years. She blamed me, which is understandable as I was partly at fault. Our egos are always going to put blame elsewhere, rather than our taking personal responsibility for our actions and choices. She also let me know I was a "nebbish," which is Yiddish for a small, insignificant man.

Stepping back from the harsh attack I just received and working with the principles of non-judgment and forgiveness, I chose to respond in a different way. For one thing, I did not need to be angry anymore, and did not need to become even angrier after the full frontal assault just launched at me. With prayer, meditation and working the exercises in *A Course In Miracles,* I was able to respond differently and truly get to a place of forgiveness, and release and let go of the negative and fear-based emotions I was feeling. The unfortunate end of this relationship became a perfect opportunity to apply the principles of forgiveness and not be judgmental with her.

I did send her one last email. I told her I was sorry for the faux pas, as I did realize I had unconsciously sabotaged the relationship right before we left. One of the faux pas was being judgmental with her parents, who did not approve of me since I was not a fundamental "Christian." In their belief, a Christian is only one who believes in the conservative, fundamental doctrine of Christianity. You are not really a Christian if you practice more mainstream Christianity, let alone New Thought Christianity. In their view, they will be in the front row of heaven, and hope their daughter will at least be in the balcony. Aware of some of my beliefs, they worried for their daughter's afterlife.

As they were somewhat cool, aloof and unfriendly toward me, my ego felt justified in being judgmental in return. By being reserved and minimally friendly in return, my ego felt justified in attacking them. While reading *The Disappearance of the Universe* during the trip, I became aware of my judgmental reaction to her parents, and regretted how I acted toward them. I realized I needed to be in a place of non-judgment and unconditional love toward them, and respond with love-based and positive behavior. I also realized I needed to forgive them and to forgive myself.

Needless to say this faux pas, as well as another more serious one, sabotaged the trip right before we left. Unconsciously I set up the failure. I needed to own this. Partly I may have done this knowing how difficult a challenge it was going to be a stepparent to two boys who liked how their life was exclusively with their mom. Other fears may also have been operating.

I responded to her email differently. I thanked her for her feedback so I could recognize the faux pas and acknowledge to her that I sabotaged the trip. I told her that awareness is not judgment and I did not judge her. I assured her I was moving on, but needed to apologize for my responses to the situation. Humorously, I told her I preferred shmuck rather than nebbish to describe how I acted. I was guided by Spirit to compose and send a forgiving response to her attack on me. In a subsequent meditation using one of the Course exercises, I could truly forgive her and see her, as she truly is, a beautiful golden ray of light that is our true heritage as creations of God, no matter what our outward appearances or behavior may be.

It is so easy to go into judgment, be angry, and hold on to resentment and grudges. How easy it is to say statements like, "I don't get mad, I get even," or "There is one thing I can never forgive," or "I will forgive, but I will never forget." All are variations of the ego justifying resentment and attack. It is very hard to have compassion toward those who hurt us, whether physically, mentally or emotionally.

It is helpful, even in the worst circumstances, to remember we do not really know why someone acted the way they did, how they see their world and why their ego acted the way it did. Two of don Miguel's Four Agreements address this very issue. It is suggested we not make assumptions and not take anything personally. The ego sure wants us to assume why people act the way they do and certainly take it personally.

It would be very easy to make assumptions and react personally to what she did. My ego was certainly willing to take me there. As I was able to step back, not make assumptions, and try not to take what she did personally, I was able to become more compassionate. While not understanding why she did what she did, I can honestly look at my own part in the failed relationship. With compassion, I can understand partly why her ego would respond to perceived attack on my part. With compassion, I can look at her patterns of behavior and consider how fear and the unhealed past lead to the behaviors she engages in. Her promiscuity, her seeming ability to only connect physically, her difficulty in developing long-term meaningful relationships, her difficulty feeling safe in romantic relationships, her seeming victim drama and her practice of unsafe sex suggest emotional wounds not resolved. She made a comment once; she couldn't trust or be close to her adoptive father. The way she said it is similar to what victims of sexual abuse say about the perpetrators of abuse. It may very well be she was sexually abused as a child, which would explain much of her behavior. However, this is only an educated guess and I will never really know what emotional wounds lie unhealed within her. Nor do I need to know. With compassion, I know something traumatic is unhealed.

Forgiveness is about releasing our own negative and fear-based emotions from the past and when these emotions are projected on to present relationships. It is about releasing anger, hurt, resentment, grudges and judgments. As we forgive others we free ourselves to be in the present moment, move forward free from additional emotional baggage that only impede our own growth and development. Forgiving ourselves frees us even more to move forward with life, and choose who we want to be.

Forgiveness of others does not mean we let others continue to hurt us or stay in dysfunctional relationships. It does not mean we do not set boundaries, do not move to open and hon-

Healing and Transformation

est communication or do not share expectations so we can get to common ground with loved ones we still want to relate with. Forgiveness recognizes the other is not in their right mind. If they were, the would not have their ego attacking everyone.

Jesus demonstrated the truth of forgiveness, unconditional love and non-judgment throughout his ministry, but none more dramatically than while he was being crucified. He said, "Father forgive them, they know not what they do." He did not take what they were doing to him personally. He recognized they were not in their right minds. We excuse ourselves for not doing the same, by saying He is the Son of God. Well guess what, you are the Sons of God, too.

Forgiveness of ourselves is also about compassion. Compassion for ourselves, we are not perfect, we do make mistakes and we have emotional wounds and traumas to heal, just like everyone else. It means no longer being judgmental about ourselves and not condemning ourselves. We can take ownership of our mistakes, explore the roots of emotional wounds that need to be healed, release the old emotional hurts and free ourselves to make better and better choices of who we are and who we want to be. Forgiveness of ourselves reminds us everyone else needs forgiveness too, no mater the order of error or mistake.

A Native American prayer speaks of forgiveness so we may return to God without shame. This prayer, from the Red Cloud Indian School in Pine Ridge, South Dakota, states:

> O Great Spirit, whose voice I hear in the winds, and whose breath gives life to all the world, hear me! I am small and weak; I need your strength and wisdom. Let me walk in beauty, and make my eyes ever behold the red and purple sunset. Make my hands respect the things you have made and my ears sharp to hear your voice.
>
> Make me wise so that I can understand the things you have taught my people. Let me learn

the lessons you have hidden in every leaf and rock. I seek strength, not to be greater than my friend, but to fight my greatest enemy—myself. Make me always ready to come to you with clean hands, and straight eyes. So, when life fades, as the fading sunset, may my spirit come to you without shame.

It is challenging to let go of hurt and anger, and move to a place of true forgiveness. Yet not doing so only impedes our own healing, and prevents us from transforming our lives. Holding anger, resentments and grudges are poisons that eat us from inside. We make the mistake, at the ego level, of acting with hatred as a weapon attacking those who have harmed us. Yet, the harm we do is to ourselves.

The world we live in is a perfect opportunity for forgiveness and salvation. The adversities of life, particularly those where emotional wounds were inflicted on us, are perfect opportunities for healing and transformation. True forgiveness is the only way to break the pattern of assigning guilt to others, blaming others and not releasing the negative and fear-based emotions, which keep us trapped in our own dysfunctions, control dramas and fearful reactions to others and the world.

When we forgive others we are ultimately forgiving ourselves. As the Lord's Prayer reminds us, "Forgive us our trespasses, as we forgive those who trespass against us." When we forgive others we cancel our own mistakes and errors. In practicing true compassion and non-judgment with others, we have the same come back to us. As we forgive others we learn to be compassionate and non-judgmental with ourselves. We learn to no longer condemn others and to no longer condemn ourselves.

Forgiveness is a cornerstone of the spiritual path and is an essential process in healing and transformation. At the end of *The Disappearance of the Universe,* the Ascended Masters tell Gary Renard, "Be grateful for the opportunity to forgive each others and thus yourselves. Replace your grievances with love. Let your minds be led to the peace of God, and the truth that is within you shall come to your awareness." Not only does forgiveness resolve emotional hurt and pain, it frees us to rediscover our spiritual heritage and to remember we are spiritual beings having a human experience. Everyone on the planet, no matter how awful his or her behavior may seem to be, is a spiritual being having the human experience. Forgiveness reminds us of our truth and their truth, no matter how far we have strayed from remembering who we really are.

Chapter 11
THE GIFTS OF SPIRIT

One of the purposes of healing and transformation is to increasingly return to our spiritual heritage. While resolving past wounds and hurts frees us to make better choices of who we are and who we want to be, ultimately life is a spiritual quest. We do want to return to Heaven. As we progress through the healing process, we begin to manifest more and more the gifts of spirit, which in turn helps us to evolve spiritually. This process of enlightenment allows these gifts to return to our every day awareness and consciousness. This, in turn, further enhances the process of healing and transformation as we are guided in how to do this from other dimensional realms.

It is a worthy goal to heal old wounds so we are better able to function in the present moment without all the pitfalls the unhealed life continues to provide. When we do not examine our life and do not make the effort to heal the past in the present, we endlessly continue the dysfunctions and control dramas we previously learned. In its most devastating forms, we create serious mental illnesses. In more benign forms, we may still create occasional emotional crises that manifest in depression and/or anxiety of varying degrees. If we have not learned to heal old wounds and past hurts we become even more vulnerable to the adversities, failures and losses of life that are visited upon all of us. Unfortunately, if we do not heal old wounds and past hurts, we repeat old dysfunctional patterns in our relationships with others, endlessly recreating situations to try to correct those wounds or projecting our dramas on to our relationships, independent of what the other person is really all about.

A woman I know has had three significant relationships in which men have betrayed her. The most devastating was her husband and the father of her three children. A successful salesman, he became addicted to cocaine. In time he became verbally and emotionally abusive, finally threatening physical violence. He threatened to kill her and the children, prompting her to leave and seek a divorce. To this day he claims she ruined his life by not standing by him. With his addiction, he lost his wife, his family and his home. Financially he abandoned her and her children.

Two subsequent relationships included betrayal as these men cheated on her. They also would give her gifts of jewelry, which turned out to be fakes. Again, she was abandoned emotionally and financially.

She dated a new man to who she was really attracted and fell in love with. She could see a future with him. For Valentine's Day he bought her a special heart shaped necklace, with the heart encased with twelve rubies. He made a big deal out of getting her this necklace. Two days later she told him she was upset with him and was reluctant to share why. Eventually it comes out she thinks the necklace is a fake, or was a birthstone gift because the rubies were originally bought for someone else, and then given to her instead.

Her unhealed wounds led her to believe a scenario entirely different from what took place and the man's intentions. She actually believed the man was going to break up with her. Her reaction had nothing to do with the actual event, but the event triggered her old wounds not yet healed. We can easily do as she, projecting our unhealed dramas on to new people and new situations, until we recognize and resolve the wounds so we can be in the moment for what it is.

As we progress through the process of healing and transformation, we begin to create more "normal neurotic" patterns of behavior and reactions to life's challenges. We are better able to handle the adversities and challenges that arise, but are not quite able to take these events as opportunities to further grow and evolve. Eventually, as we do work through past hurts and wounds, we increasingly self-actualize. Thus, we are able to take the events and challenges of life as opportunities to further grow and evolve, reaching to our full potentials. Eventually we get better at authentic living, with genuine responses in the "now" moment. Not only do we begin to create our lives with a healthy psychological foundation, taking it a step further, I believe we are more capable of creating our lives as masterpieces of joy.

Each of us has the potential and is capable of creating heaven on earth. This requires living completely in the present moment, neither hung up on past failures, losses and disappointments nor constantly contemplating and planning the future. Living in the present allows us to forgive the past, forgive others, and ourselves, be unconditional love and allow the gifts of Holy Spirit to direct our lives and how we interact with others.

As *A Course In Miracles* teaches us, we learn to see others not as different, but as brothers and sisters all created by Love. We look beyond differences and seeming divisions, recognizing the unity of all humankind and indeed, of all creation. Separation and perceiving differences is what led to the rise of the ego, with emphasis on individual identity. The ego then goes on to place value on differences, to judge others and the world about us. Our collective egos create the world in which we live and the mess we have created of that world. Our injured egos focus on others to blame when life does not go well, often forgetting or ignoring our own part in the drama.

Healing and Transformation

The purpose of healing and transformation is to address our own emotional wounds and hurts. To face and to resolve these wounds by learning to release and let go of the negative and fear-based emotions attached to these painful events. As we do this, we free ourselves to live in the present moment and respond to others based on what is happening in the present, rather than through the prism of old dramas and dysfunctional patterns. As we heal, we also transform the energy attached to old wounds, freeing it to be available to us in the present and freeing it to move between the physical, mental, emotional, etheric and spiritual bodies that comprise our true reality.

As we progress through this transformational process, we increasingly live in the present moment, seeing unity in all there is and unity with all humankind. We live without being into worry or fear. We experience the peace that passes all understanding that Jesus promised us. We move into a state of waking up. We move beyond third dimensional consciousness and progress into fourth and then fifth dimensional consciousness. As we progress in consciousness, we manifest more the gifts of spirit. We enter into the Christ Consciousness, a consciousness of unconditional love, non-judgment and complete forgiveness of others and ourselves.

The importance of this process is we learn to stay in the moment. This is the key to bringing heaven to earth for our selves. Fifth dimensional consciousness is having heaven on earth. As each of us achieves this we help spread to those we come into contact with, and into the overall consciousness of humankind. Thus, healing and transformation does occur on a planetary scale.

Once this is in you, you spread it to everyone you meet. That is how heaven is coming to earth and how we return to another Golden Age. We learn to stay in the moment, staying right here, right now. It is accepting what is. It is getting beyond separation, judging differences, and finding fault and blame elsewhere.

As this energy and light is being infused into our planet at this time, it brings up all our "junk." As we increasingly enter the Photon Belt, all our unresolved issues and karmic debt comes up to be healed and resolved. In the past three years, I am continually amazed how many individuals I have significantly related to which I have had past lives with, and then had the opportunity to resolve the old hurts and wounds with these individuals. This frees me to be more in the present moment.

We are living in a time of profound change. Each of us is now given the opportunity to recognize our "stuff" and choose to deal with it. Courageously facing our past, our hurts and wounds, our disappointment and our failures, we can finally release and let go of all the negative and fear-based emotions. Living life in the present and transforming the levels of consciousness and dimensional awareness on which we are capable of functioning.

With all the transformational energy infusing the Earth at this time, the unresolved mental, emotional and spiritual wounds and hurts we carry are arising and will continue to arise. If we are unwilling to face and heal these wounds, they will overwhelm us. This is partly why we see increasing conflict and violence between individuals and groups of individuals.

The gifts of spirit naturally arise when we heal and transform our lives. We become increasingly intuitive, have more profound dreams, and experience greater levels of psychic phenomena. Our sixth sense comes more to the fore. We begin to have lucid dreams. These are dreams in which we know we are asleep; yet aware we are dreaming and even what the dream is telling us.

I experienced a lucid dream about a significant relationship, which ended in an angry way. In the dream, there was a colleague of this person letting me know that the former girlfriend hated me. In the dream, I was able to accept her feeling of hate, yet send feelings of forgiveness and peace to the former girlfriend. I understood the dream was helping me to resolve lingering hurt and resentment I still felt toward this individual.

The gifts of spirit are our natural heritage. We are meant to manifest and express this heritage. Connecting to our divine

Healing and Transformation

Higher Self comes easily as we heal old wounds and traumas, and increasingly learn to live authentically in each now moment. We learn how to connect to our mission and purpose, as we heal and transform. We release the density in our bodies as we move forward, allowing energy to freely move between all our bodies. Negative and fear-based emotions are transformed, no longer locked into our physical bodies. Some psychological traditions have known that old emotional experiences are locked into the physical body. The Bioenergetic Therapy School works directly with the physical to find and release the negative and fear-based emotions that hinder psychological growth and development. Various energy-healing systems do the same. Even therapeutic massage will tap into hidden emotions that need to be released and resolved, whether in this lifetime or past lifetimes.

As we release and let go of the negative and fear-based emotions trapped in the various bodies, the barriers between the bodies become more permeable and energy more freely moves between these bodies. Additionally, the density decreases as we begin to vibrate at higher frequencies. We move into higher dimensional vibrations. This, in turn, allows the gifts of spirit to more readily come into conscious awareness. This also allows us to more easily and readily access the gifts of spirit. This is what being born again means. It is not just a belief in a particular path or system of belief; it is a transformational process that elevates consciousness and vibration functioning.

In the restful state, we are trained, prepared, and walked through the events coming into our lives, in the not so distant future. Déjà vu experiences are reminders of the sneak previews we are given in the sleep state. Since there is much change about to take place on this planet, with increasing chaos and fear, accessing this information helps us to be ready, and more importantly, guided for what is coming next. Whether the end of a relationship, such as I experienced and shared in the chapter on forgiveness, or knowing I was going to be fired from a job I once held or being shown a vision of how the Earth may change and what it may look like in the future, our connection to our Higher Self, through the gifts of spirit, prepares us for what is coming. We become able to anchor peace and a higher consciousness into ourselves and into the collective.

The planet is being inundated with greater light energy. If our energy chakras are closed we have difficulty assimilating this light. If we are able to move this energy through us, we are able to build our light body, hold the greater energy and make the shift into higher consciousness and awareness. The result is greater bliss and higher wisdom. If we remain closed, this intensifies the fear with more turmoil and chaos. With the increased energy, the gifts of spirit are manifesting in us regardless, often creating fear and greater turmoil since healing and transformation has not occurred to sufficiently cope with the information breaking through. On a grand scale, this creates tragedies such as mass suicide in some cults. On a lesser, but no less tragic level, this results in violence and destructive impulsivity. On a collective scale, the increasing fear allows those in power to manipulate society to achieve their desires for control and greed.

Everlasting forgiveness of others and our selves releases the anger in the emotional body. We also release pain, rejection, feeling alone, feeling unloved for and other toxic emotions. As we experience what is in the present moment, allowing ourselves to experience it fully, then move beyond it, we release these and let them go. The energy connected to these feelings can then be utilized for our greater awakening and our greater capacity to experience and express the gifts of spirit.

As we heal and transform, we move into deeper, greater levels of compassion for our self and for others. As we embody greater levels of self-love and self-compassion, we develop more profound levels of understanding and awareness of why we do what we do. With the gifts of spirit we make better choices of who we are and who we want to be, taking into consideration this greater understanding of ourselves. We become more at peace, allowing others to live in their own space as well. We let go of the need to control others and the need to

Healing and Transformation

define how others should live and believe. We truly understand what freedom of religion really means.

As we step more and more into our light body, we experience the "veil" lifting so we can experience higher levels of self-awareness. This leads to becoming one-minded with the Presence-of-All-That-Is. Your higher awareness blends with your humanness, and you again know you are a spiritual being having a human experience. You again have the ability of knowingness, versus simple intellect. Increasingly utilizing the gifts of spirit as part of conscious awareness, you can increasingly consciously create yourself. The ego mind becomes increasingly less important and you embody greater levels of truth and compassion.

As we embrace increased levels of light energy, we are more aware. We can access our guides, teachers, and, personal Angels and loved ones in spirit. We can share their energies, wisdom and guidance. Gifted psychics convey messages from these entities to us in readings. Their guides and Angels, as well as your guides and Angels often specifically guide gifted healers as to what to do with the person in front of them. We do not have to wait until we are on our deathbed to "see" the Angels or our loved ones welcoming us back home, reassuring us there is nothing to fear. In my work with our elders, I cannot tell you how many times the dying have told me the Angels have been visiting them at night for the past few weeks. One cynical lady I worked with "saw" the Angels coming to get her roommate as she died, marveling at how the room filled with light and Angels. In that moment, she was transformed, the miracle of sight in that moment freeing her from her own painful past. We do not have to wait until the end of life to have the veil lift. As we heal and transform, these gifts of spirit emerge long before then.

As we reach higher levels of awareness, we simply begin to see through the veil of the individualized expression of ourselves we have been taught to believe. Do children have imaginary friends? Or, do we tell them what to believe and they stop seeing their guides and Angels, here to assist them. As we see

The Gifts of Spirit

through the veil, we again are more able to experience connection with our soul, rather than as separate from our soul.

As we reconnect with the soul, we bring our selves and others into greater love, non-judgment and trust that all is in divine order. We operate from love rather than fear. When we ask Holy Spirit to guide us, we are directed. When I was a new therapist, there were times I would not know how to help a client. I would ask Holy Spirit to guide me. I was amazed as Spirit spoke through me, having no idea what was going to be said next, providing the perfect answer or direction for that client. I suspect I am now better at blending my experience and skill with the allowance that Spirit work in me and through me at all times.

As we work to allow the gifts of spirit to emerge and be part of our lives, we learn to give up control. To surrender is to be in partnership with our Higher Self. We evolve, and everyone evolves with us. We are ascending pilgrims on this planet in this time and place. We have the most marvelous opportunity to experience ascension as a group and with the planet. We can create this ascension peacefully and smoothly.

In the ascension process the veil between the earth plane and other dimensional realities becomes thinner. Information from other dimensional realms assists us in releasing the ego, moving into a full conscious awareness that we are spiritual beings, capable of living on the Earth yet experiencing heaven. With guidance from spirit we can create the New Dawn.

There are many in the higher realms that are ready to assist us. Through the many gifts of spirit available to us, they can inspire and guide us. They can assist us to heal all time and space, to move beyond the ego and encompass greater expressions of the Divine Self in the physical domain. We can communicate with our guides, teachers, loved ones and personal Angels. We can recall past lives and "see" future realities. We begin fully expressing our selves, and become unconditional love, non-judgmental, and forgiving. Not a forgiveness that pardons others, but the true forgiveness that recognizes error as

Healing and Transformation

simply an underlying recognition we are all equally created by and loved by God, no matter the seeming level of the error.

We are living in a time of high anxiety and fear. The world seems out of control. Whether the adverse effects of the economy, terrorist activity, war, ethnic and religious strife, and escalating conflict within societies and families, we are living in challenging times. With healing and transformation, you are better able to cope with these events. You begin to learn you do not have to take on the fear of others. You do not have to feel alone and unsafe. Connecting to your Higher Self and increasingly manifesting the gifts of spirit, you are better equipped to handle the great changes that are happening and going to continue to happen.

We are in a time of great change, accompanied by greater light energy. The healing process allows us to better assimilate this increasing light energy. Moving this energy through your light body enables you to hold this energy and make the shift into higher dimensional realities. With this comes greater joy, greater bliss and higher wisdom. Wisdom such as knowing everyone is right and everyone is wrong. Without healing and transformation, you remain closed to accessing our higher self and the fear intensifies.

It is important to release the anger in the emotional body. It is important to release the pain, rejection and attitudes of others who do not understand us and seem so uncaring. As you allow yourself to feel the full range of emotions, to experience the sadness and anger, then you can discharge the feelings. This allows you to get to the place of grace, to truly forgive yourself and others. In forgiving, you experience an increase in your intuitive ability and the other gifts of spirit available to you. You are able to let go of control, a favorite activity of the ego, and allow your Higher Self and Holy Spirit to truly guide you in everything you say and do. You are then divinely led. You become peaceful in the midst of chaos.

With healing and transformation, we are able to step into elevated levels of light frequency. We increasingly move away from the darkness. The veil between physical dimensions and

The Gifts of Spirit

the higher dimensional frequencies begin to lift. We are able to communicate with and receive messages from loved ones on the other side, our guardian Angels, the Angels and Archangels, and the Ascended Masters. We receive the guidance of Holy Spirit. We connect with our Higher Self. We move to higher levels of self-awareness. We are able to become "one-minded," become one with the Presence of All-That-Is. There becomes a blending of our humanness with our higher awareness. We enter a level of awareness and vibration that allows for knowingness versus intellect. It is moving from separation and duality to oneness and unity.

With healing and transformation we are better able to consciously create. We are able to drop the human mind or the ego mind, and embody greater and greater levels of truth and compassion. This allows us to access the gifts of spirit freely available to all. The potential is within all of us. Simply because these gifts are more developed in some does not make them unique or special. Developing the gifts is part of healing and transformation, but most important is what we do with these gifts. Do we use them to evolve and to help everyone else evolve? With greater gifts comes greater responsibility to be of service to all.

As we evolve and develop these gifts of spirit we become increasingly intuitive. We have a heightened awareness of ourselves psychologically and emotionally, as well as spiritually. We remember our divine heritage. We increasingly recognize we are one with everyone else and with God. There is less belief in separation. We let go of duality. We remember each soul is on its own path and not judge how that path serves that soul's evolution back to God.

We may see our selves as individuals, yet connected and guided. As we develop these gifts of spirit, we begin to be aware we are not really separate from one another or All-That-Is. We begin to understand we are simply holding an individualized awareness, as part of the greater whole. As we become even more aware, we recognize a blending of energies. We discover there are parallel realities that exist in the experience we call time.

While aspects of the larger self may be operating in separate identities, at the soul level we are able to access the wisdom of the soul, or Higher Self. All of the experiences, we have at any time, as well as all the experiences we believe we have had in the past become accessible to us. We are able to bring into this now moment all the wisdom and knowledge we have experienced. We also access the wisdom and knowledge of the soul group to which we belong. We travel through eternity with a group of souls, learning and evolving, healing and transforming together across space and time. As we heal and transform, our wise teachers and our Higher Self become more self-evident.

Eventually, we evolve to the level of the Buddha or of Jesus, who became the Christ. The Christ Consciousness is being in the space of not judging others or experiences. Buddha and Jesus could not separate their selves any longer from the wholeness. That is why they demonstrated complete forgiveness, non-judgment and unconditional love. Where we see individuals, they saw God.

The evolved feeling of compassion is through the experience of the whole. It is not as an outside observer simply observing someone in pain any longer. It is being part of the pain with someone. It is no longer an individual experience, but an experience of the whole. In the oneness you begin to truly understand the grace of God and can no longer be in judgment of anyone or anything. You begin to understand you would never leave anyone behind. This is why we all get to heaven together. There is no hierarchy in heaven. There is complete oneness and unity, for we are all the Son of God. We cannot move forward without taking everyone with us. We remain tied to those who are still in a state of forgetfulness, who need their healing and transformation.

We begin to gain increased awareness of this truth we are all one. We gain greater levels of choice and awareness. We choose more consciously. We release the unconscious choices that come from the human mind, the ego mind, belief systems, and fears. It is letting go of control dramas, manipulative styles and limited belief systems about you and about all others. You merge more with your Higher Self.

We begin to surrender more of the human thinking. We let go the control of trying to manipulate or trying to force an outcome, to feel safe with a certain outcome or to manipulate how a fate is to unfold for us. We learn to bring our selves and others into greater love, non-judgment in the situation, and trust that all is in divine order. This is the opposite of coming from the human self. Every moment is perfect for each of us in that moment.

Whatever gifts of spirit emerge for you, these gifts help to guide you deeper into remembering you are a spirit having a human experience. They help you heal and evolve to the greater truth and understanding of the oneness of it all. These gifts guide you to make choices in genuine partnership with God, helping all to return together to heaven. In the meantime, they help you create heaven on earth in each now moment.

The healing process is to clear out the old emotional wounds so the ego no longer controls your life. It is releasing all the old negative and fear-based emotions so that you are increasingly free to live life in each now moment without the control dramas, manipulative styles and dysfunctional patterns that prevent you from having the happiness and joy you deserve in each now moment. You more maturely handle the adversities and challenges of life. You are able to heal all time and space, resolving any negative, karmic debt you have accumulated in the past. You are able to approach each event and relationship in life with the freedom to experience these things without fear and erroneous judgment. You are able to manifest unconditional love, non-judgment and complete forgiveness. Finally, you are able to walk the path of joy guided by your Higher Self, Holy Spirit, and all the guides and teachers available to you from other dimensional realms and realities.

You also begin to experience the unity of all that is. You move from duality to the recognition that we are all one, One

Sonship, and that we are equal in the eyes of God. No matter what the seeming outward appearances, within we are all part of the Sonship. As misguided as we all can be, especially as the ego directs us and as spiritual pride can divide us, the truth is we are all one in God's eye. Spiritual pride combined with the ego can lead us to believe we have the exclusive path back to God and only a few make it back to heaven.

The so-called "psychic" abilities we all have are neither good nor bad, in and of themselves. There are no unnatural powers. As awareness increases we may develop abilities that are quite surprising. Communication is not limited to the small range of channels the world recognizes. In *A Course In Miracles,* it is stated, the limits the world places on communication are the chief barriers to the direct experience of the Holy Spirit. The world's limits are placed out of fear, to maintain separation. Transcending the limits of the world is merely becoming more natural.

The new abilities of the gifts of spirit are helpful. Under the guidance of the Holy Spirit they become useful teaching aides. The importance is in how these gifts are used. They are not an end in and of themselves. They do not prove anything. They do not indicate achievements from the past, unusual attunement to the unseen or special favors from God. God gives no special favors and no one has powers that are not available to everyone.

As gifts of spirit emerge, there is the danger the ego will use these gifts to glorify itself. This is a similar danger to the arrogance of spiritual pride, which interferes with attaining spiritual attunement and understanding. As these gifts emerge, we must be careful. The purpose is for greater awareness and a greater capacity for conscious choosing. Any ability developed has the potential for good. The more unusual and unexpected the gift is the greater its potential usefulness. The gifts of spirit can be a great channel of hope and healing in the Holy Spirit's teaching and guiding. Gifts of spirit are simply letting the limitations of the human mind be lifted.

The Gifts of Spirit

As you heal and evolve, you will begin to have the inner questioning within the self. What is really me? What is someone else? What is my Higher Self? What is my human self? Where do I begin and end? All the lines of separation begin to blur more and more. You will never see yourself as wholly separate again. With heightened levels of the light within the body, you begin to lose the defined delineation of what is you and what is another. Yet you do not lose the individualized self, until such time as you return to heaven and become one with the Sonship as we once were.

At this level of healing and transformation we would never consider leaving any one behind. Ultimately, we have a responsibility to help all who are still forgetful, in turn guiding them forward as we have been guided forward. It is not enough to believe Jesus is Lord and Savior. It is also walking his path and living in the physical as he lived. He never condemned and always asked our Father to forgive. When others made errors, he would simply say "Go and sin no more." With increased awareness we make better choices. Theologies arise from the ego to keep us separated and divided. All Master Teachers have taught how to walk the path of salvation and redemption. You have to walk the walk, as they say in AA, not just talk the talk.

To walk the walk means to more consciously choose the spiritual path. Instead of choices based on the human mind, ego mind, the belief systems and the fears, choices are made with the Higher Self and the Holy Spirit. This then means embodying greater levels of the ongoing search for truth. Healing and transformation allows us to face the fears, release the fears, surrendering greater levels of belief and trust in the Divine and less control by the human experiences that ground and limit us. We begin to experience less that life is a struggle and experience a decrease in fear. We increasingly experience the positive and love-based emotions. The soul is here to further evolve itself. Gifts of spirit help the evolution. The original purpose of being in the physical densities was to blend spirit with the

Healing and Transformation

physical, and not be entrapped in the physical forgetting our divine heritage.

With becoming spiritually centered, we get to choose, in each moment, to be powerful or powerless. We get to choose to overcome forgetfulness and remember we are spiritual beings having the human experience. With greater gifts of spirit, we access our teachers and guides in other planes of existence to help us remember and more fully live with unconditional love, non-judgment and forgiveness. This is awakening the Christ Consciousness. It is finding peace in the midst of chaos. Growth is letting go of the human mind, not holding on to the ego self. Growth is finally forgiving us. We merge again into the wholeness. The ego has us believe we lose everything when we do this, but in reality we are gaining the universe.

Healing and transformation leads to the gifts of spirit. These gifts allow us to be more aware. We are able to make choices consciously, with the guidance of enlightened beings that are standing by to assist us. They gently guide us, even if we deny their existence. How much better to be consciously aware of their guidance and direction, so we experience peace and joy, and fulfill our part in the Divine plan!

Chapter 12
THE PURPOSE OF PROPHECY

One of the interesting gifts of spirit is the gift of prophecy. The future is not meant to be left to chance! As we heal our lives and the transformational process evolves, we increasingly become aware of possible futures. This helps us to continue the healing process, for all time and space. Increased awareness about possible future events, in our life and in the collective experience, means we have the opportunity to make better choices of how to respond to those potential events or make different choices that alter those events.

The purpose of prophecy is to increase awareness and, where possible, change probabilities. For instance, if you go to a psychic who tells you a loved one is about to have their transition and return to spirit, you may make better use of the time you have left with that person in the physical. You may want to heal old wounds in the relationship, forgive them personally or simply tell them how much you love them and how much you have valued having them in your life. Being given advanced warning; you can better utilize the time you have left. Making

Healing and Transformation

the most of the opportunity to express your appreciation of them and how they have benefited you in your life journey.

Prophecy did not end in Biblical times. The gifts of spirit did not cease with the advent of Christianity or any other religious tradition. Yet, those traditions are rich with the voices of prophecy. Other traditions have had their prophets as well. The ancient Greeks had a collective consciousness that allowed the oracles at Delphi to perceive future events and share them with their community.

In more recent times prophecy has emerged in various sources. The well-known "Sleeping Prophet," Edgar Cayce, gave numerous predictions of future events in the first half of the last century. He would go into a trance state and questions would be asked to him. Initially he provided physical healing readings, with thousands of readings providing diagnoses and cures, which are documented.

While in the trance state, it was discovered he could respond to other questions put to him. There are many fascinating readings that cover the lost civilizations of Atlantis and Lemuria, how humankind separated from God, the role of the Essene community in bringing forth Jesus and the concept of reincarnation. Some readings asked about future events, practical as well as more general. From this, emerged predictions about possible Earth changes, including the possibility of a pole shift.

Some of the Marian sightings have also foretold of events yet to come. Mother Mary appeared to the children at Fatima, predicting events that included possible Earth changes, evidenced by strange events in the skies. The Vatican has allegedly concealed some of the predictions. The Catholic Church did not want some of these prophecies to become public, especially if they contradict Church teaching. When Mary appeared in the Balkans, she predicted some of the more immediate events that have since tragically unfolded there.

Gordon-Michael Scallion is a current-day intuitive who publishes a bimonthly newsletter, sharing impressions he receives about possible upcoming changes. He has also been on the

The Purpose of Prophecy

radio and is currently available on the internet sharing some of the predictions. He has seen what he interprets may be a pole shift, with the sun being to one side of him, then suddenly on his other side while facing in the same direction. This is followed by intense winds that would occur if the Earth shifted its axis. He has printed a map showing how the United States may look after some of the predicted Earth changes do indeed occur.

In the recent book, *The Disappearance of the Universe,* the Ascended Masters who speak to Gary Renard offer a glimpse of future events. Unfortunately, these include a major terrorist attack on a city in the world. They also indicate there will be contact with our extraterrestrial brothers and sisters. On a bright note they suggest the stock market will hit 50,000 at some future time.

In the St. Germain literature, it is revealed that George Washington was shown future visions of the United States. These occurred while the Colonials were encamped at Valley Forge. It is said he was humbled, yet energized, by what was revealed to him, giving him the strength and courage to continue fighting for the independence of this great nation. Accounts of Washington's countenance when he emerged from seclusion, after these visions were shown to him, was one of wonderment and ecstasy.

Numerous visions of future events are available and can be found in books devoted to these visions. Most notable are the predictions of Nostradamus, who deliberately concealed his visions for his own protection at the time he lived. Some interpretations of his have been direly interpreted, with significant fear attached to them. Indeed some of his predictions may foretell disastrous events that may be yet to come. Care should always be given to the predictions of future events. It is not necessary to go into fear. Fear can bring about the dire events predicted. As with any prophecy, we have free will and can change possible outcomes with a consciousness of love and positive attitude.

For a time, there were predictions of global nuclear war and the horrors of a nuclear winter to follow. The collective consciousness of visualizing peace instead changed this from happening. Events such as millions meditating for peace on New Year's Eve every year appear to have shifted that destiny from occurring. We now know how close we came to that happening. In the mid 1980's the leaders of the Soviet Union came very close to deciding to "win" the Cold War by preemptively attacking the United States with nuclear weapons. Obviously, they were not even considering the fact the nuclear cloud of destructive radiation would have blown right back over them. Or maybe reason somehow did prevail; with the understanding there would have been no winners in such an attack. Look at all the destruction of Chernobyl, with just one reactor melting down.

Another time, the Soviet radar seemed to show an incoming missile attack from the United States. The Colonel in charge feared there was some kind of glitch and what appeared to be happening was not accurate. It turned out, the way the radar was hitting the tops of some clouds gave the impression of an attack, which was not true. His reward for hesitating was to be demoted, effectively ending his military career, yet he saved the world. So the probability of this prophecy was quite accurate at one time, but fortunately the millions who meditated for peace changed this. Healing and transformation does work, even on a planetary level.

When we heal the old wounds and traumas of the past and move forward on the spiritual path, we increasingly gain access to the gifts of spirit. We begin to have enhanced intuitive abilities that suggest possible outcomes in the immediate future, as well as more distant time. How often do we get a strong feeling to choose a particular course of action, doubt what our intuition is suggesting? Only to find out later, what we sensed was going to happen, did indeed happen.

With increased intuitive ability we are able to sense what may be coming or what course of action we can take. Learning to trust this natural ability and learning to act on these feelings

The Purpose of Prophecy

can help future events unfold in a smoother and orderly fashion. Obviously, strong feelings of caution and warning should be heeded, for our Angels and guides often protect us through the use of our intuitive ability.

We may also begin to experience prophetic dreams. In these dreams certain events may be foretold in our future or in the future of the world we live in. As we progress spiritually, these dreams may become more intense or be more vivid. We may receive strong suggestions on the course of action or direction we should take in our lives. Certain events may be foretold, giving us the opportunity to better prepare for the events, or other choices may be available to us if we heed the information given in the prophetic dream.

We are given previews of coming attractions in our lives in the dream state. This is why we later have déjà vu experiences. When it feels like you are experiencing something again, and could swear it has happened already, but it is now actually happening, this is a déjà vu moment. You "saw" the moment in the dream state, and now what you were shown is happening to you.

As we progress with the process of transformation and increasingly walk the spiritual path, we more consciously access and remember these previews. We can also take advantage of these previews to more consciously choose to follow our life path. We are reassured we are on the right path and we can more consciously choose to fulfill our mission and purpose in this lifetime.

Questions can be posed before you go to sleep at night. You can ask for answers in the dream state to direct what is the best course of action to follow or to answer questions you are puzzled about on how to proceed or what to do in particular situations.

You ask for the answers to come to you in your dreams.

As we evolve, we not only remember our dreams more clearly, but we also begin to have lucid dreams. Lucid dreams are when you know you are soundly asleep, yet are consciously aware of the dream and what the dream means, or what the

Healing and Transformation

dream is trying to tell you. Since dreams often occur with symbolic imagery, this form of dreaming accurately tells you what your subconscious mind or your higher self is trying to tell you. The subconscious mind is the part of your mind that accesses your inner wisdom and what your higher self is trying to communicate to you.

The dream state can foretell future events. The Christian Bible shares many events in which prophetic dreams occurred, and the benefit that occurred to those who listened to the messages of the dream and took the proper course of action. One example is the dream that Joseph had warning him to take Mary and Jesus and go to Egypt. Heeding the warning in the dream, they left the next day, getting out of Palestine before Herod ordered the murder of all children less than two years of age.

Several years ago I was terminated from a position as the director of a chemical dependency unit for a hospital system. Several days before I was actually terminated, I had a vivid dream in which I was forewarned of what was coming. It didn't make it any easier to go through that particular adversity in my life, but at least I was prepared when they called me in to do just that.

A particular kind of vivid dreaming is lucid dreaming, as discussed in an earlier chapter. In this type of dream we are fully aware of the dream and the message and/or interpretation of the dream. At times these dreams can prepare us for future events, revealing to us what may be coming and making us fully aware of what is coming. These dreams can also help us heal and resolve old issues, so we are ready for events that are about to take place.

Before attending a daylong spiritual seminar, I had a lucid dream the night before in which I entered the seminar room, walking past a former lover. We exchanged greetings as though there was no lingering bitterness between us. In the dream I found myself silently forgiving her. The next day in the seminar I was able to experience a meditation exercise in which forgiveness was offered to old relationships. Then the facilita-

The Purpose of Prophecy

tor came and worked with the energy of my heart center, further releasing and freeing this chakra. In the dream the night before, I "knew" I would release old relationship wounds, thus allowing further healing and transformation of my heart center.

More recently, I was shown in a lucid dream a relationship I hoped to salvage was not going to happen. It prepared me for the eventual outcome. Despite attempts to meet and resolve differences the relationship could not be saved. In a last meeting there was some hope that we had worked through differences and could try again. That very night I had a lucid dream in which she told me it was too late as she had moved on. Then her daughter came up to me in the dream, with a frown on her face, and said she didn't like me anymore. Since I was very close with this daughter, her statement in the dream stunned me. I immediately "knew," while dreaming, the relationship would not be salvaged. I awoke depressed because I knew I was being prepared for the eventual outcome.

As we evolve spiritually we become more open to the gifts of spirit that are our natural heritage. We may begin to experience visions of upcoming events in our life, the lives of others or in the future of the world. In meditation and in healing circles I have "seen" upcoming events for myself, for others or for the world. Understanding these visions helps me better prepare for what may be coming. Understanding these visions helps me make better choices of who I am and who I want to be. Understanding and heeding these visions helps decide whether certain courses of action may be beneficial or harmful.

Certainly visions that warn us should be heeded. How often have we heard stories of people who saw a disaster ahead of time, tried to warn others, and decided them selves not to take that train or plane, or travel a certain route or go to a certain place? Visions may occur spontaneously or may happen during meditation. They may show the actual event as it will happen, or there may be a sense of what may occur.

Gifted intuitives often "see" upcoming events. This is called clairvoyance. The intuitive may gaze into a crystal ball or see visions as they unfold the Divination cards. They are shown events or people that may be coming into the person's life. They can often give fairly accurate descriptions. Over the years I have consulted with intuitives and been amazed at the visions they see transpiring at a future time. Interestingly, I sometimes have to put predictions on the "memory shelf." Sometimes the vision or prediction emerges several years later.

Sometimes predictions are shared through clairaudience. The intuitive will speak to beings in the spirit realm and convey their messages and predictions to the person receiving the information. Sometimes the intuitive will literally speak directly to the being, then turn to you and tell what they are saying from other dimensions. There was a minister with this gift, I saw a few years ago, who would sit there and listen to my deceased relative, my spirit guide or other entities and then tell me what they were saying.

When going for a reading with a gifted intuitive, one is going to get information about upcoming events. A gifted intuitive or psychic knows what information to share. They may see the death of a loved one coming up in your life, but know this information is not to be shared, as you may have to experience that event suddenly. They may also know not to share such information, as you may not be able to handle what is coming. There may be a wide variety of events they see, but may not share, as you have to experience some events in certain ways.

On the other hand, the intuitive may see certain events are coming up which they may not share with you, because you may not be able to handle the information or may misinterpret how the event is going to arise. They may not be able to share certain information, as it may interfere with your free will. There are times when I am communicating with an Angel or Ascended Master through the process of channeling. Certain information that I request will be offered to me, but only if it is understood that I retain free will, and what they are sharing are only probabilities of what may occur.

Given these possibilities, gifted intuitives can often provide us with information about probable futures that can aide us in making better choices or better prepare us to handle probable events in a much better way. For instance, knowing that a parent may be coming to the end of their journey on this plane, and about to transition to other dimensional realities, being forewarned may help us to make the best use of the time remaining while they are here. We may choose to spend more time, and more quality time with a loved one. We may choose to let them know how much we love them and how much they have meant to us in our lives. We may choose to heal unresolved conflict and wounds between us, to truly practice forgiveness with them, to give our forgiveness and ask for their forgiveness. To complete this time together, with a clean slate.

The gifted psychic, Alexia, practicing in both Dearborn and Coldwater, Michigan has stated many times, "The future is not meant to be left to chance." Throughout history, prophets have spoken to their people forewarning them of coming events. Every religious tradition documents the sages of their times and places. Prophecy did not suddenly end 2,000 years ago. In our time there are many prophecies, particularly about the approaching times we are in.

There are numerous predictions about the times we seem to be living in now, with many interpretations of upcoming events. Some of these prophecies seem dire and can be fearfully interpreted. They speak of dramatic changes coming to the planet. Some speak to catastrophic change at the physical level. Numerous prophecies speak of major geological changes, altering the entire surface of the planet. In the United States alone, some of the predictions include earthquakes on the West Coast, the sinking of land as far in to the east as Colorado, land sinking in the southeast, the Mississippi River basin widening as the continent splits, with the Great Lakes eventually emptying into the Mississippi River and into a new river that empties into the Arizona region. There have been predictions of a partial or complete shift in the axis of the Earth, with the Gobi Desert as the possible new North Pole. Other predictions suggest Atlantis will rise again and there will be a new continent in the Pacific.

Other prophecies indicate dramatic climate changes, with more powerful storms. Recent hurricane seasons appear to be bearing this out, with the deadly and catastrophic destruction of New Orleans serving as a forerunner of what may be coming. Some predictions indicate it will be increasingly more dangerous to live in coastal regions, and people will begin to relocate further inland.

Climatic predictions suggest there will be rain where there were previously drier zones and more arid land where there is now abundant moisture. Some predictions have indicated the melting of the polar caps, raising ocean levels even more and changing weather patterns. Some predictions indicate the United States will become more subtropical, especially in the northwest.

Other prophecies predict major plagues that will begin to decimate the population of the planet. One has to only look at the devastation the AIDS epidemic has already reaped, especially in Africa. In recent years, the Bird Flu has emerged as a deadly disease, which has already had far reaching effects in Asia. At the time of this writing, it is spreading into the Middle East and Eastern Europe, beginning to cause panic and fear there.

War is also widely predicted in many prophecies, including the possibility of another world war. Fortunately, predictions of a nuclear holocaust appear to have been changed by all the millions who have meditated for peace over time. There are still predictions of limited use of nuclear weapons, which may be used by nations and by terrorists. Sadly, rumors of wars and wars are indeed happening in many places. Some predictions are one-third of those taken off the planet in these apparent end times will be due to war. Certainly the genocidal conflicts in parts of the world seem to tragically mirror these predictions. Unfortunately, our wounded egos even manifest in larger belief systems and actions, so war becomes a viable response to perceived attack, even between nations. Now there is talk of clashes between civilizations, such as between the West and Islam.

Given the very real probability that earth changes, plagues, and wars are upon us as the Earth moves into a New Golden

The Purpose of Prophecy

Age, how we can be ready for the changes and be in safe places? Birth is always accompanied by birth pains. The evolvement of this planet to higher dimensional realities will be accompanied by the painful realities reflected in earth changes, plagues and wars. Those souls that are not ready to evolve or choose not to evolve will not be able to survive the coming changes. Each of us has the opportunity to choose to move forward into the New Golden Age. This is accomplished with healing old wounds and transforming our lives as we engage a true spiritual path.

As we heal and transform our lives, we increasingly develop our intuitive abilities. It is our intuitive abilities that will help us to further evolve, as we are directed by our inner wisdom. As we become more intuitive, we are able to directly hear the still small voice within, which is God, through Holy Spirit guiding and directing us to our greater good. It is returning to God Within that allows us to be truly guided to our greater good, in all areas of our lives, including to where our safety lies with the coming changes.

In the times that are coming, if not already here, external authorities will not be able to help us or properly guide us. How much trust is there with government officials and their ability to handle crises? The latest events in New Orleans with Hurricane Katrina have exposed just how little preparation and response our governments are capable of providing. Sadly, our political process has so deteriorated, our leaders would rather angrily proclaim that their view is the only view that will rightly guide us rather than reach consensus and represent the views of everyone to reach solutions that represent the greatest good for all.

Another authority source that may fail us is the medical establishment. The insistence they have the only solutions to illness and that their authority is the only authority to be respected in this area, does not always facilitate the best solutions for your healing and transformation. This is not to make light, in any way; of the many valuable contributions the allopathic and osteopathic systems of medicine have contributed to our

Healing and Transformation

better health and longevity. Nor will I recommend, in any way, you discard these systems for alternative systems. Yet, there are many alternative systems that can facilitate healing at the physical level, and help with healing at other levels as well. Homeopathic and naturopathic systems offer many promising solutions to healing. The wide variety of alternative health options also contributes to healing. Add to this, healing emotional issues further contribute to healing at all levels. Energy work also enhances healing. Finally, meditation and visualization further contributes to healing physically and at other levels.

Religious leaders also may not be able to properly guide us through the coming planetary transformation. Unfortunately, many religious authorities are caught up in their own egos, following their particular faith outwardly, but not walking or living the true spiritual path. Creating fear and causing judgment does not walk the spiritual path, nor does it provide leadership for their followers to walk the true spiritual path. Insisting that their path is the only path to God adds to separation and fear.

Unfortunately, many religions as they are practiced, are ego-based structures that are the antithesis of the true spiritual path. They insist that simply believing is enough to get you to heaven, leaving out the work of dealing with your own ego, the wounds associated with it, and moving toward healing and transforming yourself into a true spiritual path. While all faiths have at their core the fundamental truths, as we know them on this planet, the wisdom imparted by the great Master Teachers have been distorted over time by the power and control dramas of the ego driven leaders of those faiths. Following their authority will not get you to heaven nor will it help you in the coming transition to the next age.

With healing and transformation we become more intuitive, allowing us to hear and be guided by the only true authority that can be trusted in this time and place. It is our connection to our inner wisdom that allows us to be truly guided, especially in the current times of change on the planet. Now, more than ever, is there the need for vision in a changing world. There will be many voices, especially authoritative voices, which will

The Purpose of Prophecy

tell you their way is the one and only way through these challenging times. There will be many false prophets as well, as warned of in the New Testament of the Christian Bible.

Guidance can be accessed in many ways. There are many ways to obtain guidance through intuitive sources. Using Tarot Cards, Viking Runes, Angel Cards and Native American Animal cards can provide information and guidance. Consulting with reputable psychics and intuitives can also be valuable sources of information and guidance. Obtaining information and guidance through individuals who are able to channel can also offer valuable information and guidance. All of these sources must be evaluated by the admonition offered by Jesus; "You shall know them by their works." The same applies to all the seeming authorities that also seek to inform and guide you.

Ultimately, knowing someone by their works means trusting our own intuition of what is being said "feels" right. We have to learn to trust our own inner guidance as we evaluate what is being said and the source of that information. Does the information "feel" right?" Does the source of the information and guidance "feel" right?" Not because someone else told you they are right or their information is valid. In the coming times, it is only through our guidance by Holy Spirit, our Inner Wisdom, God Within or the "still, small voice within" that will truly guide us. As we heal and transform, we operate from love rather than fear. Our intuition, based on love, will guide us truly.

The intuitive Alexia channels her spirit mentor, known as Alhambra. In the November, 2005 Alhambra Institute newsletter, Alhambra reminds us that life on Earth has become chaotic and changeable. There will be many interruptions that impact our lives. This will include interruptions in the flow of goods and services. Enormous changes are occurring that will make life difficult and unpredictable. Look at what Hurricane Katrina has wrought, if only for a few weeks, for the rest of us outside the Gulf Coast. Look at the rise in oil prices and the disruption in fuel supplies for the moment. In August 2004 the East Coast and part of the Midwest dealt with the power grid failing for several days. More of this is coming.

Alhambra reminds us that biblical prophecies about the ending of this time of human existence are part of a spiritual rebirth on the Earth plane. Part of this rebirth is the recognition to understand the proper relationship between material goods and pleasures, and the spiritual life. Everything belongs to God, and is part of the natural world from which it is taken, used and given value by us. With the earth changes taking place we are not being punished, but the material world is being placed back in proper perspective and not an end in itself. Remember, Jesus taught us, what profited a man to gain the world and lose his soul.

The most valuable part of living on the earth plane is to grow spiritually. Souls and spiritual growth are more valuable than any material thing. Alhambra tells us, as we move forward through this great spiritual lesson at this time, those who have sold their souls for possessions now have to learn what is important. Are pride and possessions more important than soul growth and development?

Alhambra reminds us, possessions on the earth plane are just tools to make the earth journey more comfortable. Understanding this, and we don't really own anything, we grow with the knowledge that all belongs to God. If we move through the world, appreciating what God allows us to have and using "things" for comfort in the physical plane, we grow and evolve. It is not that we can't have these things, but they must be understood and used in the proper perspective. We learn the lesson of mastering materiality on the earth plane when we accept all belongs to God and we can give it up when it goes. Many of the people I work with in nursing homes learn this lesson as they accept they came into the world with nothing and are now leaving the world with nothing materially. Remember what we take of value from this world is the love we give and receive. What we take of value from this world is the wisdom we learn along the way.

The Purpose of Prophecy

Alhambra reminds us that Biblical prophecy warns us that during the changing times there will be many false prophets. These many false prophets will come and say "come this way" or "come over here." Alhambra reminds us the governments of the world do not know the future, the media doesn't know the future of the world and the churches don't know the future of the world. When they tell us what is going to happen they are feeding their own greed, not only for money but also for power and control. Because of this corruption, everyone will have to develop his or her own relationship with God once again. These other sources have been corrupted by the material side of existence and can't be relied upon to lead the way.

People will have to allow their intuition to guide them to the gates of the new world. Intuition is our link to God, to Spirit. As we learn to trust in God's guidance through intuition and as we learn to how to trust God to show us the way, we'll make it through the coming changes.

The constant changes ahead will create constant stress. If we know the future and are able to "see," "sense" and "feel" what is ahead of us, we can eliminate the stress and make material and spiritual progress at the same time.

Fortunately as we heal and transform our lives, we gain greater intuition and greater trust in our intuitive ability. Beyond that, the future is not to be left to chance, not only by knowing what is coming, but also by proactively working to change future outcomes. By creating harmony and joy within ourselves we can connect with others to facilitate healing and transformation on a societal and planetary level. Prophecy indicates probabilities that can be altered by the collective consciousness. Already some of the dire warnings that were scheduled to happen by 1998 have been altered and lessened.

We can still choose individually and collectively to alter future events. We can begin to work in harmony with each other and with Mother Earth to peacefully and gently move into the New Golden Age. It does not have to be catastrophic. Jesus stated, when two or more are gathered in his name then change can occur. Walking the spiritual path and working in harmony to alter the consciousness of all can indeed change the world. Imagine a world in which everyone understood the spiritual principles of non-judgment, forgiveness and unconditional love. Imagine a world where everyone takes full responsibility, knowing that every thought and action, create their own future. As you sow, so do you reap.

Edgar Cayce, mentioned earlier, was a noted intuitive who gave many visions of the future. Some of his more dire predictions were expected between 1958 and 1998. Fortunately, these have not occurred. This is probably due to our collective free will changing these events, as a sufficient number of individuals have collectively meditated and visualized more peaceful change.

Mark Thurston, Ph.D. commented on Cayce's 21st Century vision in an article in the A.R.E. Venture Inward magazine. His comments appeared in the March/April issue. Cayce was partly a visionary, a prophet who described what life events were all about and where they were leading us. Thurston commented the real power of Cayce's teachings often came from his capacity to put our modest, small-scale lives into a much bigger context.

While Cayce predicted major earth changes and the re-emergence of Atlantis, he was a prophet on a much grander scale. There were ten elements of this prophetic vision, suggesting a new way of living on the earth. We have a part in bringing these essentially hopeful visions into reality. We do this with our free will, working to heal and transform our lives, manifesting this new reality. A new reality based on the living of true spirituality.

First, according to Cayce, a new medicine will emerge, a transformational healing based on holism and dealing with the energy system of the body. As previously noted, we have interconnecting bodies, physical, mental emotional, etheric and spiritual. The new medicine will integrate these bodies with physical treatments to promote the healing of the physical, methods to transform attitudes and emotions, and disciplines to keep spiritual ideals and purpose clearly centered.

The Purpose of Prophecy

Second, intuition and psychic abilities will become normal. Individuals will have personal and direct communication with the spiritual world, allowing connections to be practically applied in daily life. The healing process we are talking about helps this to readily emerge. It has happened in past times and places and can happen again.

Third, science and spirituality will no longer be antagonists. This convergence will transform culture, as research and enlightenment become partners. This will lead to a science of the spiritual world and a new sense of sacredness in the material world. As science advances, what now seems to be only taken on faith will be explained. What we now understand to be miracles simply obey universal laws we don't yet know let alone comprehend.

Fourth, dramatic geographical changes will take place, including significant changes in weather patterns. We are already experiencing this with greater numbers and intensities of storms. The tsunami in the Indian Ocean and recent earthquakes also suggest this is beginning to manifest. In North America, the seasons are changing and what were once gradual season changes are now abrupt changes with extreme changes in temperature from day-to-day within seasons.

Fifth, there will come to pass a worldwide social leveling. This could be difficult, painful and even violent at times. Prosperity and abundance are the natural gifts of the spiritual path. Everyone will enjoy the abundance of the material world without needing more than is necessary to live a comfortable life. Material wealth gained, at the expense of others or the Earth will no longer be possible. This does not mean a lack of abundance. The spiritual path allows for manifestation to occur. This abundance will provide comfort and joy, and not be driven by overcoming a sense of lack, by greed or by correcting emotional wounds from the past.

Sixth, leadership on the international scene will move to the Orient, and according to Cayce, to central China. China will one day become the cradle of a true Christianity, according to Cayce. As the Gobi desert is the crown chakra of the planet, it is natural the Earth will re-orient in this place. Eventually the Gobi desert may become the new North Pole, pointing to Arcturus, the Christ star, as the new North Star.

Seventh, archeological discoveries about ancient civilizations will radically alter our sense about human history. According to Cayce, these discoveries will show us the ways our ancient ancestors found to integrate science and spirituality. Ancient civilizations were more advanced than we believe ourselves to be. While we are technologically evolving, we certainly are not spiritually evolving. Making our technological advances capable of being misused, returning us to a more primitive time. The Atlanteans certainly managed to do this when their civilization deteriorated and the laws of man overcame the laws of God. They eventually destroyed themselves when their technology was used against others and had power and control over others.

Eighth, the continuity of life will be fully accepted as an indisputable fact. There is no death, just a transition from one state of consciousness to another. With death we merely shed the physical body, the remaining bodies simply exist at other dimensional realities. The fear of dying will no longer exist as a central human motivation.

Ninth, the principle of oneness will again be paramount in human affairs. We are indeed all one. The oneness of God will guide all religions, the oneness of energy will guide all science, and the oneness of humanity will direct politics.

Tenth, the Christ Consciousness will reappear in earthly life. The second coming is inviting the Christ Consciousness into our daily lives. There may also be an appearance of the soul, who came 2,000 years ago as Jesus, who became the Christ. What this means is he was the first to totally and completely take on the Christ Consciousness and manifest this at all times while in the physical. This prophecy was found many times in the Cayce readings. As a young teen, I had an experience while playing in the woods behind our subdivision. Suddenly I was immersed in blinding white light. I "knew" I would witness this prophecy.

The Purpose of Prophecy

A time of great change and of great opportunity awaits us. We can no longer rely on authorities to help us move into the coming New Golden Age. We must instead rely upon our inner wisdom, accessed through intuition, dreams, coincidences and intuitive sources.

Additionally, the future is not to be left to chance. With free will properly guided through spiritual attainment, we can alter probable realities with the guidance of Holy Spirit. We can facilitate our own healing and transformation, and the healing and transformation of our planet and civilization. Prophecy can enhance the healing process and is the natural outcome of the healing process.

Chapter 13
HEALING THE COMMUNITY
HEALING THE NATION
HEALING THE WORLD

As we heal individually, we also begin to heal our community and ultimately the world. The world as it exists now is the result of all our thoughts and actions. We mistakenly blame God, or wonder aloud, how God could let all the terrible things that happen in the world exist. We fail to recognize the truth; with our collective free will we continually create the world we live in. The world is the result of the interactions of all our egos. We have been given free will, and with that free will we began to miscreate eons ago. For in the separation, our collective souls decided to create without a spiritual foundation. Gradually we forgot we are spiritual beings having a human experience. In our separation we began to create in the material realm and became entrapped in the material realm. Without God and His Will at the center of our creation, we began to miscreate, and the world in which we live evolved as a result.

Originally we all existed in continual bliss and companionship with God. This was the Garden of Eden. Heaven is a state of complete oneness and harmony with God. It is pure spirit and without form. We are created in the likeness of God. That is we are spiritual beings existing in the only true universe, which we refer to as Heaven. Along the way we got the idea of being separate. It was just for a moment, but in that moment we got the idea of creating without God. In that moment we became separate, and the universe we believe in came into existence. Yet it is an impermanent universe, everything is constantly decaying.

With separation came duality. Instead of oneness, we began to make distinctions.

Good versus evil, you versus me. All the differences we can and do catalogue came into existence. We also began to have, as part of our existence, egos, which further led to separation and the belief of separation. We began to perpetuate the illusion we are all separate. As this further evolved, we began to be in conflict about these differences, saying some ideas are better than others, and that some ideas are right and some are wrong. Over time we developed elaborate systems, to identify and reinforce differences exist and we are individual beings separate from one another.

As we developed the ego, to keep us separate and to protect us in separateness, we grew further and further apart. In time the tyranny of the ego emerged. It continually convinced us it is safe to listen only to it, and certainly not to remember who we truly are. In its tyranny, the ego sees differences, does not celebrate such differences, and rejects oneness and unity. The tyranny of the ego also enters into judgment, finding those who are different are wrong and enters into conflict with those who are different. At its worst, the ego finds some individuals and situations unforgivable. It goes even further to find some as less than human.

We begin to form groups with others who we find are like us and find fault with those who are not like us. Over time, we evolved into various groups we call communities. We see our communities as right and other communities as wrong or ours as better and theirs as worse. We also form larger communities related to the collective egos of the groups and identify with them at times. So the city, state and nation become greater communities we can relate to at times. Sometimes we connect with a regional grouping. Sometimes we connect to subgroups in the community based on ethnicity, religion, skin color, gender, orientation, occupation, and political belief or class affiliation.

We identify with groups like us, or believe as we do, and find fault with groups not like us, or don't believe as we do. We become judgmental of those who are not like us. Since the ego often has, as its best defense is a good offense, we not only find fault with differences, we also attack others who are different from us. In turn, they do the same thing and conflict arises. Conflict within and between communities reflects the same dynamics as conflict between individuals. When individuals are in conflict their egos are clashing. When communities are in conflict, the collective egos of each group are in conflict. Ultimately when whole groups clash, we have the collective egos of the larger groups going to war. Whether the clashes of civilizations which are emerging again, such as between the East and the West, or between Christians and Muslims, or the clashes of nations that can lead to world wars. It is the collective egos of these massive groups that clash with one another.

With our unhealed wounds, we form our ego identities and rely upon the ego from ever having harm come to us again. Unfortunately, this often involves judgment and attack. We see the other person as wrong and ourselves as right. Since the other is wrong, we justify to ourselves, it is okay to attack them, whether verbally, emotionally or physically.

Vengeance and revenge become "appropriate" responses to the perceived harm from another. Certainly, if their ego and its control dramas attack us, then we are fully justified in responding in kind. How often do we hear someone say, if their child were harmed they would seek revenge? How often do we say as a society that we should seek revenge on the murderer by executing them?

The logic of the ego is to see differences, find fault, and judge and to attack. Then the logic of the ego is to fully justify its reliance on negative and fear based emotions. Judgment becomes acceptable. Moral and value systems come into existence to justify judgment. This is not to say there is not intrinsic value in moral thought, but not to justify judgment and attack. Moral values can and do help us discern differences and see some choices and actions as harmful and destructive. Carefully thought out moral value systems can and do help us make better choices about who we are and who we want to be. They can, and do, help us to operate with more positive and love based emotions.

Often judgment and un-forgiveness go hand in hand. Once we justify someone else is wrong, it becomes easier to say what he or she believe or do is unforgivable. Even our religious systems state some sins are unforgivable. How else can concepts such as excommunication even exist? We even project our egos onto God, believing there is a hell and a soul can be lost forever. We say God gets angry and can be vengeful. We say God punishes us with adversity and misfortune and can, and does, punish whole groups of people for being wrong. We say God takes sides, excluding some of God's souls, and favoring one group over the other. Each religion becomes the one and only exclusive path to heaven. One woman told me her parents were concerned about her because she did not participate in their chosen path. They said they worried when they got to heaven they would be in the front row and she might only make it into the balcony.

Recently another acquaintance told me emphatically, she believed Jesus was her Lord and Savior and the only way to sit at the right hand of God was to believe this. Without this belief you would be lost and not know God or experience heaven.

The ego fully justifies some actions or beliefs are unforgivable. In parts of the Muslim world, to not believe as they do is unforgivable, you are an "infidel," and it is then acceptable to murder you. This is not the exclusive province of Muslim extremists, as many religions have justified murdering those who

Healing and Transformation

are not their kind of believer. The tyranny of the ego knows no bounds.

The ego also rejects unconditional love. The ego always sees things as conditional, including love. Needing to see differences and offering judgments, it is hard to imagine we are to love, even the unlovable. Jesus made no exceptions in his love and expects no less from us. God loves us so totally and completely we cannot even begin to imagine such a love. So we project judgment onto God, seeing Him as angry and vengeful. We have come to believe that God would condemn any misguided soul. We can't imagine, since God gave us free will, He will not punish us for miss-creating.

It becomes easier to believe we will suffer eternal damnation, rather than know we all return to heaven together. The ego would have us believe souls can be lost, when unconditional love would never allow that to happen. Instead what happens, is we can continue to miscreate until we get tired of suffering, then we can choose to return to God. This is the whole point of the parable of the prodigal son, as God never stops loving us and patiently waits for our return.

The tyranny of the ego keeps us in separation. In separation, there is no room for non-judgment, forgiveness or unconditional love. Not only do we do this in our everyday relationships, but also we extend this to our community, to our nation and to the world. War is the collective tyranny of the ego judging others, finding their offenses unforgivable and attacking in anger and fear.

The spiritual path is the opposite of the ego driven path. The spiritual path emerges as we learn to be love. As we heal and resolve our own past emotional wounds, we are increasingly able to walk the spiritual path. We begin to see unity, when before we could only see separation and difference. As we begin to manifest non-judgment, forgiveness and unconditional love, we again see the unity and harmony in all things and in all individuals. Every being on this planet has at least a glimmer of light within them. The darkest individuals still retain the light of God within them, which connects all of us together.

Healing the Community, the Nation and the World

The power of redemption and salvation lies in the light that is within, no matter how hard we work to cover it with ego driven choices.

There are many who may deceive us appearing as light workers serving the Living God. Yet, God knows what is truly in each heart. He knows when we walk the spiritual path and when we don't. We may judge others with our egos, never knowing the truth that abides in the person we judge, and condemn. Even those who seem to have chosen a path of darkness are not condemned, but simply have to face the consequences of their choices and resolve their karmic debt.

Many individuals who have near death experiences report similar occurrences. There is a sense of moving through a tunnel and coming to a wall of light. At the wall of light are all their loved ones who are on the other side. They are greeted and welcomed back into the spiritual dimensions. After a period of time, an Angel appears and we receive a life review. A three-dimensional replay of our life plays before us, showing all the consequences of our actions, both positive and negative. It can be very painful as we see the hurt and pain we caused others. It is the "judgment" for that lifetime. The Angel helps us with this review, as she is totally loving and forgiving, even as we judge ourselves. Despite the many errors we make, we are shown what we learned, what we could have learned and what we failed to learn.

Since each lifetime has its purposes and lessons, we are shown what we accomplished and what remains to be accomplished. We then go on to other experiences, or schools, to continue to learn and evolve. We may need a "spiritual sleep" to cleanse our soul, or we may simply need to have our soul cleared with light before it can move forward. The later is what some understand to be purgatory. Then, with a clear slate, we move on to evolve and grow. At some point we come back into third dimensional worlds, trying again to manifest the spiritual path in the physical realms.

The Ten Commandments were given as guidelines on how to manifest the spiritual life in the physical dimensions. In

Healing and Transformation

Conversations with God, they are re-defined as the Ten Commitments. When we follow the spiritual path, these naturally emerge as the manifestations of the spiritual path. Fully understanding these commitments allows for correction of the ego's belief in separation and condemnation. As we learn to operate from positive and love based emotions these commitments readily manifest in our lives.

The ego sees the Ten Commandments as rules of conduct. The ego fears the violations of these rules, and the belief a vindictive God will punish us for all the transgressions that occur. Systems of fear arise describing God as unmerciful and ready to condemn anyone who violates these laws. As commitments, there is a covenant with God that as we walk the spiritual path these commitments naturally arise and operate in our lives. These commitments become freedoms, not restrictions. As these commitments manifest, we come to know we are on the path back home to oneness and unity with God.

The ten commitments become signs, indications of the healing in us is such; we now walk the spiritual path. In doing this we find God again. So when we love God with all our heart, our mind and our soul we no longer put any other god before God. Not any of the material temptations of the physical world, nor any priority or pursuit, which motivates us more than being one with God and following the spiritual path.

Not using the name of God in vain means not calling on God for anything but connection and unity with Him. We no longer concern ourselves with the wants and desires of the material world to the exclusion of God. It is having God first and foremost in our heart, mind and soul. By understanding the power of words and thoughts, and how these create our reality, then what we say, think and do, create the kind of world we live in. With the spiritual path, we do not think of invoking the name of God in an ungodly manner.

Remembering to keep a day for God is no longer staying in the illusions of the ego and no longer staying in duality and separation. Learning to dedicate some time to remembering God and our spiritual heritage, we come to understand every moment is holy, keeping a time for God until we recognize all moments are holy. We remember who we are. We are spiritual beings, increasingly living completely with positive and love based emotions as our guide.

Honoring our father and mother is first honoring our Father/Mother God in all we say, think and do. It is honoring our parents, for having given us life, which helps us to honor everyone. With unconditional love there are no exceptions. From our ego mind, we cannot even begin to imagine the possibility of honoring everyone, for in the separation we judge some to be unworthy, especially if they are "sinners," "evil" or "infidels." The hardest part of being love is everyone is worthy of love, even those the ego labels as despicable.

Not murdering is not willfully killing without cause. It is neither terminating any particular incarnation nor changing any life energy from one form to another without the most sacred justification. There is a new reverence for all life forms, including the animal and plant kingdoms, to impact them only for the highest good. This includes a reverence for Mother Earth, understanding and respecting her as a living being.

Not committing adultery is not defiling the purity of love with dishonesty or deceit. Not stealing is not taking a thing that is not our own, including not cheating nor conspiring nor harming another to have something. It is not being untruthful and telling lies in any form, especially bearing false witness against anyone. It is not desiring the committed relationship that someone else has, understanding all are part of the unity and not wanting to separate out what is joined together for a couple within that unity. It is not being jealous of the good fortune of others and wanting what they have, understanding ultimately, everything belongs to everyone.

Ultimately, in walking the spiritual path, one no longer desires to do the things the ten commitments stand against. It becomes impossible to have murderous thoughts, to desire what belongs to others, or be dishonest and deceptive. Placing God first and walking the spiritual path leads to true freedom. We no longer desire to tell others how to be and how to live their

Healing and Transformation

lives. We can joyfully share this path we have found, and you can walk this path. It is a path of love, not coercion or manipulation. It is not a path of fear.

As we heal and transform our lives we increasingly walk a path of joy, a path of divine re-connection to our higher self. We move from separation to unity. We see differences as positive, a part of the fabric of life that creates unity. One of the ideals of the United States of America is the creation of unity through diversity.

As more of us heal and walk the spiritual path, the more we create communities of peace, love and joy. Eventually we create a planetary transformation honoring peace, love and joy for all. Conflict will simply disappear as individuals walking the spiritual path increase.

We are currently in a time of great polarization. This is the natural outcome of ego dominating thoughts and actions. The ego's best defense is a good offense. Ever vigilant, it seeks to protect us by scanning the world for potential threat and getting the other person before they get us. However, since the ego comes into existence based on our emotional wounds, it very often misinterprets what others do based on the perceived potential of threat.

Collectively we do the same things. We join groups of others. In adolescence we join various subgroups. We become loyal to our group and become suspect of the motives and behaviors of other groups. In many of the same ways, as in adolescence, we identify with other groups we "belong" to in the larger communities we exist in. We identify with our groups and oppose their groups, and disapprove of the other group or groups. We take on the labels of class, gender, race, ethnicity, religion and community.

Inevitably, conflicts begin to occur in groups and between groups as we judge others, find offense in their behaviors or beliefs, become conditional in our love, and are unforgiving of those who offend us or do wrong as we see it. We become self-righteous in our view as we condemn those who think and feel differently.

The ego perpetuates the defenses, preventing the healing that needs to take place. We stay in dysfunction and endlessly replay the same dramas. Then we wonder why we don't experience much happiness and joy in our lives. Eventually, we may tire of suffering, and work to address and heal the underlying emotional wounds and begin to walk the path of joy. Whether from this lifetime or other past times, we decide there has to be a better way to live and function in the world. Whether we get into therapy, explore alternative healing modalities, attend transformational seminars, read and apply self-help books, listen and learn from Dr. Phil and others like him, attend religious seminars or retreats, read and apply metaphysical truths, learn to meditate and listen to the "still small voice within," or develop self-awareness in some other way we can begin a process of healing and transformation.

As we heal and begin to walk the spiritual path, we begin to manifest the ten commitments. We begin to experience the peace, which embraces all understanding. We become less judgmental, unforgiving, and conditional in our love. We no longer have a need to be protective and defensive. We no longer need to react to the smaller and larger dysfunction of others. We no longer contribute to fear and instead respond from love. Consequently, we bring peace to every encounter we have with others. We bring respect, love and joy to others. Everywhere we go we spread peace and joy.

When you walk the spiritual path, you will begin to notice others respond to you differently. People will smile and greet you, even perfect strangers across ethnic and racial lines. You can travel anywhere in the world and people will react to you in a friendly and positive way.

Instead of polarity, you begin to demonstrate you can honor others even when you differ in viewpoint from them. There can be respect and civility in your interactions with all others. When Jesus said to turn the other cheek, he meant we don't have to react to other's behaviors. We have the choice to walk the higher path. We don't have to take personally what others do toward us. Since each of us walks our own unique path, we don't really know why people do what they do. We really don't walk in their shoes. The choice we have is to do our best, to honor what love would do and what Holy Spirit would have us do in each situation.

As more of us walk the spiritual path and live the ten commitments, we begin to heal our community. We can work to create harmony and peace with others. We can move beyond divisiveness and the desire to win while someone else loses. We can create common ground, living with others in peace and harmony. As we create a consciousness toward greater oneness with God, we create a greater oneness with others and with all life.

Since our nation is a collection of communities, the more we heal and transform our communities, the more we begin to heal our nation. There is tremendous division in our nation right now. We are divided in many ways, with great polarity in what we should do as a nation and how we should treat one another. Our collective egos have created discord and disharmony. As groups, we justify attacking one another just like we do individually when we let our egos be in charge. We act as though anyone who disagrees with us is less worthy of respect and dignity. We feel justified in attacking others for believing differently than us. We have forgotten the spiritual ideals this nation was founded on.

America is a unique experiment in the recent history of the world to honor freedom of thought. It goes against the tyrannies of the world that previously existed, whether governmental institutions or religious institutions. Freedom of religion is a particularly powerful part of this idealism. Each person is free to believe what he or she wants or to not believe at all. Even each person within Christianity is free to believe what form of Christianity he or she wish to follow. There is no one-way to believe or follow.

The founding fathers were very aware individuals who attempted to create a government that was a servant of the people. They also tried to create a government with checks and balances to prevent the tyranny of the majority, at the expense of any and all minorities. Our egos are very good at trying to impose our will on others. We do this rather than work to become aware of the inner emotional wounds the ego is protecting us from, and from potential new emotional wounds life can send our way. When we become aligned with groups wishing to attack or control others because we speak for the majority at that moment, we allow our individual egos to occupy our minds with anything but being aware of the emotional wounds within that need to be healed.

There is a huge difference in advocating for a particular idea and selling others on the merit of your position, versus denigrating and putting down other ideas or personally attacking others for having a different position. We have become so polarized we can't imagine it is okay to agree to disagree. We say we believe in free speech, but find ways to curtail free speech, especially in the name of political correctness. We somehow think it is better to be polarized and win at any cost, rather than work to common ground, which will require give and take and may require compromise.

In the meantime, individuals whose real interest is in power and control, rather than being servants of the people manipulate us. Our political parties have gravitated to the far left or far right, believing they are absolutely correct and the other side is totally wrong. Even the representatives of a particular district or politically defined boundary forget they represent all the people, not just the majority that elected them. Our collective egos allow us to be manipulated by politicians with the notion there are absolute truths in how to govern. The common good, representative of all viewpoints, is lost in the polarization that has evolved. When particular religious viewpoints are added to the political mix, the collective egos of self-righteousness further create division and polarization. It is the ego mind wanting to tell everyone else how to live, rather than let each have their own freedom to choose how they want to live and what they want to believe.

What would happen if our collective egos are healed and we begin to operate out of love rather than fear? Imagine a

Healing and Transformation

world in which there is a sense of community based on what emerges as the common good, deciding a particular course of action, while respecting not everyone agrees. Imagine a world in which a consensus emerges based on letting all viewpoints be heard; with respect and dignity for all, even with those we disagree. Imagine a world in which we really can agree to disagree while working for the common good.

This nation was conceived by men of spiritual principle, understanding and ideals. They were guided by Ascended Masters who helped lay down a blueprint for democracy. This nation is meant to be a guidepost for an eventual world government that is spiritual in nature. We have not lived up to our ideals very often. With power comes corruption. Shakespeare had it right when he said power corrupts and absolute power corrupts absolutely. It takes great spiritual strength, and the humility that goes with it, to work toward the common good of all. As our collective egos heal we will create a nation that once again lives up to its ideals. The nation we have now reflects our collective egos based on fear and the need for power and control. As we heal and evolve, we will no longer be easily manipulated by politicians and other leaders trying to influence the world we live in. We will intuitively know who to vote for and who to follow. We will be able to discern who has integrity and who has evolved spiritually. As Jesus said, "You shall know them by their works." It truly is not just talking the talk, but also walking the walk.

Since we collectively create the world we live in, as we increasingly heal and transform our lives, then local, national and global healing will occur as well. As a species we will evolve. We will achieve ascension and the world we live in will reflect the fruits of living the spiritual path.

Imagine a world in which we practice good karma. The following was sent to me in an email. It was written by the Dalai Lama. I find it valuable in understanding how to live the spiritual life. Good karma includes the following instructions for life:

Healing the Community, the Nation and the World

1. Take into account that great love and great achievement involve great risk.
2. When you lose, don't lose the lesson.
3. Follow the three R's: respect for self, respect for others, and responsibility for all your actions.
4. Remember that not getting what you want is sometimes a wonder- stroke of luck.
5. Learn the rules so you know how to break them properly.
6. Don't let a little dispute injure a great relationship.
7. When you realize you made a mistake, take immediate steps to correct it.
8. Spend some time alone every day.
9. Open arms to change, but don't let go of your values.
10. Remember that silence is sometimes the best answer.
11. Live a good, honorable life. Then when you get older and think back, you'll be able to enjoy it a second time.
12. A loving atmosphere in your home is the foundation of your life.
13. In disagreements with loved ones, deal only with the current situation. Don't bring up the past.
14. Share your knowledge. It's a way to achieve immortality.
15. Be gentle with the earth.
16. Once a year go someplace you have never been before.
17. Remember that the best relationship is one in which your love for each other exceeds your need for each other.
18. Judge your success by what you had to give up in order to get it.
19. Approach love and creating with reckless abandon.

Imagine applying these same ideas to the larger community we live in. In time a true spiritual renaissance can evolve.

The United States of America is designed to follow spiritual ideals, and to be a beacon of light and hope for the world. We incorporate into our culture many varying cultures and eth-

Healing and Transformation

nicities, weaving a rich tapestry of universal man as we evolve. America represents the ideals of brotherhood, unity and harmony. It represents the ideals of freedom, equality in opportunity and pursuing happiness. It represents the ideal of spirituality, with freedom to pursue, in any way one chooses, to manifest this in our lives. It represents the ideals of libertarianism, with little intrusion by government into our lives. It represents the ideals of people truly governing themselves in a representative democracy, not people in power and control dictating how we should live and believe. It represents the ideals of government serving the common good of the people, not the special interests. It represents the ideals of citizens choosing to take time from their careers to serve the community or nation, not professional politicians only concerned with re-election and serving special interest groups that fund their campaigns.

There are times when America has risen to our ideals. Unfortunately, there are too many times we have fallen short of our ideals. As we heal and transform, we evolve to a more spiritually enlightened nation, once again becoming a beacon of light and hope for the world. Our government lags behind the good of its people. The national response of ordinary citizens to Hurricane Katrina give pause for hope that we are evolving toward a time in which the ideals of America once again shine forth for all the world to see.

Our prosperity and abundance are in large part due to the generosity of the American people, for as we sow, so shall we reap. As we move back to the spiritual ideals of this nation, we show the world the possibility of differing people living in peace, harmony and unity while respecting differences. Spiritual evolution will do more to bring peace and harmony to the world. As the Old Testament of the Judeo-Christian Bible says, "Those who live by the sword will die by the sword." In the short run, it may seem like the forces of darkness will prevail, but in truth the light always shines away the darkness. As we collectively heal and transform our lives, our nation will once again reflect spiritual ideals and guide the world to global peace, harmony and unity.

When large numbers of like-minded people meditate for peace, great changes occur. We can and already do change the world. Some of the dire prophecies predicted for this time have been modified or cancelled. We are responsible for our world and how it is. As love replaces fear, a global community will emerge based on positive and love based emotions and thoughts.

We are being propelled to a new global reality whether we like it or not. Waves of increased light energy are infusing our planet to evolve toward higher dimensional realities. We are partly in charge of the planet's evolution, but part of the process is in accordance with the divine plan. If we fail, to bring healing and transformation to our lives, we will certainly not move forward with the planet's evolution. Those souls who can't go forward will go to other third dimensional worlds to continue meeting their karmic debt in the densities where they must still learn. Each of us has a choice in this now moment, to embrace healing and move to a spiritual path, or return to other third dimensional worlds to meet their negative karma. Eventually each soul tires of suffering and turns back to God. Why not choose to do this now? Why not join the great adventure unfolding on this planet now, helping to heal and transform ourselves and the world, moving to a peaceful ascension into greater awareness and light; greater connection with God.

We have the opportunity to help participate in and guide the planetary transformation unfolding. This time of polarization on the planet is part of the birth process into the New Golden Age. We can catastrophically enter this new golden age, or the process can be more gentle and benign. We can evolve our consciousness through healing and transformation and be part of the grandest opportunity in the history of the universe, to achieve ascension through a gentle transformation facilitated by the collective consciousness moving onto the spiritual path.

As one of the Astara lessons shares, God sends His Light into the world, activating physical matter, and the human form emerges. This is the breath of life, by our Creator, into this planetary world. A physical vehicle emerges in which we can be

Healing and Transformation

spiritual beings having a human experience. It is the unity of the masculine and the feminine that creates our physical form. God is male and female, positive and negative. The physical universe exists because of this polarity. God is both Mother and Father, the negative and positive poles of the same principle, the Great Cosmic Source of all, the Cause that is behind all.

The masculine principle of energy combines with the feminine principle of formation, allowing evolution itself as the manifestation of energy through form. We have the capacity to manifest energy into form. As we evolve we become more capable of doing this. Jesus demonstrated this continuously with his miracles. He did this as a healed and transformed being using energy to manifest new forms. He fully integrated his physical, mental, emotional, etheric and spiritual beings to create. He suggested we could do this too.

The planet is now evolving to the point where many of us will be capable of doing these things. This helps to peacefully shift this planet into the next dimensional realities. The energy of God is ready and abundantly available to us to perceive as we grow and expand our conscious awareness.

The Astara lesson continues with the coming of the Christ Spirit first manifested by Jesus; God released His astral form into the planet earth and became the "saving blood" of the planet. The earth moved from involution to evolution, leading to higher planetary vibrations helping to make possible higher and better forms. Thus, humanity is on the verge of evolving physically, as well as mentally, emotionally and spiritually. The feminine principle, now anchored permanently into the planet with Venus passing between the earth and the sun, when producing form becomes a positive element as it absorbs into itself the masculine Properties of the God Light.

With the arrival of the Aquarian Age, new forms of humanity will emerge. This production must come through women. The balance of the feminine becomes important, as woman is the channel through which will emerge the new forms of man.

These evolving physical bodies will better house the indigo light souls coming to the earth now.

The physical earth, along with her etheric and astral spheres, is passing into higher vibrations. She is moving into fourth and fifth dimensional vibrations. This is why time is more fluid and seems to have sped up. With these higher frequencies only souls able to manifest in these higher vibrations of the new age will be permitted to rebirth onto the planet. Thus, the thousand years of peace manifests, as promised. Healing and transformation allows you to currently participate in this great awakening and to return for more adventures on an evolved planet. All the more reason to embark on the journey of healing and transforming your life, to participate in this accelerated opportunity to evolve spiritually and ascend with a planet, shaping that very ascension process.

The "sacrifice" of Jesus meant giving his astral form into the planet to absolve much of the negative karma, or astral currents, humankind had created to that point in time and space. This gave spiritual strength and direction to many souls to be saved for this life wave. This helped us to proceed into the Aquarian ethers of the New Golden Age.

You get to be part of an evolving life wave of souls with an evolving planet, allowing Adam Kadmon to once again manifest in the physical. In harmony with Nature, our physical forms will evolve so greater levels of consciousness can be experienced in the higher frequency, physical dimensions. Thus, ascension is completed and we return into the unity and bliss of heaven, reunited in companionship with our Creator. The masculine and feminine combine in a unity of creation, as the light of this union descends into ever-denser substance, creating a new world and a new life wave of humanity. At this moment, we are in the beginning of this great adventure of co-creation with God, as we heal and transform our lives, and collectively heal and transform our communities, nations and world.

Chapter 14
RETURN TO THE SPIRITUAL PATH

There is intrinsic value in healing old emotional wounds. By healing and transforming our lives we increasingly live in the present, freely responding to each new situation unencumbered by ego perception based on past hurt, embarrassment or humiliation. We begin to live with authenticity and integrity in each now moment, able to bring our very best to each and every situation and individual. We can increasingly live with joy, happiness and peace. We begin to understand we do not have to take others' control dramas, manipulations, verbalizations and behaviors personally. We stop making assumptions about why others do what they do. We begin to communicate and relate to others with direct, open and honest communication. We operate from love rather than fear.

Thus, the opportunity exists with healing and transformation, to begin to walk the spiritual path. It is not an exclusive path; it is many paths that reflect the one path. It is a path in which we begin to practice complete forgiveness. It is a path in which we begin to practice unconditional love. It is a path in which we begin to practice complete non-judgment.

Walking the spiritual path is striving to re-connect with the Higher Self. It is the action of doing, which is putting into action, rather than just believing. It is a saintly path, although it is not a path of perfection, for we are still human. As we walk this path we forgive our past, we forgive others and we forgive ourselves. That is what complete forgiveness is about.

In my healing work using hypnosis, we are able to uncover the deep emotional wounds, beginning the healing process at a more intense level. As we release the negative and fear-based emotions, we are able to replace these with healing light, love, joy, peace, happiness, and most importantly forgiveness. As clients forgive themselves and others, a great peace comes over them. They no longer carry the emotional wounds and there is no need for their ego to vigilantly guard against future wounds. The more we are able to do this, the more we are able to walk the spiritual path, continuing to heal and forgive. Ultimately, we are to forgive the world. At some point in the healing process we want to walk this path, a path of spirituality and a path of joy.

As we begin to walk the spiritual path we begin to see the world the way Holy Spirit sees it, as a perfect opportunity for forgiveness and salvation. On the spiritual path we begin to concentrate on our own lessons, no longer concerning ourselves with everyone else's lessons. We stop telling others how to live and stop judging what they do, instead focusing on making better choices about who we are and who we want to be as we face and deal with what we are here to learn and do.

As we begin to walk the spiritual path, we come to understand we are in the world but not of it. We do not get caught up in all the interacting dramas. We do not get caught up in material possessions and desires. We can enjoy these things and live quite comfortably, but not be ruled by them or only motivated in acquiring these things. We can live and survive in the world, but exist at another level. We can live in the third becoming fourth dimensional world, but strive for fifth dimensional consciousness and existence.

We can be like Peace Corp workers, living in the different world and culture of the people being aided, but yet not be of that world because we do come from a different experience and context. The world of monks and cloistered nuns were places that individuals could seek God while existing in this world. Yet, they were not of this world. They withdrew to communities in which they could contemplate and meditate on God. They could follow a particular spiritual path in the community that served as a refuge from the world while being in the world. Whether Buddhist or Christian, some seekers could move beyond the world of everyday experience and survive without being of it.

Returning to the spiritual path means being on the path, and continuing the process of healing and transformation, continuing to evolve to oneness and unity with God. Heaven is not a place; it is a state of being. It is without form, for God and heaven is without form. To get there we must walk a path of forgiveness, unconditional love and non-judgment. It is not enough to believe in a particular theology; it is a path that must be walked.

It can be a exhilarating feeling, to simply believe in someone or something, returns you to heaven and oneness with God. It is a powerful thought, in which simply believing a particular individual is a Lord and Savior gets you to the right hand of God. At the level of duality and separation, it is possible to believe such a heaven exists and that only those who believe are worthy to enter and only they will be admitted. If such a belief helps one to live a better life, be kind and good to others, and making the world a better place, then a greater good is served.

However, there are greater levels of understanding and consciousness that are more challenging to embrace and a path more challenging to walk. By continuing to heal and transform, it becomes easier to walk such a path and accept the wisdom of the spiritual path. It becomes easier to connect with our inner wisdom, and to listen to the "still, small voice within," whether we believe it is God, our Higher Self, the Holy Spirit, Jesus, Buddha, Krishna, Moses, Mary, or Mohammed.

The spiritual path is about concentrating on our own forgiveness lessons. If everybody concentrated on his or her own forgiveness lessons instead of everyone else's, the world could be transformed in a moment. The parable of the prodigal Son is about all of us doing our own work on our own path, embraced and welcomed home to our true reality, as we remember we are spiritual beings having a human experience. Although the prodigal son walks a path of dysfunction, it is his path to learn the lessons he has to learn. Tired of suffering, he finally begins to walk his spiritual path back home to God. Yet, it is his lessons that help him return to the path. Once again it is not for us to judge another's path, but to focus on our own.

Learning to listen to the "still, small voice within" is learning to walk the spiritual path, for then we are truly guided to live and be the spiritual being we truly are.

One level of consciousness is dualism, a level of thinking most of the entire world believes in, even among most that follow the spiritual path. All spiritual paths are necessary, as teaching of dualism must eventually lead to the teachings and practices of semi-dualism, non-dualism and eventually, pure non-dualism. It is at the later level we completely experience the Love of God. Dualism is the thinking of subject and object. It is the thinking of separation. This is the thinking the ego is most comfortable with, for it is obvious at this level that there are differences. It is obvious to the ego mind, at this level, differences can be and often are irreconcilable. There is good and evil. There is yin and yang. There is morality and immorality. There is the right spiritual path and the wrong spiritual path. There is the right religion and the wrong religions. In every conceivable way the ego can define differences at the level of dualism.

The next level of consciousness and thinking, or learning on the spiritual path, is semi-dualism. At this level we accept God is Love. This creates a challenge, if truly believed, because if God is Love can God also be hate? If God is perfect Love can He/She somehow be imperfect? If God is the Creator, can She then be vindictive and vengeful against what He created? If God is perfect, can She create a flawed and decaying world? Can He create disease? Can She create adversity? Would He allow disasters and adversities?

The answer to these questions is, of course not. This level of thinking removes us from a hidden, but terrible fear of God. At a deeper level in duality, the fear of a vengeful and wrathful God because we took a moment in Heaven and decided to separate from God. When we separated from God, thoughts of fear entered in, and we have dreaded God will vindictively punish us. Thus, the spiritual ego was born. With semi-dualism, we still think of separation as defined by having a body, with God and the world still outside of us, but there is now a sense that God is not the cause of our situation. Since God, or Perfect Love, can only be responsible for good, everything else must come from someplace else.

This leads to the next level of consciousness and learning, which is also a level of spiritual sight. It is a state of mind of non-dualism. This is the concept of oneness or unity. It is unity that sees all as one, yet still recognizes it as oneness with the mind that created the need for duality, or separation, to begin with. The Buddha mastered the mind, recognizing the mind created the illusion seen at the level of duality. When the Buddha said he was awake, he realized he was not actually a participant in the illusion, but the maker of the entire illusion.

The final step on the spiritual path is where our mind, the maker of the illusion of separation, chooses completely against itself in favor of God. This is pure non-dualism. It is complete oneness with God. It is complete oneness with everyone and everything, moving beyond form, back to heaven. That is why there is one Sonship, hinted at by the sense of unity. This is where we remember we are all part of God. This is how we can behold the Christ in each person. We all go to Heaven together, because we really are only one. The seeming separation of duality is an illusion we created, in that one moment, to be separate from God.

We invest great energy in believing in duality. We manifest this duality to stay in a state of separation. The ego works hard to see this duality, and invests great energy in perpetuating this level of thinking. This is why healing the emotional wounds lead eventually to transformation. As we learn to forgive others, and ourselves we eventually learn to forgive ourselves for the moment we chose to be separate from God.

In the moment we chose separateness, the fear then arose that what we did is unforgivable. The fear arose that God was extremely angry with us and we would pay, with punishment, from an angry and vindictive God. Ultimately, all the dramas we play out in life reflect this fear. Ultimately, all the emotional wounds perpetuate the belief in duality, and perpetuate the ego's defensive stance toward others and the world. Because the ego believes in attack to protect our individual integrity, then conflict, control dramas, manipulations, and fear-based actions emerge repeatedly.

Lacking forgiveness and being judgmental, we live at the level of duality and create the world in which we live. Then we blame God for what we created, asking how God can create such things. Subconsciously, we perpetuate the fear that first arose at the moment we chose to be separate. In our dysfunction we actually re-enact the original separation, the moment we cast ourselves from the "Garden of Eden." God did not cast us out, we cast our selves out!

As we begin to heal and transform, we no longer live with the tyranny of the ego. As we transform, we move away from un-forgiveness and judgment. We move away from conditional love. As we begin to walk the spiritual path, we begin to forgive others and our selves, we become non-judgmental and manifest unconditional love. We begin to listen to the "still, small voice within," or Holy Spirit or our Higher Self. We begin to take on the Christ Consciousness, which is a level of spiritual consciousness, which is not the sole province of the man Jesus, who became the Christ. He walked the spiritual path to show us how we can do the same thing. He became the Christ, and we are also to become the Christ. This is another reason he said to us, "These things you can do, and even greater things than these you can also do."

Healing and Transformation

The ego is a psychological concept and it is a spiritual concept. As a spiritual concept it represents the separation that began with the one tiny, mad moment when part of the Christ Mind said, "What if?" In that moment we began to see differences. We began to split into seeming individuals, and in that moment we began to experience fear. The ego, as a spiritual concept, had to see differences, and thus began the descent into duality. The spiritual ego loves differences, the better in which to perpetuate separation, despite all the misery that results. The psychological ego then springs into being to further enhance the notion of separation. It operates through various defense mechanisms, to protect the individual from further hurt, embarrassment and humiliation, to create and perpetuate judgment and to practice conditional love.

The spiritual ego creates special relationships. There are special love relationships, and special hate relationships. As we return to the spiritual path, we understand love is unconditional and completely and equally applied. It is applied equally, not only to our loved ones as the world defines it, but to all, since we all spring from the same source. We are all guided within by a light we often, if not always, ignore. When we stay busy with what the ego defines as special love and special hate relationships, we avoid seeing and understanding the unity in all of us. When we see unity we apply unconditional love equally to all.

As we return to the spiritual path, it becomes even more important to concentrate on our own lessons in forgiveness, and not everyone else's. We really do not know how or why the path, others take in life, blesses their soul's growth and development. This is another reason we are not to judge. It is already hard enough to wonder why we face the adversities and challenges of our own path. It is hard enough to see how adversities and challenges are ultimately there for us to learn our own lessons and progress with our own soul growth and development. As we learn to align with our Higher Self, or with Holy Spirit, only then do we see the world the way Holy Spirit sees it. The Holy Spirit sees the world as a perfect opportunity for forgiveness and salvation.

Returning to the spiritual path is asking for guidance. We ask for access to the Holy Spirit's entire thought system. Jesus was able to access the Holy Spirits' thought system, could see through the illusions of the ego, and could achieve the state of pure non-dualism. He saw each person as perfect and able to complete his or her part in the divine plan perfectly. In time, each of us has our part in returning to the spiritual path, fulfilling our part of the divine plan, and then we all return to Heaven at the same time. It is in the application of true forgiveness, along with the guidance of our Higher Self, which eventually leads to genuine happiness, peace and Heaven. Returning to the spiritual path is taking responsibility for the power of the mind. It moves us away form the ego that wants us to feel special and apart. We wake up, because we overcome our ego and completely live attuned to Holy Spirit.

Returning to the spiritual path is waking up to our true reality. It is not the ego, or the personality we adopt in each lifetime. It is remembering we are spiritual beings having a human experience. The human experience does include healing the emotional wounds and making better choices of who we are and who we want to be. Ultimately, it is returning to the spiritual path. Learning to live with non-judgment, unconditional love, and complete forgiveness.

Returning to the spiritual path requires practicing and ultimately being true forgiveness. It cannot be conditional forgiveness. It cannot be forgiveness of only those closest, by who are safe to forgive. It is everyone and every situation. Most importantly it is also forgiveness of our self. It is the application of true forgiveness that will lead to genuine happiness, peace, and finally Heaven.

The ego wants to hold onto grudges and resentments. The ego tries to convince us that certain actions are unforgivable. The ego finds endless ways to categorize what can never be forgiven. The drunk driver who kills someone, the child molester, the murderer, the ruthless ruler, the terrorist, the abusive

Healing and Transformation

spouse; all are obvious examples. More subtly, it is the neighbor who yelled at your child, the parent who angrily accused you, the boss who unfairly fired you, the raging relative who spoke to you in such an unkind manner or the person who took credit for your accomplishment. The ego is very good at finding fault and assigning blame, and saying these things can never be forgiven.

Anyone who judges us can affect us, according to the ego and its seemingly protective position. Nobody can really judge us, for they truly don't know the path we walk, the wounds we keep working to heal and why we do what we do. Lincoln had it right when he said, we can only please some of the people some of the time. As we walk the spiritual path we really are no longer affected by what others think or how they judge us. It is their opinion, based on their own dysfunction and ego driven thought system. We really cannot be hurt. On the spiritual path we can show others we are whole and they can be too. If you show them they cannot hurt you and you do not hold anything against them or your self, then you are on the spiritual path. This is what turning the other cheek is about. We don't have to react to others' behaviors, nor hold it against them and respond in retaliation. We can choose another path, another response and total forgiveness. Think how powerful it was, as Jesus was crucified he stayed centered in his truth, practiced complete forgiveness, and did not attack those who attacked him.

The ego loves to attack. It loves to attack others to make us important and to diminish the importance of others. The ego believes in separation, in judgment, and in finding fault. At its worst, the ego even claims that God is on their side. The more important question is, "Are you on God's side?" Are you on the side of pure love?

As we begin to walk the spiritual path, we no longer try to control others. The spiritual path understands what our mission and purpose is in life. Each of us has a specific mission and purpose in each lifetime. We also have general missions and purposes. In particular, we are not to cause harm to anyone. We are not to interfere or hold back any soul's advancement. It is our general mission and purpose to enhance and facilitate all souls' growth and development.

Life is not about keeping score. It is not about how many friends we have or how accepted we are by others. It is not about having plans or being alone. It is not about who we are dating, how many dates we have or how many partners we have. It is not about sex, as wonderful as that can be. It is not about family, career, how much money we have, the car we drive or the 'toys' we acquire. It is not about appearance, what we wear, what we do for leisure or the music we listen to.

Life is not about the color of our skin, the ethnic group we belong to, or the religion we follow. It is not how smart we are or how we do in careers or the kind of career we have. It is not about what we accomplish in the career. It is not about the clubs we belong to or the sports we participate in. It is not about representing ourselves, what our resume states, or who will accept the written you.

Life is about who you love and who you hurt. It is about who you make happy and unhappy. It is about keeping or betraying trust. It is about friendship regarded as sacred or used as a weapon. It is about what you say and mean, maybe hurtful and maybe heartening. Life is about whether you participate in gossip or spread rumors, or speak with integrity and choose not to be involved in gossip and innuendo. It is about discernment rather than judgments. It is about who you have ignored or you have been attentive to. It is about jealousy, fear, ignorance and revenge, or their opposites. Life is about carrying inner hate or inner love. Most of all life is about using your life to touch other hearts, rather than create harm for another's soul growth and development.

The spiritual path is choosing to touch the hearts and minds of others in a positive and loving manner. Each of us is on a spiritual quest, not just in one lifetime but many lifetimes. On the spiritual path we offer miracles. Miracles mirror God's eternal Love. By offering miracles we remember God. We may never know the lives we touch by sharing our love and wisdom with others. Yet, we change the world as we practice the gifts of spirit and offer healing to others, by healing ourselves. Ultimately, it is by healing ourselves that we heal others and the world. By releasing unforgiving thoughts, unloving feelings, and judgments of any kind, we release our selves and all go to Heaven together. Each healing cancels karmic debt, saves many future lifetimes, collapses the illusion of time, and changes future potentials that are negative and destructive.

Understanding everything is consciousness; the thoughts and actions of individuals affect consciousness, which creates reality. Just one person can change future realities by influencing the consciousness surrounding a future event that is building. This is why Jesus emphasized, when two or more are gathered in his name the world can be changed.

Some future realities are so strong it may take a global shift in consciousness to change them. Probabilities such as a third world war or Earth changes may require many of us to have such a shift in consciousness. As long as we hold on to old paradigms, such as false masculinity or lack of balance, negative probabilities may emerge. Notions of un-forgiveness and the need for revenge, currently fuel the many wars on the planet. Seeming clashes of civilizations, as each believes they should, tell everyone else how to live and how to believe.

Thoughts systems that insist there be an Armageddon create the reality of catastrophic war and the use of weapons of mass destruction. True freedom and true responsibility allow each soul to walk their own path and learn their own lessons. The healing process allows each of us to move away from the tyranny of the ego, which collectively creates movements that could manifest in destructive actions. The ego driven belief that it is okay to kill someone in the name of God is the ultimate proactive ego attack on others. As we heal, we release the need to have the ego in control. We become part of walking the spiritual path that leads to the peace that passes all understanding.

Gordon Michael-Scallion shares in his newsletter *Intuitive Flash* (May/June, 2005), our planet has a collective consciousness, which contains all the Earth has experienced. Wars, pollution and millennia of hate in certain regions, like the Middle

East, add to the consciousness of the planet. Forces attempt to maintain balance. When this cannot occur, chaos and destruction take place.

Some of the future scenarios have already been altered by the shifts in consciousnesses that are taking place. As we become more aware and as the spiritual path, more benign outcomes become possible. Ultimately, a peaceful transformation of humanity and the planet remain possible. We can achieve ascension, moving into higher dimensional realities, without catastrophic change. Each individual contributes to this happening by working to heal and transform his or her lives.

In the same issue of the *Intuitive Flash*, Cynthia Keyes writes about consciousness, stating we actually have more power than we realize to keep love and compassion as dominant forces in consciousness. She states that although we cannot see it or touch it, it continually influences us, as we also influence it.

She shares what we often refer to, as the collective unconscious is a kind of cosmic thought bubble surrounding the universe. It is a library of sorts, holding all the knowledge, of all the past, present and future events. It is an invisible etheric consciousness that permeates all that is, all that was, and all that will be. We each contribute to this consciousness. We each can change this consciousness. When we heal and transform our lives we influence this collective consciousness in a positive way. As we release the negative and fear based emotions we have carried for all time and space, we heal and change past, present and future lives. We move closer to Heaven. We manifest the miracles, which alter time and space for our selves. This is what unity is all about. We are each part of the collective, and as one, we return to Heaven as part of the unity we ultimately are and exist within.

She shares how each and every one of us, all souls, is part of this consciousness. All of our existences create the universe and the world we live in. Wonderfully as we walk the spiritual path, we change consciousness and we transform and heal the world, and even the universe, we exist in. There are many levels of consciousness, both in the physical dimensions and in the spiritual dimensions. All levels affect us, and we affect all levels. As we heal and move beyond the ego, we can and do heal all time and space, for ourselves and for all others.

Every thought, every emotion, every action affects the world of consciousness. We blame God, but we create the world we live in, and we can change the world we live in. We get a sense of this collective consciousness when major events happen. Think of the consciousness, positive and negative, we had with 9/11, Hurricane Katrina, or the massive tsunami that hit the Indian Ocean in December 2004. Think of the power of the fear, yet, then the power of the compassion and effort to help others in need. Think of the moments you are suddenly intuitively aware when danger or harm comes to a loved one. Jesus reminded us of the power of change that can occur when "…two or more are gathered in my name."

As we heal and walk the spiritual path, we then in turn join with others doing the same thing. There can be an overwhelming outpouring of love and compassion that can change the direction of consciousness, from fear and negative based expression to positive and love based expression. This then touches all who are more open to the force of love, enabling them to further develop their spiritual attunement and increasingly walk the spiritual path. As more walk the true spiritual path, the world heals as we advance peace, unity and compassion.

As we walk the spiritual path we become aware of God working in and through us. We do this with humility and grace. Only God is real. Since God created us in His image and likeness, that is as spiritual beings, that is the only part of us that's real. This reality includes complete freedom.

In the moment we thought "what if?" we detoured into fear. This is the moment we forgot to laugh, and forgot our joy. This was the moment of the Big Bang, when the universe came into existence. The moment of what if is the moment we had the thought that was not of God, not of God's Love.

Despite the seeming separation that took place, we did not lose our creative power. Unfortunately, with fear, the ego became the director of this creative power, rather than perfect unconditional love. We began to miscreate. Our world and universe resulted.

Since God is the answer to every problem, healing allows us to realign with our true creative Source. We become God's love in the physical world. This is the first Christ Consciousness. However, with the ego and fear, we stopped creating with love. We started thinking thoughts that were not of love. We created the world we live in, and we continually create our life path.

With healing and transformation, we are able to live on the Earth but think the thoughts of Heaven. In alignment with our Higher Self we allow Holy Spirit to heal us of all the illusions of the ego. The world is a thought system based on fear. Yet, we can live in this fallen drama by identifying with spirit rather than the physical. As we walk the spiritual path we understand our real body is our light body. We can be in the world but not of it. Yet, we also transform the world to become more like us.

Our task on Earth is to know the truth, that we are spiritual beings, that we are light bodies. The vengeance of the ego would have us believe it is okay to attack, to destroy, to defend and to believe in lack and limitation. It is to believe in a body that will die, and with it our identity. Walking the spiritual path reminds us we are not a body, but are a spiritual being having the human experience.

Walking the spiritual path is knowing the potential of the Christ Consciousness. This is what the second coming is all about, a return to the recognition of our true heritage. Jesus the man became the Christ by completely aligning himself with the Christ Mind. He remembered he is a Son of God, so that we could remember too.

The potential through the Christ consciousness is to know no limits, that health is real and to know there really is no death, just a transition to other dimensional realities. Walking the spiritual path goes beyond good intentions. It is willingness to walk the path of joy. It is a willingness to walk the path of love. It is a willingness to see others as God sees them. It is a willingness to let Holy Spirit guide us. It is the willingness to align with our Higher Self. With this comes the limitless possibility for good. This was so lovingly demonstrated by Mother Theresa, who saw God in every poor dying soul on the streets of Calcutta. I love her statement, "We can do no great things, only small things with great love."

Each of us has more power than we realize to keep love and compassion as the dominant forces in consciousness. As we live each day in unconditional love, complete forgiveness and non-judgment, we transform our corner of the world and affect the whole world, in turn. Every act of kindness, every loving thought, every smile and kind word, every moment of gratitude, and every moment of appreciation for the gifts of spirit we possess and manifest create the New Golden Age coming now. With increasing positive and love based consciousness, the greater the goodness, peace and unity that can and will emerge. Each little effort changes the world. We really do heal and transform one another. The action of returning to the spiritual path, walking the walk, creates the increasing unity, which is our true heritage.

Chapter 15
LIVING THE SPIRITUAL LIFE

Healing our lives allows us to begin to walk the spiritual path. Transformation is living the spiritual life. Living the spiritual life is putting into action what has resulted from the process of healing our lives and the transformational process that results from healing. It is not about what we believe, in as much as, it is about doing what we believe. In the Edgar Cayce Reading 1825-1 it is stated, "Give that which awakens within the minds and hearts of others…purity that touches even to the lips of God." As we live the spiritual life, we demonstrate by our actions, there is a better way to live. We can talk about what we believe in all we want; it is what we put into action that really matters. There is no hypocrisy when we do what we believe. It is not enough to say, this is the way back to Heaven, or to create ascension. It is walking the walk. This is why Jesus said; "You shall know them by their works."

Interestingly, a new Baylor University study on faith found a wide variety of beliefs in God, in America. The study, was cited in a column by Deb Price, printed in the summer, 2006 (*Venture Inward*). Most Americans agree God does not favor a

Healing and Transformation

political party, and that Americans are quite diverse in their thinking about God. For starters, Americans don't agree on who God is. The Baylor Institute for Studies of Religion finds that Americans can be divided into four groups based on our views of God's nature and behavior. Thirty-one percent believe in an angry, punitive, authoritarian God very involved in the world. Twenty-three percent believe in a benevolent God whose power is felt as a force for good. Sixteen percent see God as critical but disengaged, delaying punishment until after death. Twenty-four percent say God is a distant creator who got everything started and then bowed out. About five percent of the population is atheists.

Spirituality has always been a core American value. Spirituality focuses on how we connect with a higher power, and how we live a spiritual path. The founding fathers of this great nation understood the potential spiritual significance of America. America was not just meant to be a democracy, but was to fulfill a spiritual destiny as well. The Ascended Masters, and particularly St. Germaine guided them. They understood the need for freedom of religious expression, and not having any one faith or theology gain official endorsement. The idea that we are a "Christian nation" misses the point entirely of what the founding fathers were attempting to accomplish. The founding fathers were interested in spirituality, not a particular religious thought system, understanding the sacredness of the individual and recognizing the God connection within us all.

They were aware of the Iroquois League of Nations and their idea of the Great Law of Peace. This is the assumption that the transforming of the individual into a consciously spiritual being was a basic goal of life. The founding fathers sought to have America be a place where we could heal and transform our lives, within the freedom of a community of souls honoring each walking their own path of spiritual transformation and growth.

The founding fathers understood the spiritual ideal of liberalism, a frame of mind that honors the individual spirit and perspective. This most closely resembles the Gnostic gospels that honored knowing God within and discovering that connection to your Higher Self, rather than relying on a theology or religious belief system. Theology and religious beliefs, in and of themselves, are valuable. They attempt to explore what life is all about from a religious perspective. However, walking the spiritual path is doing the work of healing and transforming, to rediscover the spiritual reality of each of us, and furthering the journey back to Heaven. Each of us has the opportunity to have our own personal experiences of spirit, rather than rely on external sources to tell us what these experiences ought to be.

Meditation becomes a valuable experience to hear "the still small voice within." With healing, we are better able to shut off the chatter of the ego, become still, and gain the direction and guidance Holy Spirit has to offer. New Thought Christianity arose out of the ideal of its practicality and creative optimism matching America's cheerful self-reliance. Meditation is an important part of this form of Christianity, which when practiced allows the inner wisdom of Holy Spirit or the Higher Self.

True freedom is allowing each person to have his or her own spiritual experience. The trouble with the ego thought system is it wants to tell everybody else what to do or how to live. The paradox is the ego's unhealed guidance only leads to separation, conflict, and remaining stuck in the material world. One can cheerfully believe they are on the one and only path back to heaven, but walking the spiritual path is the action of forgiveness, unconditional love, and non-judgment.

Living the spiritual path is choosing peace, harmony, long suffering, brotherly love, kindness and patience. Doing this is as if we are taking hold of the hand of God. It is living so that when we look in the face of others we see the reflection of our God. The soul of every one is the image of God. For God is in each and every one of us, no matter how they appear to be and no matter how destructive the path they have chosen to be in the material world. No matter how caught up in the destructive and dysfunctional patterns of the ego, both spiritual and psychological, the spark of divinity lies in each and every one of us. No matter how dark the energy of another person seems to be, there remains a light within, connected just like you and me, to God.

While the results of the Baylor survey reflect how the question is asked about what God is like, the majority of people do not see God as Pure Love. He is not seen as unconditionally loving, completely forgiving, and nonjudgmental. Despite the efforts of many Master Teachers to suggest what God may be, the religions that have evolved from those Master Teachers, eventually teach of a God of fear. This is not surprising, given how our egos operate by attacking others and judging others as a way to seemingly protect us. If we do this with one another, would we not ultimately project our ego belief systems onto God? It is unfortunately a short leap of thought to then believe one form of faith is the right way to think and believe, and that all others are wrong. It is a short leap of belief to attack others for not believing our own chosen path. So God becomes an ego defined belief system. A particular theology becomes the only right way to believe and act, rather than an attempt to understand the mysteries of creation, and meaning and purpose to life.

It is certainly easier to believe something, than it is to live it. Having the right belief negates the need for responsible living based on universal truth. Instead we can just seem to take responsible action to follow "the" chosen path. Add self-righteousness and the ego can really run amok. At its worst, it leads to violence and killing others for not being the right kind of believer.

We live in a world and a universe that honors the idea of separation. Everything is designed for us to continue the belief in separation. The ego lives for separation. It thrives on separation. It allows us to make judgments and to hold onto resentments and grievances. It keeps us from understanding there really is unity, we are all one, and we all go to heaven together. Instead we can play out an endless drama of separation.

Busy with the endless drama of separation, we do not have to let our Higher Self be in charge, and place the ego where it belongs. We do not have to walk the spiritual path. We certainly do not have to do the hard work of facing and healing our emotional wounds, so we can transform our lives and begin to walk the spiritual path. Until we do walk the spiritual path we will not exit the karmic wheel of life. We endlessly play out the drama of separation, lifetime after lifetime until we become weary and turn back to God. Inevitably, we will tire of suffering and long to return home. As we heal the emotional wounds, and decide not to live with the tyranny of the ego, we once again begin to walk and live the spiritual path. We then put into action unconditional love, forgiveness and non-judgment.

The ego tries to convince us that our problems are the problem, and uses the seeming separation of every one and every thing to verify the seeming reality of this world. The ego keeps us from facing the inner wounds and underlying feelings of guilt by seeing others as to blame. The ego takes comfort in attacking others for the "wrong" ideas and "wrong" thinking, in which they engage. This keeps us from true forgiveness of our selves and of others. We even create Jesus to be the wonder body that is different from us and very special, thus keeping everyone else different and not special. The truth about Jesus, as our elder brother, he was able as a man to see the face of Christ in each one of us and remember God. By aligning completely with Holy Spirit, he became one with God. Walking the spiritual path is for us to do the same thing.

Living the spiritual path is completely forgiving the world, seeing the innocence in others and in our selves. This is the essence of complete non-judgment. To be able to see again the unity in all things, and especially the unity of all of us.

In *The Disappearance of the Universe,* we are reminded to extend forgiveness to our brothers and sisters, as God extends forgiveness for us. When everyone has completed his or her forgiveness lessons, God will take the last step and welcome the collective prodigal Son home into the oneness of Heaven.

Walking the spiritual path is not easy to accomplish. What is important is to strive to be on the path. It is beginning to manifest a saintly life. This recognizes our humanness, and is not perfection, while striving for perfection. It is striving to forgive

Healing and Transformation

our past, to forgive others, and to forgive ourselves. It is to forgive all time and space.

Forgiveness is very powerful in healing our selves and releasing us from the tyranny of the ego. In my hypnosis work, we regress the client back to the source of the emotional wound. We then recognize the entire negative and fear-based emotions attached to the memory. We visualize, imagine and see the negative and fear-based emotions being released. We then visualize, imagine and see the positive and love-based emotions replacing the departed negative and fear-based emotions. This includes forgiving the other person or persons, and forgiving ourselves. This process powerfully releases the emotional wounds. At times, it accomplishes in a few sessions what would otherwise take many sessions of therapy or other lengthy self-help healing processes to accomplish.

As we progress with the work of healing, we then want to walk the spiritual path. Healing and transformation go hand in hand. As we progress with this process, the seeming differences give way to the greater understanding we are all one. As we progress, we have more spiritual experiences. We become more loving, more peaceful, more forgiving, and more responsible for our lives. We recognize the folly of judgment. We experience increasing joy.

In *The Gospel of Mary Magdalene* by Jean-Yves Leloup, Mary Magdelene notes, it is only sin that we create with our sickly imagination. Remember sin means error. With the poor use of our senses, intelligence, and emotions we become disoriented. We forget we can and should be guided by our Higher Self. Through disorientation, we pervert our selves, society, and universal order itself. It is these distortions, the result of our unhealed self and its ego, which lead to miss-creation. As noted earlier, we do create our world. The world we create is an arrested perception of the world. We then take these relative perceptions as real, mistaking our perceptions and interpretations of reality for Reality itself. According to the Magdalene Gospel, Jesus taught:

> It is you who make sin exist,
> when you act according to the habits
> of your corrupted nature;
> this is where sin lies.

Corrupted means we believe what the ego perceives, rather than recognizing the true reality, we are all one.

In her gospel, Mary Magdalene indicates that people are spiritual beings, sin is not real, and the material world will dissolve. Salvation lies in discovering within ourselves the true spiritual nature of humanity. This is the unity that transcends the seeming separation and duality, at the most basic level of consciousness in the world of materiality. Understanding our spiritual reality within, we begin to overcome the deceptive entrapments of the bodily passions and of the material world in general.

We engage in endless judgments based on distorted perceptions, and miss the spiritual path. We see the faults in others and miss the faults within ourselves. Jesus tried to teach us to be open to, and connected, to our Higher Wisdom within us. To do this we have to let go of judgments, not only of others but also ourselves. We can live authentically in the now, living, loving, feeling, thinking, hurting, crying, laughing and loving. If we are not "sick" we can stop blaming our childhood, our parents, society, the Church, the evil world, and our selves as well. Jesus reminded us, as we judge, we will also be judged. There is no use for blame, towards others or us.

What we think, say and do can either take us further away from God or bring us closer. This is the deep and transformative question to ask ourselves. Do our actions awaken the God in us, where truth, goodness and beauty are One? Or, do we take ourselves further and further away with bitterness, aversion, lies, ill will and violence. Not just physical violence, but also mental, emotional, and spiritual violence. We choose the path we walk, and that is our true freedom. With healing we increasingly attune to and walk the spiritual path. Directing our selves through the heart of sickness and suffering toward increasingly living the spiritual path back to Heaven.

The Master Teacher, Jesus, was the first person to completely walk the spiritual path and live the spiritual life. He was completely aligned with Holy Spirit. He demonstrated a pattern of spiritual fulfillment, which is applicable to us all. It is rediscovering the awareness in each of us, at the soul level, there is an imprinted pattern of the mind waiting to be awakened by the will of the soul's oneness with God. It is a pattern in each of us, regardless of religious or personal beliefs. It is a Christ pattern, in perfect accord with God, and waiting to be brought forth and find expression on our lives. Regardless of her Catholic belief, Mother Theresa amply demonstrated this throughout her life. While she honored the teachings and values of the Catholic faith, what she actually did was live the spiritual life. She remembered she was a spiritual being and saw, in all that she ministered, they too were spiritual beings. She did not judge, but instead extended unconditional love to all.

We are all sons of God. Jesus was like each one of us, and ultimately each one of us is destined to be like him. That is why he stated we could the same things he did and even greater things than these could we also do. That is also why he reminded us we are not of this world. He emphasized we are all one.

Living the spiritual path is not about religious conversion, denominationalism, or rapture scenarios. Jesus is a supportive elder brother who demonstrated a pattern, which is within all of us. As we heal, we are able to transform our lives, living the spiritual path. As an elder brother, he showed us the gentleness of the things of the spirit. These are love, kindness, long-suffering, and patience. These are by treating one another by and through the spiritual actions just stated. We do share a common spiritual heritage, despite our diversity. We are all sons and daughters of the same God. We are all destined to return to Heaven. We all go as one.

The way we all go as one is through the process of ascension. It is a rising of our lower self to become one with our

Higher Self. The spiritual life is uniting with our Higher Self, to the Divine Spirit within. Every material act, and impure thought of the lower self, separates us from the Higher Self. Naturally, through the unhealed emotional wounds, we stay stuck in the defensiveness and dysfunction of the ego, keeping us from the light within that takes us home.

The ego thrives on the idea of separation. Living the spiritual life is recognizing the true unity returning us all to Heaven. The seeming coincidences in our lives are continuing opportunities to see the truth and operate from Holy Spirit and not from a divided self.

We have a choice. We can continue to dwell in dysfunctional patterns of behavior. We can continue to dwell in gender, cultural and ethnic roles. We can continue to dwell in control dramas. We can continue to dwell in neurotic patterns of behavior. We can continue to let the spiritual and psychological egos control our lives. Or, we can choose to heal and transform our lives, walking the spiritual path instead.

We are living in a time when we are increasingly and truly beginning to feel Spirit. Duality is beginning to fade away, although there are many who cling to separation and their particular belief. In fear, these individuals have to believe their path is the only path and the right path. They even go to the extreme of justifying the killing of others to promote the belief in separation. But when we kill others in the name of God we are only killing a part of our selves. We can endlessly play out this drama over time and space, or we can begin to see the unity in all things, and forgive the parts of our selves we judge to be lacking in others. It is inevitable the knowingness of unity and living the spiritual path is coming to all of us. Healing allows us to get on the spiritual path right now, and not waste one more moment in separation, judgment, fear and dysfunction. The future is the past healed. We can and do heal all time and space.

We experience deep anger at times. The emotional wounds are deep. Healing the past allows these wounds to become inconsequential scars. We can take stumbling stones, including those within, and turn them into stepping-stones to our greater good. The divine plan is a plan for self-realization and ascension. The ego plan is ultimately one of self-destruction. Taking responsibility and loving ourselves again, allows us to live the spiritual path. We are no longer victims. We become creators, not miss-creators.

The spiritual life is allowing the divine to meet our humanness. As we heal all things, the divine readily emerges again. Healing is ultimately forgiving the world, for the world is a reflection of what we see. As we forgive the world, we begin to see the divine again. We are responsible for what we see. We choose the feelings we experience. We decide the goals we want to achieve. Everything that seems to happen to us, we asked for at some level. Every thought creates a result. That is why integrity of thought is so important. When we transform our lives, we again see the divine in all things, and we receive the divine in all things. When we see everyone as a brother or sister of light and love, we respond differently, even to their mistakes and dysfunction. We do not have to participate in their dysfunction, we can respond differently. We do hear stories from time to time of how loving and forgiving responses changed a person's life. When we let Holy Spirit guide our actions and thoughts, we do respond differently. Holy Spirit always knows the right thing to say and do. Living the spiritual life is letting Holy Spirit guide you in each and every moment.

In living the spiritual life, we give the world the best we have. Even though it may not be enough, we give our best anyway. Giving our best is between God and us. Psychological growth sets the stage for the spiritual growth, allowing us to bring our very best to each and every situation. As our Higher Self guides us, we awaken spiritually and achieve greater awareness. With healing, we remove the roadblocks that interfere with this awakening and awareness to take place. With the increased awareness and subsequent connection to our Higher Self, we can bring our very best to each and every situation. Not concerned with outcomes, we continue to be guided to do what best serves others in each and every situation. The seeds we plant in others may not manifest for thousands of years.

A positive and healthy emotional life is dealing with the traumas of the past. It is working on experiencing and expressing our emotions in healthy ways; all are ultimately part of achieving soul growth. As we live the spiritual life, we have the freedom to choose to move on. We can acknowledge the dramas we tend to express; yet we can deal with them and move on. Even under the most trying of experiences, the adversities we all have to deal with, we can continue to show mercy, grace, peace, long-suffering, brotherly love and kindness.. When we live the spiritual life we bring hope and cheer, joy and love to our selves and to others. We become one with the Spirit of God. We accept His presence in all life, by being caring, loving, healing and supportive.

Living the spiritual life is an understanding there is only one presence and one power in the universe, God the good, omnipotent and available to us all. The spiritual life embraces diversity, knowing there are many spiritual pathways. Each pathway is right for that particular soul.

Living the spiritual life is being in the world, but not of it. We can partake in and enjoy all the material world has to offer. We can enjoy the beauty of this world and all the pleasures it has to offer. We can also face and deal with the many adversities life in the physical dimensions present to us. We can and do face the everyday challenges of life. Yet, the spiritual path is such that these positive and negative experiences are not the be all and end all of life. Instead our focus is on bringing peace, joy, happiness and forgiveness to this world. It is walking the path of joy and reaching, once again to Heaven. It is creating Heaven on earth.

Any one person does not contain the energy of God. It was not just contained in Jesus or in any other Master Teacher. There are many paths to God. Holy Spirit holds in trust what we might have been and what we can become. Holy Spirit has the Divine Plan to help us become that person of divine possibilities. There is a mystical aspect of us, the place in you and me, which is the one begotten Son. There are no exclusions. A client of mine recently said to me, "If God is in all of us, how can God kill a part of Him Self?" And, of course He cannot.

We are a shared power with God. There are no problems that do not have solutions. There are no problems so large that they would overwhelm God. With God, living the spiritual path, we can get beyond the illusions of fear. We can get beyond separation, and all kinds of fear and hatred. We are one, and recognize we are one; part of one Sonship. We can accept the oneness of all humanity.

Love will transform the world. As we live the spiritual path, we open our hearts and ask God to use us. This is truly what it means to be reborn, returning to the truth of spiritual beings having the human experience, attuned to and aligned with our Higher Self. God is born in our hearts again. This is the Holiest of Holies, accepting God in our hearts, and then sharing that love with others and the world.

As we fix ourselves, as we heal and transform, Divine Love flows through us, and we become a radiant light. Together we become rivers of light in the world, overcoming the darkness and dissolving fear. As we move into the center of our hearts, we die to what we were and we are born into who we can be. As we share that light energy, we become beacons of light and hope to others, helping them to heal and move forward to rediscover their own inner light.

As the Lord's Prayer states, on earth as it is in heaven. True religion is that which helps you attain union with God and express Divine Love. Live the spiritual life. Doing the healing work frees you to become one with God, see the unity in all life, and return to the divine source that is all.

* * *

Healing and transforming our lives provides us with a wonderful opportunity to achieve ascension in this life, and to no longer return continuously to the physical plane. As we heal the emotional wounds, and learn to no longer be guided by our egos, we move forward on the transformational journey to enter and live the spiritual life. We truly begin to manifest complete forgiveness of others, our selves, and the world we live in. We truly begin to manifest unconditional love, the agape love that sees God in all and recognizes no matter what mistakes and miscreations others present to the world, we do not have to stop loving. We can love with the total love God continually gives to us. We truly manifest non-judgment, understanding each individual walks the path, which provides their lessons and helps their souls to evolve.

On her web site "Remembering Wholeness," Carol Tuttle (www.rememberingwholeness.com/tuttle.html) presents the following, which best expresses what healing and transformation can accomplish:

"In every moment and every day of your life,
You have choices.
The choice is to struggle more
or to create more freedom and joy.
Thoughts create;
Therefore, whatever you believe in you will experience.
If your focus is on the negative
then you will experience life as getting harder.
If the focus is on the positive
then you will experience life as getting easier.
The universe simply gives us whatever we believe.
Change your belief and you will change your life.
If you believe you are anything less than wonderful,
powerful, appreciated and honored
then you are believing a lie.
Realize that you are a wonderful, perfect,
learning and growing,
and doing the best you know how.
You are loved.
You are already whole.
You have just forgotten your wholeness.
And in the forgetting you stumble and make the mistakes
that you are meant to learn from.
We come into this world with the sole intent

on remembering who we are;
our gifts, our glory, our power and our God-Self.
God loves you,
and you are worth all He has to offer.
Regardless of your actions, in spite of your weaknesses,
you deserve God's love;
All you have to do is ask.
Ask God and His angels to assist you
in creating a new life.
The heavens want to assist you in increasing
that which brings you more joy.
The challenge of our time
is not how much more pain you can endure,
Our new challenge is how big can you dream,
how much joy can you hold,
and how long will you let it be that way?
Whether you believe it or not
you are the creator of your reality.
Start partnering with God
to create a reality that brings you joy.
God loves you, and His sole purpose
in creating you was to help you
learn how to create a joy filled life.
Remember…the light you had and the truth
you knew before you came here,
It is still in you. It is still you.
Remember!"

May all the joy, peace and love that are your divine heritage increasingly dominate your life as you heal, transform and live the spiritual life. With healing and transformation we increasingly join with others in forming rivers of light that lead others away from the darkness. We increasingly create a harmonious world that recognizes the unity beneath the diversity, and takes us into the New Golden Age. We heal our selves, and we heal the world. We all go to heaven together. It is hard work and requires tremendous honesty and self-examination. It means taking complete and total responsibility for our life, no longer being a victim, releasing control dramas, old gender roles, and all dysfunction. We begin to self-actualize at all levels and truly walk and truly live the spiritual path, becoming one with All-That-Is.

Light and Love!

REFERENCES

A Course In Miracles, Foundation For Inner Peace
Alexia, Alhambra Institute Newsletter, The Alhambra Institute, Dearborn and Coldwater, Michigan
Eric Alsterberg, Ph.D., Life IS An Adventure: a Guide to the Path of Joy
Edgar Cayce, Association for Research and Enlightenment, Virginia Beach, Virginia
Wayne Dyer, Ph.D., Real Magic
—, The Sky's The Limit
—, Your Erroneous Zones
John Gray, Men Are From Mars; Women Are From Venus
Harville Hendrix, Getting The Love You Want
Robert A. Johnson, HE: Understanding Masculine Psychology
—, SHE: Understanding Feminine Psychology
Sonja Lyubominsky, Time Magazine (01-17-05), article on Happiness
Abraham Maslow, Toward a Psychology of Being
Phillip McGraw, Ph.D., Relationship Rescue
—, Life Strategies

References

Jamie Sams & David Carson, Medicine Cards: The Discovery of Power Through the Ways of Animals
The Christ, New Teachings for an Awakening Humanity; 1994/95 Update
Leonard Pitts, Jr, Columnist, Miami Hearald
M. Scott Peck, The Road Less Travelled
Deb Price, Baylor Institute for Studies of Religion, Venture Inward Magazine, Summer, 2006
James Redfield, The Celestine Prophecy
—, The Tenth Insight
—, The Secret of Shamballa
Gary Renard, The Disappearance of the Universe
—, Your Immortal Reality
Don Miguel Ruiz, The Four Agreements
—, The Four Agreements Companion Book
—, The Mystery of Love
Jamie Sam, The 13 Original Clan Mothers
Edward Shostrum, Actualizing Therapy
—, Man, The Manipulator
Gordon Michael Scallion and Cynthia Keyes, The Intuitive Flash
St. Germain Foundation
Mark Thurber, Ph.D., ARE Venture Inward magazine
Carol Tuttle, www.rememberingwholeness.com/tuttle.html
Neale Donald Walsh, Conversations With God, book I
—, Conversations With God, book II
—, Conversations With God, book III
—, The New Revelations
—, Home With God
Marianne Williamson, Enchanted Love
—, The Healing of America
—, A Return To Love
Jean-Yves Le Loup, The Gospel of Mary Magdalene
Gary Zukov, The Seat of the Soul

CPSIA information can be obtained
at www.ICGtesting.com
Printed in the USA
FSOW01n1153010317
31414FS